Plundering Eden

Plundering Eden

A Subversive Christian Theology
of Creation and Ecology

G. P. Wagenfuhr

CASCADE *Books* · Eugene, Oregon

PLUNDERING EDEN
A Subversive Theology of Creation and Ecology

Copyright © 2020 G. P. Wagenfuhr. All rights reserved. Except for brief quotations in critical publications or reviews, no part of this book may be reproduced in any manner without prior written permission from the publisher. Write: Permissions, Wipf and Stock Publishers, 199 W. 8th Ave., Suite 3, Eugene, OR 97401.

Cascade Publications
An Imprint of Wipf and Stock Publishers
199 W. 8th Ave., Suite 3
Eugene, OR 97401

www.wipfandstock.com

All Scripture quotations, unless otherwise noted, are my own translation.

PAPERBACK ISBN: 978-1-5326-7742-7
HARDCOVER ISBN: 978-1-5326-7743-4
EBOOK ISBN: 978-1-5326-7744-1

Cataloguing-in-Publication data:

Names: Wagenfuhr, G. P., author.

Title: Plundering Eden : a subversive theology of creation and ecology / G. P. Wagenfuhr.

Description: Eugene, OR: Cascade Books, 2020 | Includes bibliographical references and index.

Identifiers: ISBN 978-1-5326-7742-7 (paperback) | ISBN 978-1-5326-7743-4 (hardcover) | ISBN 978-1-5326-7744-1 (ebook)

Subjects: LCSH: Human ecology—Religious aspects—Christianity | Environmental protection—Moral and ethical aspects | Nature—Religious aspects—Christianity | Ecology

Classification: BT695.5 W34 2020 (print) | BT695.5 (ebook)

Manufactured in the U.S.A.   MAY 12, 2020

For our goddaughter
Chiara Goodman

Contents

Preface

THIS BOOK IS PART of a developing theology for a radically new period of human history, perhaps something of a final chapter. I've never respected doomsday apocalypticism. There have been major catastrophes in human history, but then again human civilization has never been so "advanced," the human species never so numerous and interconnected, and the whole of the planet so fragilized. Theology has tended to see the people of God as on the side of good, often through the belief that God is at work through human civilizational development, and at work in the human political arena. These views are quickly becoming unsustainable. But where do Christians and others turn in this time? What price will theologians be willing to pay to save the world? For me, I believe we must face tomorrow with resolution and the desire to take responsibility for our destructiveness, confessing that all have sinned, and that the depth of this sin goes even to the point of the destruction of much of God's creation on this planet in the pursuit of what we have believed to be the good. Christian theology, I believe, has the only plausible answer for why we are in this situation, and the only plausible solution—true reconciliation with the Creator in Christ.

I was part of the "Earth Club" as an elementary school child in the early 1990s, where I learned ecological propaganda. I grew up in suburbia, but loved going with my father to the wildernesses of Colorado to hike, ski, and bicycle. Over time, I began to critique the practices of the people of my heritage for whom the wild exists as "public lands," or the "land of many uses." At the same time I began an apprenticeship as a software engineer during most of my teenage years, and living constantly at the forefront of the rapid years of the personal computing and internet expansion.

Having read the Bible with an independent mind, I came to be haunted by a major question as a late teen: why does human civilization oppose the curses of God as seen in Genesis 3? In a sense, my major theological question has always been discerning the creation of God and the creations of humans. As an undergraduate at Wheaton College in 2002, I asked one of my philosophy professors my big question, to which he responded I should read Jacques Ellul, which I did not do until later and almost by accident. In 2005 I took a month-long course with the National Outdoor Leadership School (NOLS) to learn to become an outdoor educator, with a focus in glacier mountaineering. Christians were not well respected by my leaders because they were perceived to treat the wilderness as their own property or backyard. I wanted to challenge that, at the same time I challenged the instrumentalization of the wild even by those most eager to promote it. After over a decade of many solo experiences in the wilderness of Colorado and a few in the not-so-wild places of the UK during my PhD, I developed a more thorough self-critique of how I *used* the wild. While family have sometimes feared my solo excursions, and my wife jokes that one day I will be rewilded, it has been in the last five years that an interest has turned into a passion. No other writing has touched my spirit as this. No other aspect of human sin has filled me with such anger and sorrow. I began filling notebooks with ideas for a "Creation Manifesto" complete with revolutionary ideas for how the political world must change. That work is still in notes. But it led me to this more foundational theological work, which does not remain theory only. I am now working to make some of the vision of Part IV of this book into a reality in my own context.

I would like to thank all those who have helped me with this project: my father, Kolin Wagenfuhr, for introducing me to the wild as a child, and who has proven to me the potential for the imagination to be transformed by our long discussions of theology; Dr. Amy Erickson, who is of like mind, an insightful reader, and responsible for expanding the research of this book; Dr. Steven Bouma-Prediger for his reading of a draft and offering excellent suggestions and encouragement; Dr. Michael Morelli who also offered close editorial suggestions; the community members of The Embassy, for experimenting with realizing the ethic of this book; and my wife, Ainhoa Prieto Wagenfuhr, for listening to my private lectures, revelations, supporting ecological lifestyle changes, and seeking the same kingdom vision. I also thank those at Wipf and Stock who have worked with me through this third monograph with Cascade.

Introduction

The Cosmic Parasite

PARASITE. THAT WORD CONJURES up images of nasty creatures and deadly viruses. A parasite is a living thing that thrives by taking nutrients from another lifeform. Often this happens in such a way that the host creature suffers. Parasites give nothing back. Sometimes parasites derive so many nutrients from the host that the host dies. Similarly there are invasive species. An invasive species enters a stable ecosystem and radically disrupts it, leading to an unsustainable situation in which it might even choke itself out of nutrients, after having outcompeted native plants or animals. Symbiosis, on the other hand, is when two different types of creatures help one another thrive. Symbionts are better together.

But what if we consider the world and all of its living things together? Let's call it "creation." What if all of creation groans because it has been infected with a virulent parasite, or with an invasive weed? What if this parasite rapidly adapts and develops incredible strategies and techniques of resource extraction? If it did, it would not only exploit the creation, but would also compete with itself for an increasingly limited set of resources.

This parasite of which I speak is, of course, humanity. Calling humanity a parasite is incredibly offensive. I hesitate to say it.[1] We could build a mountain of evidence to establish it as a reasonable hypothesis. Humanity plunders the whole of creation, subjecting it to profound suffering.[2] Anthropologists have noted that humans are the "world's most

---

1 Richard Preston calls humanity such, suggesting that Ebola and other viral diseases may be the immune system of the earth reacting to the parasitic damage of humanity. See *The Hot Zone,* 310.

2 Rom 8:19–23.

successful invasive mammal."[3] But it's not as though humans have usually intended the destruction they have caused. Humanity isn't like a lion eating an antelope, specifically choosing which one to hunt. Rather, humanity is like a worm that sucks its host dry. The worm just eats the way it knows how. Humanity is living the way it knows how, even if the consequences are the death of its host, which will inevitably lead to the death of the parasite itself. Almost no one has intended to lead humanity, or the creation, to its present state of affairs. It just happened that way as humans have pursued their own common good.

How did humanity become a parasite upon the earth? Is that just our nature? Are we destined to roam the stars, perpetuating our species by feeding off of thousands of worlds until they are left behind as barren husks? I'm certainly not the first one to imagine this. The idea of a cosmic parasite has become a science fiction trope. The difference is that science fiction usually imagines this cosmic parasite as having evil intent and a monstrous appearance. We're usually the good guys. But some major public figures in our time are suggesting that it's time to colonize other planets (e.g., Mars) to ensure the survival of our species in the seemingly inevitable event that the Earth becomes uninhabitable (Elon Musk, Jeff Bezos, or the film "Interstellar").[4] From any outside observer's perspective, it certainly looks like humanity acts and thinks like a parasite—pursuing its own good at the expense of all else, refusing to change in order to preserve its native habitat. Two of the most wealthy and forward-thinking people in the world at the time of writing are investing incredible resources on travelling to barren, frozen rocks to save "humanity"[5] while significantly contributing to the ills of the earth through their business practices. How did we get to such levels of absurd power with almost no notion of responsibility?

Imagination

Having grown up in Colorado and having trained to be a wilderness expedition leader and educator, I feel like my natural environment is the mountains, forests, snowfields, and meadows—"outside." I put "outside"

---

3 Scott, *Against the Grain*, 70.

4 Stone, "Jeff Bezos Wants to Send You to Space Too."

5 That is, a tiny privileged minority taken as a token representation of the whole species.

in quotation marks because this is a book about perception and imagination. Have you ever paused to think about the fact that nature is *out*? For some reason we believe that the natural world is outside of us. It is different. It is alien and other. This is more true now as the majority of the human species live almost their whole lives "inside," at least inside a city. *In* and *out*—these are profound words. They convey safety and danger, tame and wild. One is controlled, the other uncontrollable. Indeed, we call unmanaged land "wilderness."

This book is about how humans perceive creation/nature/the universe. It's about how the human ability to perceive and imagine is fundamentally broken. It's about the consequences of this broken perception and imagination. Then it offers a path to a renewed perception and imagination that offers hope to a dying creation.

We know very well what the consequences of this broken imagination are. Climate change and its dire consequences are on the news daily. The UN in 2018 gave one of the most extreme warnings to all of humanity that it must radically change its ways within just over a decade, or the losses to the planet will be entirely irrecoverable. Recently, some have revised that date to a time before this book's publication. By the time you read this, it may already be too late. The time for climate change skepticism is over. Of similar importance, though by far less tied to film-worthy disaster, is the problem of soil depletion. The UN's Food and Agriculture Organization (FAO) estimates that there are now fewer than sixty years of harvests remaining for the world and one quarter of the entire earth's surface is now degraded.

But this isn't a book about how bad things are. Nor is it a litany of rage against former generations who brought us to this brink. There are a lot of ideas swirling around about how to fix this problem. Some, as above, argue for planetary colonization, believing that we need to become a "transplanetary" species. Others will highlight solar and other sustainable power sources as the solution to our carbon dependency. Carbon taxes are being discussed and voted upon. The most radical suggestions come from "transhumanists" who believe that humanity should use all of its present and future technologies to break out of the confines of biology. More moderately, ecomodernists are arguing that technology will help us decouple our species from dependence on natural environments. These are technological, political, and economic dreams of salvation. That is, they provide something like a magic bullet that will solve human problems. But they are all dreams of salvation, rooted in a broken imagination.

The mythical heart of each of these fields will be investigated as we find that there is no simple solution to the ecological problem. In fact, political, economic, technological, and urban imaginaries are all contributors to this broken imagination.[6]

A Peak Bagging Imagination

How does this broken imagination work? Let's take a brief example about human imagination in our time: "peak bagging." In Colorado there are fifty-four mountains over 14,000 feet in elevation, called "fourteeners." It is a popular recreational achievement to try and "bag" every one of these mountains. This phenomenon goes well beyond Colorado, of course. Mount Everest has now become something of a circus. Putting a mountain in your bag, conquering it, is how many in our time help themselves feel like they've achieved something profound. I did my first two fourteeners when I was well under ten years old, on the same day, so some of them are of trivial difficulty.

There are many layers of imagination at play in this example. There is the seeming profundity of an arbitrary measurement: 14,000 feet. If the USA switched to the metric system it would ruin this list of peaks. After all, who cares what is 4,267 meters or higher? The list would have to grow to include all peaks over 4,000 meters. Measurements are something we imagine as meaningful markers of value. Bigger is apparently better. In Colorado there are much lower mountains that are more technically challenging to climb, but they remain relatively untouched by peak baggers. Measurements somehow convey value about the "outside" world, even when we know that these measurements are a human construct. We create meaning and assume that the meaning is "out there." This is *projection*. We make a mountain important because we have measured it. But the construction of meaning lies in our imagination, not in the mountain itself.

Apart from arbitrary measurements, peak bagging demonstrates the value of conquering the wild. Mountains are perhaps the most powerful symbol of wilderness. They are big, imposing, create their own weather patterns, and can be treacherous for many reasons. Climbing a mountain

---

6 An "imaginary," used as a noun, is a term widely used by the philosopher Charles Taylor. By it he means a collective way of understanding the world. This is not the same as a "worldview" because it is not simply about shared perception, but about shared creative imagination.

is usually considered an act of conquest. The fact that people keep lists and check a box of which ones they've climbed shows this rather well. This isn't an act of participation, of joining in the outside, it's a sallying forth from the protected castle walls of the city to assault the strong towers of wilderness, and retreat. Peak bagging is a way of achieving a victory that brings honor, but doesn't seem to harm. It's an achievement. But this only works against an enemy. That enemy might be a challenge. Peak baggers are not intentionally the enemies of a mountain, of course. But practically speaking, the more people who set forth to bag a peak, the less honor the act conveys. At the same time, an increase in traffic can and usually does result in significant damage to the mountain's flora and fauna. Mount Everest is covered in rubbish. To offset this, trail builders and maintenance crews have to transform the mountain, creating structures to enable more sustainable and less damaging trails. But once humans begin to manage the wilderness, even to prevent their own damage to it, it is no longer wilderness.

The wild has always been an enemy to the myth of civilization. Peak bagging and other outdoor recreation in the wilderness simply represent the end of a long line of conquest of civilization. The great irony is that peak bagging is only valued and possible in an era where the wilderness poses a very small amount of threat to an individual's safety. The likelihood of death is far higher driving a car than climbing a mountain in Colorado. Peak bagging is popular because it is relatively safe and relatively easy, which means a lot of people can participate. Peak bagging creates a mountain zoo, or interactive mountain museum. How much truer is this for National Parks in which one does not have to leave the confines of an automobile to see wild things? These maintain a semblance of the wild, while actually remaining quite tame.

Because the wilderness is fully conquered, we have legally designated wilderness preserves. The wild must now be protected from humans, because it is endangered. That hasn't managed to change our perspective that it is something to be conquered, even if only in a recreational way. All of this is because the wild is outside. But now the roles are reversed—instead of building walls around our cities against the wild, we have legal walls to protect the wild from our cities. The great outdoors must be saved from the sprawl of the even greater indoors. However, even the legal walls of the Wilderness Act of 1964 only preserve wilderness as an "enduring resource" for the American people. Managed, protected, or owned wilderness is no longer wild.

Chaos, Cosmos, Creation

A major theme that this book traces throughout is the structure of the world in the storied human imagination, which constructs stories of order arising from disorder, or cosmos (κόσμος) out of chaos (χάος). Human imagination sees the wild as something other than itself. The wild is alien, different, other, threatening. It perceives the world as chaotic and in need of conquest or colonization. In order for humans to create value, they have to *impose, impress,* or *make an impact*. That is, they have to put their self-image onto the external world. This is always a violent action. This impact or impression can happen with other humans. We "make an impression" on people by doing something out of the ordinary and putting our image into their minds in a lasting way. These words all convey the act of something hard and solid penetrating something soft in such a way that the soft thing changes by the encounter.

Humans have seen the world outside the safety of their "inside" as chaotic. It is a disorderly place. It is unpredictable. It is dangerous. It is the place where humans are not in charge. Chaos is the state of affairs that alters humans. Chaos imposes something on us. Cosmos, on the other hand, is an orderly reality. Cosmos is always constructed, whether by the gods, or by humans. Cosmos isn't just the building of a city, it's also the building of intellectual systems of thought. Cosmos does not come naturally. Every myth of creation involves some act of disorder being made into some kind of new order. And many creation myths view humanity as the great fulfillment of the bringing-into-order act. Humans are cosmic beings—they demand order. Where disorder exists, they will violently impose their order. The problem, as we will see time and again, is that chaos does not exist, nor has it ever existed. Chaos is nothing more than the failure of the human imagination to make sense of everything around it. What is uncontrolled is incomprehensible.

On the other hand, cosmos certainly exists. It exists as the massively *simplified* structures that humans build, both in our minds and in concrete. But cosmos has to be built, and it is built, as in many ancient myths, out of the corpse of chaos. Scholars of religion have a special German word for this, *Chaoskampf,* meaning chaos-war. Humans, like their gods, war against a perceived chaos by building an ordered reality that fits within their ability to understand. Hence, we drain marshes, flatten mountains, and build square and level city blocks. We do not generally inhabit the wild forests, but clear cut them and create agriculture. Forests, marshes, deserts, mountains—all of these have been symbols of a chaotic "outside." Land is valued only for human purposes. Human civilization transforms varied landscapes into vastly more simplified systems of human control with steel, timber, and concrete. Humans are the great enemies of true diversity, even as this has become a sacred word in our time. We love sameness, because it is understandable, controllable, or legible.

In response to this complex of *Chaoskampf*, there is a third alternative: creation. Traditionally, the Judeo-Christian God does not create cosmos out of chaos, but out of nothing. There is no *Chaoskampf* for God.[7] Creation is created and ordered, but not violently. Creation is peaceful and good, as symbolized in Eden, not a wild monster against which humans must war. But this does not last. Creation is lost. Eden is plundered.

Hope and Misanthropy

Calling humanity a parasite is difficult. So before we get into deeper discussions it is important to say that humans are not, in their essence, evil or despicable. Even though I will argue that humanity throughout history has acted in parasitic ways, I do not believe that this is because we're acting out of ontological determination. I do not think that humans have "selfish genes."[8] This is a pseudo-scientific theory justifying human parasitism. We must avoid the twin evils of misanthropy and anthropocentrism. Neither hate, nor deep self-love will lead us to analyze the situation or ourselves accurately. As we will see, even the idea of a fixed self to love or hate is a problematic aspect of ecological devastation. Hope does not lie within our human ability to fix or change things. Our attempts at fixing and changing things are precisely what gets us into trouble. The root of the error is in the mind, in our reason, in our ability to perceive the world. This bears a dark fruit in the whole person. The error is seeing chaos when we look at creation. There is a solution to this problem, and it is profoundly hopeful. The apostle Paul believed that all of creation suffers unwillingly by human evil, but that there is hope that the creation itself will be set free from its slavery to corruption.

The only force of chaos in the universe is humanity. But the God revealed in Jesus Christ is not in the business of *Chaoskampf*, but in

---

7 It is true that some of the Hebrew Bible uses *Chaoskampf* imagery, but it usually does this to convey a message that God has *not* struggled like the pagan deities.

8 A theory advanced by Richard Dawkins in *The Selfish Gene*.

emptying himself to submit to the violence of human cosmos, in order that he would attain a great victory—the defeat of the human cosmic mindset. The challenge offered in this book will simply be this: humanity must die to itself and all that it values, in Christ, for the sake of creation. Humanity must become a new creation and perceive afresh God's good creation. "Whoever wants to save his own life will lose it. But whoever loses his life for my sake will find it."[9]

Shape of the Argument

This is a book in four parts. Part I looks at present ecological reality and shows how humans are currently behaving as cosmic parasites. Part II is a philosophical and sociological account of human epistemology. Its main point is to show that human structures of thinking are broken and cannot achieve what we believe we are capable of achieving. Part II also introduces the "myth of civilization," to show how the broken human imagination necessarily leads to ecological disaster. Part III is a theology of creation and ecology. The biblical narrative offers a coherent account for why human imagination is broken and provides a plausible solution. Part IV applies the biblical narrative to contemporary practice. It offers a theory and strategy for the renewal of the mind that enables reconciliation with creation.

9 Matt 16:25.

Part I

Cosmic Parasites

CHAPTER 1

Evidences and Questions of Parasitism

THE NOTION THAT HUMANS are parasites is bound to raise objections. It seems incredibly counterintuitive to what we believe and think about ourselves. Human civilizations have, for as far back as we have surviving cosmological myths, believed that they were on the side of good and order. But we will briefly look at some scientific studies that strongly suggest that humans are *currently behaving* as parasites. We will then explore the more philosophical questions, like whether this parasitism is a metaphysical problem, an accident of history, growing pains of a species closing in on transcendence, or an epistemological problem that may be healed.

Climate Change

Although climate change is a prevalent conversation in politics and the media, there remain misunderstandings of the theory, which has not changed in decades. Basically, specific molecules in our atmosphere interact with solar radiation in specific ways. Some of these molecules are called greenhouse gases, such as carbon dioxide and methane. These molecules absorb heat energy produced by the sun, energy that otherwise would move back into outer space. The higher the concentration of these gasses in the atmosphere, the warmer the global average climate becomes. Not all of these gasses behave in the same way. Methane is far more potent than carbon dioxide, which means that it takes a fractional amount of methane to cause similar warming as carbon dioxide. This warming effect has significant consequences for all life forms on the planet who have adapted themselves to a specific temperature range. It threatens to raise sea levels by melting water that is stored on landmasses in the form of ice. By warming the oceans, it threatens to intensify natural weather-related disasters, and to disrupt an extremely complex weather system. Warming will likely produce vicious feedback loops which will lead to runaway warming. A major source of the problem is easily identifiable, but extremely difficult to change because human civilization across the globe has become dependent on the use of energy through burning of fossil fuels. Hydrocarbon combustion produces carbon dioxide, and thus nearly all methods of transport and energy generation for electricity have been dependent on the production of greenhouse gasses. This civilizational dependence has meant that there is a significant motive to deny the reality of the problem, and if acknowledged, to take responsibility for changing it. It is worth noting that carbon dioxide and methane are also products of natural processes of digestion and composting that occur in animals and in the soil. Fossil fuels are ancient stores of decomposed organic material sequestered away out of the regular lifecycles of ecosystems. Hence, their use leads to artificially reintroducing vast amounts of carbon into the lifecycle of ecosystems, which produces unintended consequences. However, another major source of climate change is land specialization, chiefly for meat production, which eliminates carbon processing forests while itself producing more carbon and methane.

Humans have unwittingly altered the climate for millennia. One interesting, though contested theory of the Little Ice Age holds that the near elimination of pre-Columbian civilizations in North and South America by European diseases led to a period of prolonged global cooling. The reason is that these pre-Columbian Native Americans engaged in slash and burn agriculture, which involves the use of fire for clearing agricultural space.[1] The reasoning is that the massive reduction of fires and massive forest regrowth reduced the concentration of carbon dioxide in the global atmosphere, which in turn led to notable and significant cooling.

Unique to modern times is the incredible scale at which combustion is used for nearly all aspects of modern life and the corresponding rise in global population. While slash-and-burn agriculture can be a parasitic practice that sometimes leads to complete desertification of an area, indications are that ancient practitioners of this form of "shifting agriculture"

---

1. Scott, *Against the Grain*, 39.

used it in sustainable ways. Today, however, the evidence has significantly mounted to show that climate change is already having disastrous effects, and that radical change must come within a decade to prevent the possibility of runaway and potentially civilizational-level disaster.[2]

Parasitism is seen not simply in these unintended consequences of the Industrial Conversion.[3] No one intended for climate change to happen. And that's part of parasitic existence. Parasitism is demonstrated, perhaps best, by the confidence humans have in adopting new ways of living, creating new techniques and technologies, with minimal consideration of the costs. Parasitism is evident in the way of thinking that simply follows the research, the product, the market, the people. It is a specific and conscious denial of responsibility for future results of present decisions, intended or unintended. As we'll see, one fundamental aspect of human history and imagination is the consistent and conscious desire to reduce its sense of responsibility, often to nothing.

But the problem of parasitism is not restricted to parasitism itself or the unintended consequences. The problem lies primarily in the human imagination. This means that the proposed solutions to the problem do more to reveal parasitism than often the problem itself does, the most obvious examples of which are those that continue to avoid responsibility and seek quick-fixes. These are found most clearly in ideas like carbon capture technologies. Such technologies aim to extract carbon dioxide from the atmosphere. The companies currently developing such technology specifically aim at enabling the continued use of greenhouse gases by reducing their harmful side-effects, while crucially making a financial profit. Other parasitic responses involve the move to renewable energy in solar and wind. Rather than seeking a reduction of consumption as a key component of change, the move to renewable and "clean" energy sources will inevitably increase consumption, leading to more and more land transformed for the purpose of energy production. Unintended consequences, such as the death of birds by wind turbines, are written off as part of the price that must be paid. Similarly, skyscrapers are

2. Details about the threats and the underlying science are readily available on the United Nations website, for example.

3. I purposefully rename the "Industrial Revolution" here because this term, along with the technologically based historical narrative of progress and development through a series of revolutions, is better understood as a transformation of the imagination (conversion). We will spend more time later critiquing the narrative of technological development.

responsible for billions of bird deaths per year due to collisions.[4] If one person systematically killed billions of birds, that person would clearly be prosecuted as a sadistic animal torturer. If our skyscrapers do the exact same action with the exact same result, it is simply a sad reality. Parasitism comes in the distribution of responsibility. Although no one person can be held responsible for these bird deaths, that does not mean no one is responsible. Architects, builders, developers, owners, tenants, all engage in a systematic killing of birds. That's simply one moral cost of building. This small example is instructive for the way in which the vast costs of civilization are ignored by distributed responsibility.

Because we all use energy derived from fossil fuels, whether we like it or not, we are all culpable for the problem. We contribute to climate change simply by participating in the world, the more so the more "developed" we are.[5]

Efficiency is another excellent example of parasitism. Increased fuel economy, for example, has not reduced carbon emissions in the transportation sector. Instead, they have increased. Efficiency simply creates room for increased consumption. People tend to consume what is available and feasible to consume without thought, foresight, or future planning. As our population size and way of life have become entirely dependent on complex technologies of efficiency, minor problems tend to become exaggerated. Population sizes become more fragile the closer they are to the carrying capacity of a system, and technologies of efficiency are not aimed at increasing the reliability of the system as much as they are the productive capacities. Such is the case with industrial agriculture, which has become dependent on a very few number of cultivars specifically engineered for annual average yield and thus ironically fragilized.

Much of the language around climate change focuses on the environment or the climate. Indeed, the very phrases that have been used, "global warming" and "climate change" are themselves evidence of a parasitic imagination in that they imply a victim-blaming attitude. The problem, we are led to believe, is that the earth's climate is warming. That is a symptom of a wide variety of human problems. Climate change, as deniers often note, has always occurred. What has not always occurred is

4. Estimates peak at about one billion per year in the United States, projecting to global amounts would be difficult but would certainly double the estimate at very least. Loss, "Bird-Building Collisions."

5. Throughout this book I will avoid taking seriously the language of development, which I will explain as the book progresses.

the human capacity to make the climate change by normal, everyday behaviors. The focus of a parasitic imagination is on the external world. But climate change is not an environmental problem, it is a *human problem* that victimizes the wider environment. That means solutions that focus on the climate are irresponsible. Solutions must focus on humans and our behavior.

Such lack of responsibility is seen further in bad-faith "green" advertising. For years hotels have explained that they are "going green" by asking customers to reuse towels and bedsheets for multiple night stays. If the hotels were concerned with reducing their environmental footprint in earnest, they would condemn the travel culture and industry that has created their *raison d'être*. In any case, not washing linens reduces costs which are not likely passed on to conscientious consumers, thus increasing the profit margin. Hotels, tourism, and travel are part of the problem, and it is duplicitous for them to, in any way, consider themselves as environmentally friendly. But many industries do this, industries whose very existence is predicated on environmentally unhealthy human behaviors. This is a further example of parasitism, the appropriation of a consumer trend toward environmentally friendly behaviors to aid in profit-making.

Soil Depletion

But climate change is well reported. More interesting, and perhaps more disheartening is the incredible destruction to the health of soil globally. Again, the United Nations has compiled scientific research to get a picture of this. In 2015 they estimated that the earth had only 60 years of harvests remaining before the soil of the planet was too depleted to sustain much of any human life on the scale we know it now.[6] This has some to do with climate change, but is largely caused by agricultural practices. "Going green" by the elimination of combustion-based energy would not make an appreciable difference to this problem. The root issue is industrial farming practice that specializes all aspects of farming to achieve maximal yield with minimal labor inputs through its use of chemical fertilizers, pesticides, and herbicides. Monocropping, in which a field is planted with only one type of crop, is similarly a major factor in soil depletion. Also daunting, soil can take up to 1,000 years to regenerate,

6. See the Food and Agriculture Organization of the United Nations at http://www.fao.org/soils-portal/en/ for latest.

meaning that there is no real shortcut to fixing this issue. Once soil is depleted, poisoned, or desertified, it cannot be repaired easily. There are no quick-fixes for the loss of arable land.

Industrial-scale monocropped fields exist, not because they are more productive, but because they produce bigger profit. Small scale family farms produce higher quality and quantity of goods. Smaller farms are 200 to 1,000 percent more productive per unit area.[7] But they take larger labor inputs and thus remain uncompetitive with genetically modified crops farmed on an industrial scale. Because industrial farmers often do not own their own farms, they have little vested interest in the health of the soil. They may have to lease most of their equipment, seeds, animals, and even methods from major corporations. This leads to a scenario where land is no longer loved by anyone, but is exploited as a resource for corporate profit.

Parasitism is seen in the desire for corporations to patent and own genetically modified seeds that have "terminator" genes (genetic use restriction technology or GURT) that make seeds only useful for two generations, forcing farmers to buy rather than save seed.[8] Soil depletion is partly rooted in the desire for profit. Those who live on, own, and operate their own farms have significant vested interest in the welfare of the soil. When the scale increases significantly, so too does responsibility and care for the land. Profit is parasitic, as we will see in this book. But the profit-mindset is a problem of the imagination that sees meaning only in the increase of value in competition, which necessarily devalues others.

Some argue for increased intensity of farming to support a growing global population. Human population demands methods that meet their food needs, with little regard for the fact that human population levels, like all other species, increase to the carrying capacity of an environmental system, such that improving agricultural yields actually increases population levels and decreases food security for vulnerable populations who increasingly become supported by foreign aid. This may lead to the nightmare scenario in which soil depletion peaks alongside the peak human population, which will statistically maximize starvation and suffering. Now we are back to the problem of failing to anticipate potential consequences before adopting civilizational-level transformations. This, in itself, is a form of parasitism, a failure of a managerial imagination to

7. Rosset, "The Multiple Functions and Benefits of Small Farm Agriculture."

8. Currently the Convention on Biological Diversity of the United Nations recommends against these. See https://www.cbd.int/agro/gurts.shtml.

live up to its own self-understanding and effectively manage an incredibly complex world.

While specific human cultures have engaged in ecologically destructive agricultural practices from time immemorial, we now face the consequences of industrializing parasitic agricultural practices. It will end up being no one's fault, but a fault of the system we have built for ourselves.

Species Destruction

As a final example we take a third United Nations report in which it is claimed that humans will be responsible for the extinction of over one million species, an event unknown since the time of dinosaur extinctions.[9] Not only is the destruction of other species by human activity in and of itself parasitic, many of these species are vital for the survival of the food chain upon which humanity depends. One of the foundational concepts of ecology is that all things are connected. From a Christian point of view, theologians talk about the "community of creation." Any species that is responsible for the destruction of a million other species, which destroys the others out of no ill intent, looks to be parasitic. When we factor in that humans believe themselves capable of rationally guided decision-making, it means that humans are doubly culpable for speciecide. Again, if we are capable of behaving in ways that would save a million species and we do not act to prevent such a possibility, we are entirely culpable for this. For the Christians reading this book, that means we share in the blame of systematically destroying the creatures that God has called good. This makes us unqualified evildoers. But this is a third-degree murder. That is why parasite and parasitism are the proper words for the way our species is behaving. Murderers or genocidal maniacs are consciously choosing their behaviors, parasites are not. But that does not make us any the less responsible for this situation.

Part of the problem with our modern situation, as we will see in this book, is that this situation is aided and abetted by a number of parasitic philosophical beliefs humans have come to hold. Our belief that we are only responsible for the choices we make as individuals, not as corporate entities, means that no one is responsible for making changes

9. https://www.un.org/sustainabledevelopment/blog/2019/05/nature-decline-unprecedented-report/.

or preventing such an epochal elimination of species diversity. This is the belief that I am not personally cruel to animals, nor do I personally intend the death of any species, yet I choose to live a normal lifestyle, so I am not guilty of these deaths. But the system that threatens the death of these million species is our shared responsibility.

These three examples of scientifically validated disaster show that humans currently act as parasites. We, in modern times, are responsible for what could be the end of most life on the planet. To put that into perspective, anthropologists estimate that *homo sapiens* is about 200,000 years old. It is within a span of the last 500 years that human population has expanded from less than 500 million globally to now over 7 billion. That expansion was from 1 billion in 1800. Humanity has transformed the world for the worse in catastrophic ways impossible only 300 years ago. Far less than 1 percent of our species' history involves this approach to cataclysm. That being the case, I will contend that the root issue is not particularly modern, modernity has only given the means and imaginative capacity for this scale of destruction. So then, what is the problem? Why do humans behave parasitically?

Parasites by Nature?

One response will be that we are simply living out human nature. Are we not simply the species that pursues innovation no matter the cost? Did we evolve to be this way, to have a "selfish gene"? The concept of a selfish gene is Richard Dawkins's way of explaining parasitism as natural or evolutionary. But, says Dawkins, humans are distinct, because they can resist their selfish genes through cultural values and techniques like contraception. So, even with Dawkins we can conclude that evolutionary biology cannot fully account for human behavior. But he sees resistance to genes as a valuable task that humans alone accomplish. Even evolutionary biology does not seem to be the major source of human parasitism.

But perhaps humans are parasitic by nature and those cases where humans behave otherwise are exceptional. If this is the case, we must be willing to accept the consequences of this argument. It means that there is nothing that we can do to change. Moral arguments that appeal to nature often end up justifying necessity, which is pointless. Necessity is not a moral concept, because morality implies ability to do otherwise. As

Immanuel Kant put it, the "ought" implies the "can."[10] Where there is no "can" there is no "ought." That's not how morality really works in practice. Morality itself is part of the broken imagination that believes there is a will separable from its environment that can simply choose radically implausible behaviors by rational deliberation. But the point is, if humans have evolved to be the way they are, then there is no moral problem. We are parasites by nature, and so we might as well celebrate that fact and do everything we can to make sure we are able to squeeze the last drops of life out of the earth while it supports us, before we move on to find other planets to suck dry. I do not believe this is a compelling narrative. It is pseudo-science. I am not convinced that humans are parasites by nature, if for no other reason than that our imaginations are capable of thinking differently.

Parasites by Historical Accident?

If we are not parasites by nature, then perhaps it is simply an accident of history. Perhaps we have simply not yet transitioned from animals dependent on an ecosystem to gods who are independent and can control different ecosystems. This is, by far, the more compelling and common imaginary that science fiction produces in our time. The idea is that we are simply not yet quite well-developed people who will abandon our barbaric heritage of dependence for an enlightened future of environmental independence. The premise that we may currently be capable of terraforming Mars and colonizing it suggest this. This is, what we might call, "scientism." It is an "ism" because it is a belief system, a mythos, a cosmology. It is not science proper. It is not based in any rigorous research into human patterns of behavior or human "development" in different eras and places. Rather, it is the continuation of Hegelianism in which *Geist* reaches self-awareness. Numerous thinkers have proposed similarly progressive visions of history throughout the twentieth century, and theologians have been among their crowd. And it finds fulfilment in transhumanism in our time. All of these held a view that humanity developed as a species over time and was headed toward a goal of maturity, a goal many believed was reached in the twentieth century. It is perhaps more difficult in the 2020s to hold this view than it was in the 1930s, 50s, or 90s. It is important to understand that this philosophical/

---

10. Kant, *Religion within the Bounds of Mere Reason*, 6:50.

religious belief does not derive from scientific method, but from a selective agglomeration of scientific imaginative ideas. It is rooted more in a Judeo-Christian eschatological cultural remnant than it is in careful description. Hegel and Marx held this notion of necessary development, and it is not surprising that it remains in spite of the twentieth century's plethora of counterexamples of human technological and political savagery in the most highly "developed" nations.

But it is still a compelling idea found in the beliefs and narratives of highly public figures. It is compelling because it is full of hope. Progress is necessary. It has to happen. All we need to do is remain hopeful that things will get better, and they will. Tomorrow will always come, and though there might be setbacks along the way, we will end up a superior race of humanity than our forebears could have possibly imagined. We will colonize the stars, like Star Trek. We will fix any problem that comes our way. We will become gods through technology, eventually acquiring a life separate from our mortal bodies, thus becoming immortal. We will not be confined to any environment, least of all the environment of human mortal flesh.

Conclusion

Common objections to the notion that humans behave as parasites are not based in evidential arguments, but in belief systems that demand this not be the case. The evidences for human parasitism are numerous, though only three were very briefly presented here. We can name a number of other common examples even from everyday life: littering, leaving shopping carts in the middle of the parking lot, driving cars within walking distance, surface strip mining, industrial meat factory farms, single-use plastics, and domestic violence. All of these involve the passing off responsibility onto others and actively damaging the lives of others for the sake of personal gain or convenience.

Part II

Cosmology and the Human Imagination

In Part II we look at the sources of human parasitism. I argue that it is not human nature that is problematic, but a broken imagination or *epistemology*, to use the philosophical term. Epistemology is the study of how and why humans know what they know. As we'll see, the imagination plays a major role in this process of creating knowledge. We first look at how the human imagination works in relation to its environment before turning to see how this imagination has worked its way out in history through the "myth of civilization" and then in modernity with five brief chapters on various interconnected aspects of the modern cosmos.

CHAPTER 2

Cosmization

How the Imagination Builds a World

As we begin our journey of discovery into why humans act as parasites, we must first look at how the human imagination constructs an ordered world. The chief human problem is a broken imagination, an inability of the human mind to perceive the world rightly and therefore to formulate strategies and plans that are capable of achieving the desired ends.

Cosmization: Creating an Ordered World

Worlds (not planets) are built or ordered in human understanding. This is what is called "cosmos" in its original Greek sense. The cosmos is an imaginary and ordered world. Sociologists talk about "cosmization" as the process by which a culture builds a world of meaning. Let's try to be as clear as possible about this. The social construction of reality, an important theory that developed in the mid twentieth century, does not mean that there is no "objective reality" "out there." This is not the cowardly postmodernism that says, "you do you" or talks about "your truth." Those are statements masking power through moral pressure to conform. The social construction of reality means that we cannot know reality without the shared human imagination coming between reality and us. We must construct a world within the world. This is a *cosmos*. Cosmos is ordered reality. Its opposite is chaos. Chaos is not nothingness, it is simply the lack of boundary and definition, which we'll discuss later. We know that all peoples of human history had to create explanations for the structure of the world, as they experienced and understood it. Whether it is the nine worlds connected by the world ash tree, Yggdrasil, in Norse cosmology, the flat disc floating on waters under a great colander-like vault as in the ancient Near East, or the pale blue dot of Carl Sagan and modern astrophysical cosmology, we all come up with a way to explain how everything fits together. It is vital to understand that there is no "true" cosmology. No one is capable of accurately describing reality, because all possible ways we come to understand things as humans is necessarily bound to particular places, times, and relationships. There is a belief we will continue to encounter that says that truth requires excarnation or the loss of specificity and locatedness. This is a parasitic belief.

Again, that is not to say that everything is an illusion. It is only to say that no one, not even God, has some "neutral" perspective. All people are subject to forces outside of themselves, and this is what people often call "reality." We will call it "creation" throughout this book. But, everyone and everything has a perspective. In that sense, it is not stupidity that led people to believe that the sun revolved around the earth. It was common sense, and still is. We still speak of the sunrise and sunset, which is a geocentric way of thinking. It makes sense because that's simply how we experience it. If we lived on a spaceship outside of the orbit of any of the planets or moons of our solar system, the sun would seem fixed with the planets orbiting around it. But, from the perspective of the Milky Way galaxy, the sun is not stationary, nor at the center. Nor is the Milky Way stationary either. Who's to say that the center point of the universe's expansion is the real center of it all? All that we can know comes by our perspective, and that perspective is modified by the instruments (like telescopes) that we use. Where our vision ceases, so too does our imagination. That the earth goes around the sun, rather than the sun around the earth, is not functionally relevant to the vast majority of humanity's daily life experience. Indeed, the sun really does go around the earth from the earth's perspective. It's simply that such a model does not produce the most simple astronomical model. Copernicus and Galileo were controversial figures, not primarily because they challenged the Bible or religion, but because they decentered the earth, and thereby humanity, and threatened the very order of the cosmos as it was then understood. It just so happened that in their society at their time, Christianity had pride of cosmological place and the church functioned as guardian of cosmology, much as some self-appointed scientists do today.

The notion of the center is vital to understand how people create a cosmos. For ancient people the center was often their local temple or holy site. Sociologists of religion talk about an *axis mundi* that is present in nearly all ancient religious beliefs. In many cultures this was a world tree, like Yggdrasil. For the Greeks it was said to be a cave in Delphi that was called the navel of the world, likely with the umbilical attachment to the earth's source of power implied. The center was the source of power and the sacred. The closer one gets to the divine power pouring into or out of the earth, the more successful one will be. Thus, many ancient cultures had specific rites for consecrating a space before settling a new city, and the temple or shrine would be the first thing built. Many cities were built near sources of power. In the ancient world a source of power was pretty obvious—mountains (they have storms and lightning), springs (water going up instead of down), a massive and ancient tree (like the world tree), a cave (gateway to the underworld). These sources of power had to be redirected and harnessed through the act of consecration and construction of a shrine or temple.

The realm outside of the protection of the power that radiates from one of these sites, and even one of these sites before consecration, would be the realm of chaos or un-order. Construction—the building of walls, fences, and cities—is perceived throughout human history as cosmization. Building buildings builds the cosmos. This is not a practice humans have now abandoned or outgrown. The rejection of paganism by Christianity did not eliminate holy sites, pilgrimages, and relics as sources of power. The rejection of Christianity for materialist secularism has not eliminated celebrities, the sacredness of the city, the desire to urbanize the world, and to colonize every way of life different to our own. Ecologically speaking, the results of this will become more and more evident as I develop my argument. As a foretaste I will simply say that cosmization is inherently ecologically destructive. Why that is we will save for later. The important point to understand is that humans have, so far as we are aware, always engaged in the process of cosmization, or the construction of an imaginary and simplified world that makes sense. Thus, we need to look at the imagination and how it operates in order to understand cosmization.

Sources of Imagination

The imagination is not able to create something out of nothing. It must work with the material it has received and imbibed from experience and instruction. Most experience and instruction is not done consciously. We are often unaware how much children are learning at every moment. Psychology has opened large windows on the vitality of every aspect of child development. Each act of anger, separation, abuse to a child, can create major determining factors for the rest of a person's life. Schooling and intentional instruction represent only a few of the sources of imagination. Much of the content for imagination seeps into our minds without our ever knowing, which means it is not consciously chosen. The way we see things, the way we interpret things, the way we speak about things is highly conditioned. Take the word "memory" as an example. As a concept is has different meanings to different generations. For premodern generations memory is tied to story and relationships. We know this from the many premodern stories we have. Memory in the Hebrew Scriptures is related to events that prove character and consistency to commitments. For generations born after the year 2000, memory is storage. Because computers have so impacted or infected our imaginations, we have begun to see the world as a computer would. Modern memory is factual, photographic. Ancient memory is expressive and evocative. We see memory as something to be used and filled for tasks. Humans have invented clever ways of storing strings of bits and bytes, zeros and ones, and they have taken to calling this "memory." The storage of zeros and ones specifically organized has almost nothing to do with what humans have historically understood memory to be. Computer memory is a metaphor, part of an imaginary. But, when that imaginary takes on a place of prominence in daily life, the metaphor runs the risk of inversion. This is seen when people begin to think about memory as storage, as limited, as merely electrical pulses in the brain similar to the electrical pulses in semiconductors. Once we begin to see computer memory as primary, we have fundamentally altered the structure of the cosmos. We no longer live in the same world as our forebears because our imaginations have unconsciously shifted.

Many of these sources of imagination are determined for us. We do not choose the vast majority of what we experience, or how we learn. And here is where big misunderstandings of cosmization come about. We tend to believe that we choose what we believe and how we see the world, as though there were a range of prepackaged options out there that we get to choose from. We'll see this come into play when we examine the modern concept of identity and authenticity later. But people who grow up together believe very similar things. Where they tend to disagree is rarely related to the deep structure of the cosmos, otherwise they would not be able to communicate much at all.

This also means that those who grow up in an urban environment will see the world in fundamentally different ways than people who grow up in a rural or wild environment. Urban environments have major determining factors. Space is at a premium, which not only increases the incidence of disease, but also requires different notions of property and territory. The very existence of a city requires social hierarchy because its economy is only possible by a working or slave class that produces surpluses for the benefit of urban specialists and the idle ruling class. These are major factors of the imagination and are integrated into the shape of the cosmos, as well as into the myths that help create and justify the shape of the cosmos.

The city, economics, politics, social identity, religion are thoroughly integrated and mutually dependent sources of the imagination. All of these involve specific determinants that do not lie within the realm of choice and that profoundly influence our construction of the cosmos. We are "thrown" into the world, as the philosopher Martin Heidegger says. We are born into an already existing imagination that has been handed down from generation to generation. This is not to say we are fated or totally determined by destiny or some other reified and projected sense of doom. We are free—free to live into our determinants and imagine alternatives. This is not the kind of radical freedom that is often absurdly imagined when people talk about the freedom of the will. There is no such thing as a radically free will or a blank slate of a mind.

The Language of Cosmos

Constructing cosmos happens in imaginary and concrete ways simultaneously. In the realm of the imagination, cosmos is largely linguistic. We have no other way to communicate the structures of reality apart from language because the cosmos is itself a construct of language. Language is not simply our way of interpreting reality. Our lived reality *is* linguistic, or *hermeneutical*.[1] That's really what an imagination is. It is a story, a world constructed by words. It is poetry and art. Above all, cosmos is a symbol that we live within.

A Storied Existence

The most basic way to think of cosmos is as a story. Stories involve characters, including a main character. Our lives are first-person stories told by ourselves. I cannot escape my own flesh, nor should I want to. Our cosmos, our shared-storied, imaginary world, is a communally constructed third-person story. In order to tell a story larger than an autobiography, we must participate in a grand project that involves removing the main character from everyone's personal story. We have to buy into versions of the cosmos as told by godlike narrators. The best historians are always conscious of doing just this. They are radically simplifying innumerable first-person stories precisely by removing the main characters and their unique perspectives. The historian tries to find common threads, usually the largest determining factors and events that shaped all the people of a time and place.

History is obviously a story. In fact, the word "story" is simply a shortening of the word "history," which comes from Latin *historia*. For us today, however, history is only one subject of study among many others. All fields of human study are storied, even mathematics. That isn't to say that mathematics involves the telling of stories, as though it were all those "story problems" from childhood math class that involved trains leaving stations at certain times. The realm of pure mathematics seems to be beautifully exact, universal, objective, and the most non-storied type of thing there is. But even pure mathematics is storied. What would mathematics be without Pythagoras or Euler? There are always the individual, first-person life stories that lead a mathematician into that field of study. Those life stories are inseparable from the math itself if the math is to have any meaning or fit into the cosmos. Just because a theory can be understood without reference to the one who discovered it, does not mean that it has *meaning* without the necessary first-person perspective that makes it have meaning.

Stories of meaning are often called myths. In older ancient Greek (like Homer), the word *mythos* (μῦθος) simply meant a word, narrative,

---

1. See Gadamer, *Truth and Method*.

or story. It only later came to mean a false story in contrast to a *logos* (λόγος). We'll continue to use the word myth without implying that it refers to a false story. What we really care about here is whether the story is *meaningful* to those who lived by it. I want to give historical and modern peoples the benefit of the doubt. No rational person lives by things they believe to be false, by definition. The cosmos makes sense to the people who live within it.

So, cosmology—the telling of a story or giving an account about the cosmos—is story by definition. Ancient cosmologies are weird to us. Odin sacrificed himself to himself by hanging himself on a tree so that he could get knowledge of runes that might help him prevent the death of the gods at Ragnarök. That is dark stuff, but the story that is told about Odin reveals a great amount about what pre-Christian Germanic and Scandinavian peoples believed about their cosmos. Likewise, the stories we tell today explain a lot about the shape of our cosmos. Even if those stories are scientific in language, instead of involving gods sacrificing themselves to themselves, they are narrative accounts nonetheless. They involve characters performing actions over time that somehow give meaning and structure to human existence.

The Big Bang is a story that scientists tell to make the data they have fit into something coherent. It is a hypothesis. It is untestable by the scientific method, of course. The Big Bang is myth. It is cosmology at its finest. And it is the exact same type of thing that a story about how gods drive a chariot carrying the sun around the sky every day is. Each of these stories fits the data of a people in a place and time. The Big Bang narrative could not have been told in nearly any ancient society. It just wouldn't make sense. Where hard science inevitably blurs into the realm of mythmaking is when people treat the Big Bang as fact that has *meaning* for personal life. It becomes a determinant in my first-person life story. It enters my imagination and starts to change the way I see other things. Thus, it is possible that people assign a miniscule value to the earth as a pale blue dot. Carl Sagan (1934–96), the eminent astronomer and popularizer of science, engaged in mythmaking, which is cosmology, and his imagination has spurred many others to think in similar ways. That myth has massive—and massively negative—ecological implications, but we'll get back to ecology soon. At this point it is important to be reminded that cosmology is not a description of objective reality as it is. It is a human cultural creation of a structure of meaning through story. That story can, at any moment, be made entirely implausible by some major unforeseen event or reality. Mass starvation due to soil depletion will be a chaotic event that will require cosmological changes.

So, reality is storied. In order for our lives to have meaning, we must be able to integrate our first-person narrative with other elements. The world becomes unreal when it has no room for our first-person narrative, when we cannot integrate into it. Narcissism is the error of thinking that one's first-person story is the story of the cosmos, and thus expects all others to integrate to this. Normalcy involves those who are able to integrate their first-person narrative into the shared cosmos. As we will see shortly, however, that only comes by a kind of violence.

Definition and Simplification

Story is the big picture. Individual words are what a story is made of. There is wisdom in ancient Greek where both *mythos* and *logos* conveyed the sense of word and story. The two cannot be separated. Each word implies a world, and the world is made of words.

Words are defined. The opposite of "definite" is "infinite." Finitude means having boundaries. That's how words work. Words are boundary markers. They fence in meaning, corralling it within a specific area. That means words are only ever as precise as they need to be to communicate a shared meaning. In order to define words, we have to simplify experience and boil it down to a series of sounds or grouping of twenty-six letters (in English).

The more simple something is, the easier it is to communicate, manage, control. The more ambiguous something is, however, the more potentiality remains within for shifts, changes, and ranges of meaning. We might say this is why songs and poems tend to have lives well beyond their situations when precise forms of communication do not. The best works of art strike a balance between what they communicate precisely and what they leave intentionally ambiguous. If a work of art is preachy, it is overly specific and communicates an exact theme that doesn't invite the viewer or reader to participate. When a work of art is too abstract, most people simply can't engage with it at all.

Words, like works of art, are symbols. Neither the twenty-six letters, nor the range of phonetic sounds English has convey meaning in themselves. Words have to symbolize something. The careful fencing in of meaning by a word is exactly how a symbol works. A word becomes a sign, a pointer to something else. This is important because, when we consider how a cosmos is constructed, we need to be aware that it involves important simplifications and limitations. Words are not neutral. They are controlled and used by agents to have a certain effect through defining the range of possibility. This is precisely what cosmization is on a macro scale. Cosmization is the definition or simplification of reality.

Adapting to Reality

We live by myths, some of which we are unable to perceive. Children are rapidly able to adapt to, and understand new environments. In many ways, they are the best cosmologists. We talk about children and their imagination as a quaint feature of childhood that we mourn the loss of as adults. But the childhood imagination represents the necessary adaptations of a child to a new situation. All situations are new to children at some point. For adults, the number of new situations that challenge our beliefs grow fewer and fewer. For the elderly, change becomes nearly impossible due to a kind of imaginary inertia. Jacques Ellul notes that children are not geniuses for being able to learn computer programming at a young age. They are simply far more able to adapt to new languages and ways of thinking, and computers themselves are infantile or highly simplified.[2]

We adapt to the world we receive. We inherit stories of why things are the way they are. How did white people get to be here when it wasn't their native land? I learned that in fourth grade. In my case (Colorado), the answer was gold, and the settlers were invariably portrayed as adventurous and lovable rogues. The explorers, Kit Carson and John C. Fremont, were bold individualists. These are the stories that form a people. But these are living stories, even though they are about real figures of history. The values these stories give can vary greatly. The forces of postcolonialism have revised these stories by remembering and presenting other voices on such figures.[3] This is more obvious with men like Christopher Columbus. The historical fact that he engaged in criminal conduct, even to the law of Spain of his own day, was always there. It was generally ignored because it did not fit the value of the myth that was being told. He was brave, bold, entrepreneurial, exceptional, crafty, scientific, a prophet

2. Ellul, *The Technological Bluff*, 282.
3. An excellent example is Brown, *Bury My Heart at Wounded Knee*.

of an age of reason. Now among postcolonialists he is a racist, rapist, slaver, violent criminal whose own theory of geography was disproven by his own expedition. We might say that there is raw material in the story, the man himself and his recorded deeds. But this material is almost never presented as neutral. Columbus is either a man to imitate or the exact image of toxic masculinity and colonialism that all people should revile.

We have all received the man Columbus and the many places named after him. We must adapt to that world, and we are the ones who tell these stories of adaptation. This is true for all ideas, places, times, generations, and even physical realities. Transgenderism is one radical modern example in which something that has been given and accepted as fact in nearly all previous human cosmologies, that is, the binary male-female nature of reality, has been reinterpreted by integration into a reality so modified that this view seems, to some, outmoded and morally wrong. Ancient peoples saw nature and the gods as existing in male-female sexual relationships. Ancients viewed seeds planted in furrows of the earth as male seed being implanted into a woman's womb. The link is obvious to any farmer. But to those who live in an entirely constructed environment, where individual choices are believed to be the primary determinant, such imagery is an unwanted imposition of limitation. Sexuality is not for reproduction in a technological environment as it was in an agrarian one. Sexuality is not even a biological determination for those who live in an environment where nearly all biological determinants are seen as malleable and manageable. Transgenderism as an ideology is possible and plausible only within a specific environment. It is not a great liberation. It is a particular adaptation to a different environment. It is the creation of stories that help create meaning and value in a particular world. It is part of a cosmology that is rooted in the given realities of life for a specific people at a specific time. As we will see, it is part of the cosmology that produces transhumanism as well.

Transforming Reality

And yet, not everything is given or unchangeable. Certainly, change has accelerated dramatically in the last few centuries, and this has led to rapidly changing beliefs. Now even decades have characteristic beliefs, whereas we would previously have had to classify centuries as prone to certain beliefs. Reality can be adapted to fit our values. We do not simply make up stories to fit the world we live in; we also change the world to fit our stories. Technology is the most obvious example of this. Technological progress is not necessary, it is chosen. The ancient Greeks were technologically capable of having their own industrial revolution. They possessed the requisite craftsmanship and corporate intelligence. But that would not have been of great value to them. Their cosmology would not allow them to become servants of machines. Thus, their machines were almost entirely relegated to toys and diversions.[4] They would not *convert* to industrialism, so there was no revolution.

Politics and economics are other examples of how we change reality by our very beliefs about it. We believe that humans are equal in our time. That changes a lot of things about how we modify the reality we live in. We build particular kinds of cities with vast tracts of suburban sprawl to concretize our belief in at least seeming to be equal. We also believe in anonymity, in the choice of relationships. So again, we build suburbs, gated communities, and isolated apartments. The Pueblo Indians could not have had a more different belief, and so they created villages in which nearly everything was built into one big unit, similar to other extremely ancient cities like Çatalhöyük in modern Turkey.

Economically we can point to slavery as a major point of belief that shapes reality, and a reality that is shaped by belief. As James C. Scott notes, "It would be almost impossible to exaggerate the centrality of bondage, of one form or another, in the development of the state until very recently."[5] Adam Smith rejected slavery, not simply because he believed in equality, but because he saw it as economically one of the worst systems possible. For Smith, who inverted the traditional relationship between politics and economics, slavery had no reason to exist. Politics should serve the market, and thus freedom of trade and freedom of individuals to pursue their own economic benefit would lead to the common good. That belief has transformed the world in ways that are hard to overstate. But Smith did not invent that belief whole-cloth. He had influences. And more importantly, he lived in a time and place where his ideas were plausible. Smith saw himself as doing for economics what Newton did for physics.

4. Heron produced a viable steam engine. The Antikythera mechanism, discovered in a shipwreck, is a complex mechanical clock/calendar/computer that was able to predict eclipses and the movement of constellations. There were large-scale contraptions for use in theatres that enabled actors to fly, for scenes to change mechanically on a set time-schedule, and much more.

5. Scott, *Against the Grain,* 155.

The Dialectic of Cosmos

Thus, cosmos is formed by belief, and our beliefs are formed by our experience of cosmos. This dialectical relationship is the vehicle of change in our world and our beliefs. Belief is bound up with cosmos. The two cannot be separated. Each cosmos implies a range of plausible beliefs. And beliefs imply a plausible cosmos where those beliefs can be instantiated, or turned from idea into reality.

But this dialectic is also responsible for resistance to change. Take climate change as an example. There are large groups of the American population that reject the reality of climate change, or at least reject human responsibility for it and its disastrous consequences. Few ask what seems the obvious question: *why?* Why do people distrust the heavy weight of international science on an issue that cannot be ignored? Part of the reason, beyond propaganda, is that the belief in human-caused climate change is simply implausible in their own cosmos. Even when they have experienced and noticed warming over their long lifetimes, their belief system is incompatible with the idea that they share part of the responsibility for that warming. Living as a small person in a small town, simply working in a small industry or on a farm, it is incredibly difficult to conceive the size of the global population and the combined effects of small contributions by such a large number. Furthermore, they may not have significant contact with the size of the corporations and the wealthy who share a much larger weight of responsibility for climate change. This is combined with a strong individualism that holds that individuals can and should only be responsible for themselves; a belief incompatible with the idea of systemic and shared guilt. There are other factors that play into climate change denialism, but this dialectic goes significant distance to explain a belief that is at odds with the scientific majority. Politicians who support this denialism usually do so for rather different reasons.

Resistance to change is rooted in being well-adapted to a cosmos as it has been conceived. Rural peoples experience less change and less rapid change. They are therefore generally more resistant to change. The cosmos changes at a different rate outside of the city. Urban peoples often seek change, because it is by being change-agents or leading "disruptive" corporations that one becomes rich, famous, and meaningful. Thus, experiences help form cosmos, just as the cosmos shapes experience. In this way, a cosmos tends to be self-confirming and self-reinforcing. Those urbanites who have never been to rural America simply cannot believe reports of its injustices and oft-times third-world living conditions.

In order for change to occur within this system I've described, there must be an experience of chaos. If this chaos is able to be integrated with some modifications to the cosmos, the change will be minor and often gradual. When the cosmos is simply unable to cope with the gravity of chaos, collapse or revolution is likely. This chaos is well documented throughout history. The collapse of Czarist Russia is an excellent example of combined losses in war, oppression, and famine leading to the ruin of the empire.

Ecologically speaking we have not yet arrived at a point of dramatic chaos. Indeed, many people in developed nations experience little by way of shock to their cosmos on this front, so well-tuned is the system of ecological exploitation that its results are almost entirely hidden from daily life. This means radical and proactive change is unlikely. Gradual change is potentially possible, but according to nearly all scientific estimates, the time for gradual change is past. Great change does not arrive through moral effort or hand-wringing, however. Morality is integral to a cosmos and it structure. This helps describe the incredible resistance to the calls for change that the scientific community has put forth. No one willingly changes their ordered world for anything else until it is no longer feasible to maintain, and even then there is an amount of inertia that will resist even after feasibility is gone. In fact, there will be conscious and moral resistance to change. Morality rarely drives human behavior. More often morality follows from structures of plausibility within an environment. The draconian result of this is that, for ecological change to happen in the requisite time, there likely would need to be a politically manufactured crisis by a vanguard party that was intentionally designed at disrupting the plausibility of the global energy system, or scapegoating it to such a degree that violent recriminations would be encouraged. As it is, global military systems work hard to protect the vital oil and gas infrastructure on which even they are almost entirely dependent.

So, the cosmos is both formed by experience and forms experience. It is in a continual dialectic for which no one is entirely responsible, nor entirely blameless. As we construct a world, we are formed by the world that has been constructed, which in turn informs what we value and thus what we seek to construct in the future. All of this has to be storied to create meaning, hence the notions of chaos and cosmos.

Chaos and Cosmos

We do not construct worlds for no reason. Every story of the creation of order requires some notion of disorder, out of which order might be created. Cosmos is the opposite of chaos. Just as we saw that words define, or create boundaries, this is what cosmos does with chaos. Chaos is often reified, or turned into a thing. In ancient mythology it is usually personified as well in the form of a monster or evil god/goddess: Ymir, Tiamat, Leviathan. Chaos is the undefined or uncontrollable material out of which the ordered universe is created, often associated with the sea. For current scientific cosmology chaos is the state of affairs prior to the Big Bang, when all matter was compressed into an infinitesimal singularity. Cosmos formed when this singularity exploded. This current cosmology shares the exact narrative framework as ancient ones that sound incredibly fanciful to us today. Some cosmologies talk about a time before time, about another realm, about a yawning-gap or a formless void out of which order comes by separation.

The story of chaos being formed into cosmos is also the narrative structure of literature and life stories. Resolution in narrative is found in the establishment of an order where before there was disorder or threats to order. Superhero graphic novels, comics, and films are some of the most obvious examples of this. But fairy tales with their happy-ever-after endings are also classic examples of the chaos-to-cosmos narrative arc. Dragons feature heavily as enlarged, fire breathing, and flying serpents who are the prime evil or force of chaos in the literature of many cultures. But supervillains can play the same role of monstrosity for contemporary fantasy or science fiction literature. Indeed, supervillains are often made to be so by the infliction of monstrosity upon them through disfigurement and consequent social rejection. Monsters are embodiments of chaos because they break the rules. They are physical aberrations that can do things no normal person or beast can. But they are also morally aberrant or deviant, often in connection to their physical deformity. Demons and demonic possession have played similar roles in attempts to explain deviance from normality. This chaos is socially uncontrollable power.

When it comes to narratives of empire, nation, and civilization, chaos takes on a few possible forms. In times of war against similarly armed opponents, the enemy is demonized or made monstrous, e.g., Nazi Germany. This dramatic simplification is vital to enable the systematic killing of both combatants and civilians, as well as in the justification for the atomic bomb. When an enemy is not advanced or armed, the form of chaos they take is of savagery and backwardness. The enemies of civilization are often those who are most ignorant of its supposed benefits and who must thereby be forced into modern living. This form of narrative led to immense numbers of deaths in the twentieth century when we consider the great failures of Soviet forced collectivization and purges and Mao's Great Leap Forward (18–56 million deaths) to name but two examples. This is the driving narrative as well behind colonialism and modernization campaigns. Even the contemporary concept of "developing" as opposed to "developed" nations shows this cosmizing narrative. We have this idea that one is not-yet-fully cosmic, whereas the other is, and this narrative legitimizes a system of patronage and postcolonial interventionism both through national aid and NGOs.

Chaos and cosmos are intimately related to morality. It would seem to our minds immoral to withhold foreign aid, or to not help people modernize their nations. The "developing" world is understood as a world of chaos that duty requires us to cosmize. This moral duty is inherent in the notion of a cosmos, but it requires some type of disruption to accomplish. To put it bluntly, all cosmization is colonization by the powerful of the powerless and "we" are morally obligated to colonize the powerless. This is so because we are seemingly incapable of standing outside of our cosmos and imagining alternatives in which our way of living and our beliefs are not the same as objective reality. Instead, we believe that others live in some kind of unreality, or less-than-fully-civilized reality. Some recent research has shown, however, that human flourishing is not historically based on the level of civilization. Instead, this civilizing narrative has been a purposeful argument by those in power to mobilize their people for civilizational crusades. Julius Caesar argued for the imposition of Roman civilization on the "barbarians," most of whom obviously did not want to submit to his authority. James C. Scott, with other anthropologists in support, notes that "barbarians" had, on average, a higher quality of life than "civilized" peoples. "Becoming a barbarian was often a bid to improve one's lot."[6] Even their identity as distinct tribes with specific names is a Roman imposition and simplification for "legibility."

Chaos is otherness. It is anything that does not currently fit into a specific cosmos. If it is unable to be made to fit, then, it becomes antagonistic, a threat, and therefore evil. Chaos is eliminated by the act of

---

6. Scott, *Against the Grain*, 232.

definition, that corralling of disorder by order through simplification. Judgment is inherent in definition. To judge is simply to decide or define with binding authority, either through application of pre-existing legal codes, or by fiat. In this way morality is implicit and inherent in definition. What is other *must* be wrong, in spite of modern attempts to be postcolonial and resist "othering." These are, in reality, attempts to form a cosmos with more inclusive and centralized power structures. To resist othering is to move towards uniform adoption of a singular cosmos, and is therefore ironically the most colonial/cosmic activity one can do.

That is why we need a more fundamental concept than "othering," which I will call "saming." Though not the most felicitous term, it is highly useful as the opposition of othering. Saming is when one person or group defines another in such a way that the other is incorporated within that definition. It is the reduction of uniqueness and individuality by categorization. This is the method of politics, of course, to attempt to integrate a diverse band of people into a singular definitional identity that can thereby be read, manipulated, and mobilized for purposes other than those they might have pursued on their own. Saming is unification by reduction of difference. Cosmization is the process of creating categorical definitions that reduce the diversity of experienced reality to something legible, ductile, united, controllable, and powerful. This is always a violent (in the sense of violation) act in that it must destroy or re-educate some pre-existing identity or value system with or without consent. It is notable that many historical walls, like the Great Wall of China, were not designed as much to keep barbarians out, but to keep tax-paying cultivators within.[7] This physical barrier denotes the definitional boundary of a cosmos, and this boundary is neither fluid nor permeable. The violence of saming is seen in cosmogonic myths when definitional boundaries are fixed by the destruction of a recalcitrant individual monster/god/goddess.

Chaos does not exist, then. It only exists from the perspective of a particular cosmic imagination that is unable to define and integrate this experience. But chaos is a real experience, and if powerful enough, it is able to entirely destroy the plausibility of a particular cosmos. This is likely what happened with the "collapse" of many ancient civilizations. As Scott has shown, these "collapses" likely represented liberations for

---

7. Scott, *Against the Grain*, 138–39, 233.

the vast majority of people involved and an increase of cultural diversity.[8] The only real collapse was a belief system and power structure that maintained a thoroughly hierarchical system that served the elite.

Thus, chaos is best understood as an experience of a radical other that resists saming, or categorical definition. It is a real experience, filled with fear. It is that fear of being alone in the dark without a light source. It is the fear of the void, of nothingness, of existential angst. It is the experience many young people had after each of the two world wars. It is the experience some are now beginning to feel with coming ecological disasters. It is the feeling of an irrational and implausible world that one is powerless to change.

Conclusion

In this chapter we have briefly surveyed a philosophy of how the human imagination engages in the construction of reality. We have called this constructed world a cosmos. This construction works through definition, which is the simplification by categorization of the complex individualities of experience. Definition is the construction of boundaries, of walls, sometimes even physical walls. These definitions include moral value within them. Judgment is categorization and value cannot be extricated from this. That means that in the chaos-cosmos relationship, chaos is always vilified. Rather than thinking of this as "othering," cosmization is really the more basic operation of "saming" in which complex experience is simplified or reduced to categories. This is an inherently violent and hierarchical operation. Cosmization is manifested in myths old and new with profoundly similar narrative structures. These stories speak of barbarians, savages, and the developing world as others who need to be made to be the same. This is an act of crusade, colonization, or development, which are fundamentally the same process of engaging in an overpowering of people and lands whose lifestyles and topographies are chaotic from the perspective of the powerful. This has not necessarily been historically a force for human or environmental benefit.

Ecologically speaking the results of this are profound and help to explain why we are where we are. The imagination of civilization is the problem. Our present environmental situation is not an accident of history. It is inherent to the very imaginal structure of our minds. The next

---

8. Scott, *Against the Grain*, 138–39, 217.

chapter explains that this is the case from historical literary artifacts. After that, we will examine in more detail some essential features of the modern cosmos and how they all necessarily imply environmental damage through human parasitism.

CHAPTER 3

The Myth of Civilization

NOW THAT WE'VE LOOKED at the shape of how a cosmos is formed, how our imaginations are formed by the cosmos into which we were "thrown," and how our imaginations end up forming the cosmos which also reshapes the world, we must turn to look at a common belief that has run through the variety of cosmoi in human history. Let's call this the "myth of civilization." Everyone is familiar with this story, as it is necessary to the notion of cosmos itself. It is the story wherein humanity is a progressive species that has advanced through various ages by their own wit, intelligence, and ingenuity. It is multi-faceted story as we will see. But it is a subtraction story, as Charles Taylor calls such things.[1] That is, the myth of civilization works by subtracting elements of normal civilized life of the urban elite in any given cosmos and thereby invents a prehistory to that cosmos that inevitably justifies and valorizes the present cosmos. These subtraction stories are propagandistic, however, with little knowledge or appreciation of life in previous environments. Actual historical facts are usually fatal to these subtraction stories. The myth of civilization is always told by the most powerful empires, and it is told by working backwards from an imperial norm to a subtracted savagery or barbarism.

Barbarism and Savagery

The myth of civilization begins with the concept of uncivilized peoples. Cultures have different ways of speaking of other peoples. There are Jews

1. Taylor, *A Secular Age*, 22.

and gentiles. In Han China there were the "raw" and the "cooked." There were Greeks/Romans and "barbarians," a word that was derogatory of any other language group whose speech sounded like meaningless babbling. For European colonists, aboriginal peoples were "savages." In modern neo-colonialism there are the "developed" and "developing" nations. Beyond the obviously pejorative sense in which all of these titles have been used, there lies a subtraction story about how the other peoples are not like us. Barbarians have *not yet* become civilized. There are degrees of barbarism, of course. The higher barbarians are those who are similar to the civilized nation, and who simply need to be conquered and shown the light of joining *this* empire. The lower barbarians, the "raw," are those who are savagely sub-human by their lack of settled, urban lifestyles. There is a value judgment, but also a notion of potentiality. Higher barbarians are different, but not irreconcilably different. If only they could become like us, they too would join full humanity.

As people began to develop the myth of civilization, they imagined that there was a prehistory in which all peoples were like the barbarians, and that somehow, a certain people discovered civilization, sometimes aided by the gods, as in the *Enuma Elish*, and throughout the *Aeneid*.

Civilization is—for those who tell the myth of civilization—good *a priori*. There is no need to judge it as good, it is obviously good. This is, of course, because the entire point of the myth is to explain the dominance of an empire in moral and cultural, rather than military terms. Greeks are by nature superior, and it is "right that Greeks should rule barbarians, but not barbarians Greeks, those being slaves, while these are free."[2]

This quote, which Aristotle makes use of in his own myth of civilization given to introduce his *Politics*, reveals that civilization is related to dominion. Civilization is *political*. The word "civilization" is rooted in Latin *civilis* and *civis*, which pertained to the political rights and privileges of belonging to the city of Rome. Civilization, at its root, is more about citizenship than it is about technological development. In other words, it is about who is in and who is outside of inclusion in a governance or power structure. This is clear from the word *politics*, rooted in the Greek *polis*, or city-state. Because of this, anthropologists like James C. Scott describe peoples as state or nonstate peoples. State peoples are those who are governed by an established hierarchy in a fixed and stable center. They are visible, and "legible." Note the importance again of the

2. Euripides, *Iphigenia in Aulis*, 1400.

notion of a center, as we saw with cosmologies. The capital, or head (from Latin *caput*), is the center of the cosmos, as the king/emperor is the head or even father of a political people. So, the most basic aspect of the myth of civilization relates to being inside or outside of the state. Put another way, to be managed is to be civilized, to be unmanaged is barbaric. Or as Scott has it,

> "Barbarians" are certainly not a culture or a lack thereof. Neither are they a "stage" of historical or evolutionary progress in which the highest stage is life in the state as a taxpayer, in line with the historical discourse of incorporation shared by the Romans and Chinese. . . . Put clinically and structurally, "barbarian" is best understood as a position vis-à-vis a state or empire. Barbarians are a people adjacent to a state but not in it.[3]

The myth has to have more depth, however, than simply belonging to a state. The story of Enkidu in the *Epic of Gilgamesh* is instructive. Enkidu is Gilgamesh's comrade given by the gods to teach Gilgamesh some humility through Enkidu's eventual death. Enkidu begins as a wild man. As sent from the gods he is at home with the beasts. He eats grasses with gazelles and drinks with cows. He is hairy like a beast. And he ruins the work of hunters by helping the animals escape human traps. So, he must be civilized. This is done by having a prostitute sleep with him for the span of a week. The charms of a woman civilizes the wild man, which saps him of much of his strength and speed. Enkidu loses his hairiness. His animal friends no longer recognize him but run away. He exchanged eating grass and drinking pond water for eating bread and drinking beer. He has become "diminished" as a beast, but "godlike" by judgment and wisdom. This is the myth of civilization in one of its earliest forms.

The *Epic of Gilgamesh* is an ancient collection of tales and has numerous variants, some written more than a millennia apart. Earlier variants do not have Enkidu as a wild man who needed to be civilized. He was simply a pastoralist, reflecting a different cosmos in which the earlier version was recorded, a cosmos where planter and herdsman were not at odds. The later Enkidu is, Scott notes, "the product of the ideology of the mature agrarian state."[4] The later Enkidu described above is a legendary subtraction story figure. He is a creation of imagining a human as a wild beast. The ideology exposed by this inversion is that humans

3. Scott, *Against the Grain*, 227.
4. Scott, *Against the Grain*, 63.

must urbanize and turn to settled agriculture to have wisdom, be godlike, and thrive, even though there is some nostalgia in *Gilgamesh* about the costs of this conversion. This ideology is mythical propaganda insofar as early states especially were places of oppression and unhealth that many people strongly resisted both from without and from within. Inherent in this ideology was disharmony with wild animals. Union with a woman meant disunion with the animals Enkidu previously identified with. He joins the domus complex or the *oikos*[5] of civilization in which his role is to produce and eat bread and reproduce. Enkidu is made to eat bread and drink beer even though he doesn't know what they are. Both are products of grain crops that require significant labor inputs. They are only plausible crops for powerful states. Grains require a hierarchy of urban elites who are entitled to the grain surpluses extracted through taxation from the peasantry. Enkidu is made fully human by his participation in a civilizational system that sees the natural world as wild, not the place for humans, and in need of conquest.

Other stories reveal the myth of civilization in similar ways. A classic example is Mark Twain's *A Connecticut Yankee in King Arthur's Court* (1889), in which a nineteenth-century engineer is transported to medieval England and proceeds to colonize it with modern American technology and values. The patronizing portrayal of England in the seventh century reveals a similar subtraction method of constructing the past, while using elements of nineteenth-century America, like rationality, democracy, and technology, to create civilization in a land of barbarous superstition. Much science fiction follows a similar, if inverted path. Science fiction is often a subtraction story as well, starting with the contemporary reality and subtracting elements that seem to be regressive or onerous. This has the effect of reinforcing the myth of civilization by highlighting how far there is to go before civilization is reached. The myth of civilization must have an end point, and this is often utopia, or dystopia.

The modern definition of civilization does not primarily refer to state vs. nonstate membership. Science fiction centers on technology. The state is still present, but now nearly taken for granted as ubiquitous. There are almost no nonstate peoples remaining. Civilization now primarily

---

5. The "domus complex" is the broad assemblage of the *dom*esticated creatures in a confined settlement. This includes domesticated animals, plants, viruses, parasites, and domesticated humans themselves. It is a complex because each member influences the other in ways that differ from natural, dispersed ecosystems. Humans are not entirely in control, but are also transformed by being part of this complex.

refers to inhabiting the most developed or advanced social, political, economic, and technological order. What remains constant in this, however, is the idea that civilization is the location in which the power of human management is greatest and most advanced.

Myth of Management

Civilization is government, or human management. Civilization exists only where humans exert intentional control. This management is not limited to other humans, or to technology. Beginning with the early age of European colonization and the Enlightenment, we can see the transition of civilization referring primarily to state vs. nonstate peoples to technologically and culturally developed vs. developing peoples. Specialization has enabled management to increase by a division of labor and a division of the world. As we'll see, management is cosmization. Those epistemological methods that enable cosmization, namely categorical simplification and hierarchization, are applied to more distinct fields. In ancient embedded societies, political management necessarily implied economic, technological, and religious management in an undifferentiated unity. This meant that management was necessarily extremely limited. States were fragile, as their management was limited to political/military and inefficient taxation methods. Modern civilization has transcended the state and has increased its durability because it has diversified its management. If economic management fails, as in 2008, other areas of management can sufficiently cover the gap so that significant transformations can be consciously avoided. But whether ancient or modern, management is mythologized, or given value by its storied existence.

The myth of management involves a few key beliefs: that humans *can* manage anything in potential, that humans are *right* to manage, and that human management is cumulative, progressive, and necessary.

Belief: Humans Are Capable of Management

Humans believe they are capable of managing their worlds. This is, after all, what a cosmos is. A cosmos is a world in which management is possible because the world is understood. A cosmos only extends as far as management does. Outside of managed space is chaos. Unmanaged people are chaotic, or barbaric. Unmanageable outliers inside of civilization are made criminal, and a heightened level of management (incarceration, torture, forced reeducation, extermination) are applied to such. Examples abound, though perhaps the contemporary Chinese cultural genocide against the Uighur peoples is particularly notable, as it involves technological surveillance, concentration camps, reeducation programs, child separation, of perhaps more than a million people. These unmanageable outliers must be made to conform, to become Chinese, hence civilized. And China can do it, because of its military and economic power. Few nations have raised more than a tepid outcry, with almost none imposing any real sanctions. It would not make sense for China to simply liberate such peoples and let them govern themselves. Such decentralization campaigns have only mildly succeeded with successful wars of decolonialization.

All of this suggests that humans are indeed capable of management. But we need to look at *how* humans manage. The answer has already been given, through cosmization. But let's look at it in more detail. Management is dependent upon *technē* (τέχνη), that is, techniques, methods, or programs that are effective in and of themselves regardless of their relation to their environment.[6] It is only by the development of effective methods that we are able to govern anything, because *technē* leads to dominance not relationships. Technique creates hierarchies. The more artificial these techniques are, the more universally applicable they are, and therefore the more powerful. That is, techniques that are well adapted to particular environments are not well adapted to others. *Technē* must be as universal as possible. Like universal or categorical knowledge, universal techniques work by simplification. Power comes by the wideness of application, which means centralized authority for those who control and benefit by the technique. This is artificiality. It is abstract. *Technē* works by abstracting particularity, creating an ideal, and applying that ideal in as many instances as possible. This naturally does violence to local practices and ways of life.

Natural techniques and local knowledge, which Scott talks about as *mētis* (μῆτις), are the opposite of artificiality. *Mētis* refers to the kind of knowledge Odysseus regularly displayed, which is not quite rightly translated as "cunning." *Mētis* is an adaptation to local conditions, and a wide familiarity learned by experience. *Mētis* is the kind of knowledge that cannot be taught in theory, only by practice, like riding a bicycle. Skill in

---

6. See Ellul, *The Technological Society* for an extended description of technique.

riding a bicycle may be transferrable to other skills, of course, but each of these will still need to be practiced. *Technē*, by contrast, is applicable by almost anyone who follows the instructions. As Scott says,

> Whereas mētis is contextual and particular, techne is universal. . . . The universality of techne arises from the fact that it is organized analytically into small, explicit, logical steps and is both decomposable and verifiable. This universality means that knowledge in the form of techne can be taught more or less completely as a formal discipline. The rules of techne provide for theoretical knowledge that may or may not have practical applications. Finally, techne is characterized by impersonal, often quantitative precision and a concern with explanation and verification, whereas mētis is concerned with personal skill, or "touch," and practical results.[7]

Modernity, as a philosophical movement, has attempted to reduce all knowledge to *technē* or *epistēmē* (settled knowledge), thus eliminating *mētis*. And this has produced significant results in all fields of human endeavor, most obviously technology. A major imaginational problem is that the elimination of *mētis* results in a fundamental rejection of true diversity. This is not simply true by political integration of a people into a single empire and imperial identity. It is true also of the earth itself. Scott, in *Seeing Like a State*, does an excellent job explaining the catastrophic simplifications of monocropping, forest management, urban planning, and high-modernist utopianism. In all of these cases the results are major unintended and disastrous consequences.

The problem with the belief that humans are capable of management is that it is evidently untrue and its costs are too high. It is untrue because humans are incapable of controlling or managing true diversity, but instead are only capable of controlling simplifications or constructs. Humans do not manage the world—they make techniques that reshape and simplify the world. This means that taken to its logical conclusions, human management eliminates any real diversity. This is apparent in the narrowing of languages over the last number of centuries. It is apparent in industrial agriculture, which has significantly reduced diversity of cultivars and landraces. It is apparent in multinational corporations, which have eliminated the ability of small, local shopkeepers to do business in a local way and still make a reasonable living. Wealth is now more concentrated in fewer hands than ever before in human history, which reduces

7. Scott, *Seeing Like a State*, 320.

vast quantities of people to destitution, a simplified and technical state of existence. Apparent human management has polluted the oceans with plastics. It has also led to the probable death of over one million species, as the United Nations has reported. It is simplifying all life on earth by literally killing off diversity. In this way, human management is parasitic, and necessarily so because of its epistemological framework.

The belief in the human capability of management is also shown to be misplaced because it is dehumanizing. Technological progress, and the progress of humanity as it is normally understood, has structurally necessary human costs. This is because *technē* is the Platonic world of the Forms. It is utopia, no-place. It is the realm of pure and simple thought. And in order to create such a place, we must destroy all actual places. We do this through industrial agriculture, suburban sprawl, multinational corporations, large and centralized nation-states, and modern transportation. In order to be modern, one must become modern by giving up traditional ways of life. This is not a culture, it is the absence of a culture, given that any definition of culture will require diversity. "A technical culture is essentially impossible. To make it possible . . . technologists reduce it to an accumulation of knowledge."[8]

As technology has now constituted the nearly total environment in which the majority of the world's population has lived for decades, humans have had to adapt to technology itself, eventually to become a monoculture crop of "transhuman" machines themselves. We have always-already had transhumans. They are called "ideas" or metaphysical projections of the imagination. The idea of "woman" is an example, seen well in Greco-Roman art. Creating such a "woman" does not create anything new in reality, it simply eliminates all the particular humans who actually do live and who cannot become such a simplified woman. The very notion of the species *homo sapiens* is even more fraught. Becoming a transhuman would be to give up all particularity and story, which is entirely nihilistic and suicidal. The Buddha understood this and called it nirvana or enlightenment. This attempt at becoming godlike involves a becoming what our projection of a god is: omnipotent.

But, as with all human attempts at godlikeness, it is based in nothing more than fooling ourselves. True godlikeness, as we will later see, is not simply related to omnipotence. It also willingly bears full responsibility for such power. God, as I will argue, is unique because he has no species

8. Ellul, *The Technological Bluff*, 141.

knowledge, but particular, relational knowledge of everything, including every subatomic particle. True godhood means knowledge without simplification. To become truly demonic, then, is to gain all knowledge by simplification. This is not management, this is parasitic omnicide, the great striving after the One, the irreducibly simple, the all.

Finally, humans are not even capable of self-management. Self-management is a unique problem for *technē*. Coaching, self-help, religious rituals, diets, exercise regimes, and many other techniques exist in attempt to manage the self. The problem with self-management is that we are not capable of the radical simplifications necessary to control ourselves. The rare examples of people who are capable, like legendary monks, are people who have achieved this in extreme isolation from environmental determinants by a variety of means. Perhaps Buddhist enlightenment is the best example of this, achieved as it is through ideals of self-control and many deprivations. But this enlightenment is not really self-*control*, it is conceptual self-*annihilation*. The removal of physical particularities leads to an environment in which nirvana is possible and plausible. But for those who remain in the world, only a modicum of self-control is plausible, because being in the world means being subject to determinants and relationships. That is, being in the world is to not be its master, and thus self-mastery is systematically impossible.

The very notion of the "self" is a projection and simplification. There is no such thing as a self, as though there were some stable ideal selfhood that is attainable through some technique. A person is entirely complex and constantly changing. A person never exists in isolation, but in a huge network of relationships between places, times, people, things, animals, etc. To try and establish a person apart from historical contingency is to create an idealized form. Biographies are great examples of this; they reduce a person into a villain or a hero, by selectively highlighting events and relationships that prove a preconceived purpose. Biographies tend to give an impression of a stable identity that develops throughout the changes and experiences of a life. The idea of a single "authentic" individual is incredibly modern and reveals the massive simplifications of our imaginations. By contrast, naming practices in premodern cultures were rich and varied, "A single individual will frequently be called by several different names, depending on the stage of life and the person addressing him or her."[9] This is not altogether different from practices

9. Scott, *Seeing Like a State*, 64.

of nicknames and terms of endearment that may be used privately in an intimate relationship. This difference in naming goes hand in hand with difference in behavior towards a person based on setting, stage of life, or even mood. These indicate that a multiplicity of names are required for a person because that person does not inhabit the same role in every single circumstance. Thus, the notion of authenticity, so central to our own period of history,[10] perhaps reveals that we are on our way to a total self-disembedding, in which we cannot conceive of ourselves except in abstraction. This necessarily leads to isolation from others and from the wider environment, as that is the only possible way to "find" oneself. Authenticity is only truly possible for a being that exists *a se*, i.e., as a god. But this self-deification by radical simplification does not lead to any form of self-mastery or control. The authentic self, ironically, is only possible by the kind of dissociation that leads to a dissolution of the self. When I have become myself, I become only an idea. As an idea, any instantiation of the self is a *necessarily diminished* sample of the self. Self-management, like management of the creation, is only possible by massive simplifications and reductions that do violence to real relationships.

So, for these reasons it does not seem that humans are legitimately capable of management of almost any kind. This is not to say that management is not possible. It is only that humans are not the managers. The only one capable of management would have to be able to direct specific individuals without simplification or categorization. This is a task not possible for the extremely limited human faculties. The farmer of a single acre of wheat can hardly know each plant without simplification and categorization, even though she knows each plant is unique.

Given that civilization is management, this deals a fatal blow to the myth of civilization, which evacuates civilization of its self-appointed meaning. Nonstate peoples have seen this as they have resisted assimilation into civilization. But such resistance is now futile with the power of advanced technology. Civilization and its management is domination. The difference between ancient and modern civilizations is that systems of technique have replaced individuals and their court elites. Our masters are now faceless and non-responsible systems, which are infinitely harder to overthrow.

---

10. See Charles Taylor on the "Age of Authenticity" in *A Secular Age* and *Modern Social Imaginaries.*

Belief: Humans Are Right to Manage and Management is Good

Human management is believed to be good in the myth of civilization—good for both the managers and the managed. The managed includes other humans, as well as the creation. As good, it is also justified. I take this belief as obvious and do not need to give space to elaborating on it. Let us only look at two problems with this belief.

The first problem is that human management works by outsourcing virtue or character, thus is not good for either managed or managing humans. In order to manage effectively, we must simplify that which is managed. We have "human resources" who work for corporations. Their individual stories are relatively meaningless. Employees are disposable functionaries. In order for a single farmer to effectively farm thousands of acres, we have to monocrop and adapt our crops to our machines. We have to turn land, soil, and seed into economic inputs. But a farmer who sits all day in a GPS-controlled combine is also a disposable functionary. When we replace humans with machines, or *mētis* with *technē*, we give up a very human ability to learn new skills, and by these skills, we give up the potentiality of character or virtue. Humans submitted to function become efficient specialists, not virtuous people. Character comes by trial and testing. This is obvious to any athlete. In the absence of testing, character cannot form.[11] This is simply a restatement of the earlier dialectic of adaptation to the cosmos. In an environment that poses few challenges, there are few reasons to learn how to adapt. When food is given, or bought for nominal costs, it is not valued and is justifiably wasted. When work is not physical, physical skill and strength have no reason to develop. When courage is never required, it is never developed. This goes for any possible virtue. The more highly we manage the natural world, the less we must adapt ourselves. The most valued virtues in a highly managed world are conformity, specialization, and efficiency—exactly the priorities of modern education. Other virtues are outsourced to machines and techniques, including such basic virtues as physical strength and endurance. This militates against the goodness of human management for humans themselves. It is a deskilling of humanity. Human management is not entirely beneficial for humans. Yet, this would seem the prime motive for engaging in such management.

The second problem is that management is clearly not good for the creation. It is not mismanagement that has produced ecological disaster,

---

11. A point St. Paul understood in Rom 5:3–4.

but management itself. We've already said most of what needs to be said. Management reduces and simplifies the creation, destroying diversity. This is necessary to management given our inability to comprehend much particularity without simplification. In order to make the natural world legible we have to simplify it to a degree of our own understanding. The greater our management, the more we have to simplify. This will necessarily lead to ecological problems in the form of destruction of habitat, species, and soil, as we reduce the complexity in our imagination, and then in the world itself. As we have come to know more about the necessity of complexity and diversity in the health of ecosystems, it has meant that preservation by managing human management is the only feasible method of care.

Historical lessons reveal that the highest civilizations of the ancient world were the most ecologically destructive, but those who practiced shifting cultivation, or slash and burn agriculture, seemed to know something of the limits of their environment. This is primarily because they were well adapted to their local conditions and did not pursue universality or management. Their practices "had 'backwardness' written all over it."[12] In a sense this purposefully limited management or non-management produced highly sustainable practices with yields greater than modern industrial practices. Some diversity was maintained; land was given years of fallowing that preserved soil quality. Such sustainable practices cannot be incorporated to state management. Shifting cultivation represents a massive lost opportunity cost and waste of labor from a modern industrialist's perspective. Property is somewhat nonexistent in such a world. Polycropped fields are very difficult to tax, as they produce a variety of crops at different times and of varying value. Shifting cultivators are illegible people to a state.

This also highlights a further problem of management: it must seek to become universal. Managing people through politics cannot really be separable from economic and agricultural management. Indeed, early states arose precisely through agricultural management by the forcible settling of peoples. This required managing both land and people to produce and extract the necessary crop surpluses to support a palace (and temple) system. So, Scott talks about how management or domestication of the natural world led to the domestication of humans, whose bodies, schedules, and imaginations all turned to serve the few plant species they

12. Scott, *Seeing Like a State,* 283.

cultivated. "Once Homo sapiens took that fateful step into agriculture, our species entered an austere monastery whose taskmaster consists mostly of the demanding genetic clockwork of a few plants . . . ."[13] Management of land and people are inextricably linked, as people become accustomed to what they serve. In order to manage such a situation, techniques of managing all of its aspects are required. Thus, the goodness and rightness of managing the world necessitates the goodness and rightness of managing humans. The wider the scope of our natural management, the necessarily wider the scope of management of humans. The state was only made possible by grain agriculture. So also, globalization is only possible by greater control. Ecological justice is inextricable from social justice, because management of humans creates ecological injustice, and vice-versa, as observed by Pope Francis, for example.[14]

This brings us to a major problem of proposed ecological solutions. The greater we attempt to centralize control of human civilization in order to better manage the natural world, the more both will have to serve technique, and thus be stripped of diversity. Control cannot promote real diversity. Even if the United Nations is able to form some great coalition with the necessary political power to enforce ecologically friendly practices, it will involve empowering an elite whose very existence as elites is predicated on control. There is little reason to believe in the myth of a benevolent dictator capable of total management for the good of all, whether it be Plato's philosopher king, or modern technical political systems backed up by the force of infinitely powerful arms. As Pope Francis recognizes, such solutions will require political will and effective enforcement on a global scale.[15] Such a global government would be entirely free of accountability if it has power to enforce its political will. Political solutions may temporarily restrict the disasters of climate change or soil depletion, but there is no historical evidence that suggests such an empowerment will lead to liberty for people or the planet. As Ellul says, "To believe that dictatorship is a bridge to freedom is to perform an absurd act of faith with no rational, factual, or sociological basis, and is the ideology of pure propaganda."[16]

13. Scott, *Against the Grain*, 91.
14. Francis, *Laudato Si*, 48.
15. Francis, *Laudato Si*, Chapter 5.
16. Ellul, *Autopsy of Revolution*, 161.

Ultimately, there is no logical position from which humans can judge the goodness of their management, given that the terms of evaluation are integral to the cosmos itself. Management is obviously good, *because without management there can be no evaluation.* Evaluation is only possible by definition and categorization, which is how the cosmos is created. Evil exists only as that which is unmanaged and unable to be evaluated. It is condemned, of course, but it is not understood. If it could be understood, it would no longer be chaos. Put another way, management is the source of our ability to declare something good. Evaluation of civilization must come from outside perspectives. As this has come by foreign civilizations or nonstate peoples it is generally unable to be heard. Civilizational critiques from outside are the incomprehensible babble of barbarians.

Belief: Human Management Is Cumulative, Progressive, and Necessary

The final belief to observe in the myth of civilization is that human management is cumulative, progressive, and necessary. These three features work together. Cumulative management is integral to the myth, shown by our belief in "development." The only reason to increase *technē* is that we believe it is good and will be better. Development indeed has a cumulative effect. As the cosmos is able to incorporate more and more into itself, the presence of chaos recedes. The possibility of intrusions from outside becomes more limited. This also means that any chaos that does intrude will have to be of an incredible scale, realized in the fears expressed in the genre of disaster movies—epidemics, asteroids, globally devastating volcanic actions, sea-level rise, space-alien invasion, or nuclear war.

Management is also progressive. That is, it moves from worse to better. I keep reiterating this because it is so vital: management has to see itself as good and justified. That also means that any increase in management must be a good thing. The objection that revolutions have brought more free national regimes, as in, for example, the American or French Revolutions, is false. As with the Russian Revolution of 1917, the Bolsheviks found that increased control was necessary on the mythical road to the dictatorship of the proletariat. The paternalistic vanguard party, in order to compete and modernize with the West, and to recover the economy of Russia, engaged in incredible campaigns of violence and control.

This sort of violence was necessary and justified, as Trotsky argued.[17] The American Revolution led to greater taxation and control than had been present in the British Empire, as well as increased justification for violent and deceitful appropriation of Native American lands through doctrines like Manifest Destiny. The French Revolution dramatically increased the power and reach of the central government. To assume that the over-throw of an individual monarch or emperor is a victory for freedom is false.[18] Such a belief is only made possible by the transition of governance with *mētis* to a governance by *technē*. In France this led to standardiza-tions of language that eliminated cultural diversities that had existed un-der the monarchy. Authoritarian rule by an *Ancien Régime* style monarch involves a self-limited scope of management. Rule by system, the great invention of the eighteenth century, achieved greater and more efficient management while it also eliminated the ability to destroy the political rulership by simply executing a king or figurehead. If a level of freedom were marked by the ability to choose an alternative, the great revolutions have led to far less freedom. The irony is that the great revolutions of liberty set up systems more resilient to the very same kind of future lib-eration movement that must begin in a revolt. As Ellul says,

> With each surge of human freedom, the State grew stronger by pledging to secure the very freedom it absorbed. . . . But the very essence of that constant contradiction between intention and realization [of freedom] compels us to recognize that *revolution is finally the crisis of the development of the state.*[19]

Thus, revolutions and liberations have done little more than improve the state and reduce human liberty by creating managed rights and liberties granted by a powerful state.

So, it is difficult to identify the reality of progress. For anyone well integrated into a cosmos, it is a great challenge to evaluate alternatives from some neutral point of observation. The progressive aspect of civili-zation can be evaluated, however, provided we produce a narrative with more than two points of comparison. When the myth of civilization is told as moving from savagery to *us*, these two points can only ever pro-duce a line based on the feature we want to graph. Usually this becomes a progressive line, moving up. If we introduce further points, the picture

17. Trotsky, *Terrorism and Communism*.

18. Chomsky, *Understanding Power*.

19. Emphasis original. Ellul, *Autopsy of Revolution*, 163.

becomes far more complex. If we finally ask how we are defining the terms of the graph, the whole thing becomes a mess. Civilization is not simply progressive. It has involved numerous missteps and failures. Ecologically speaking, we may be moving toward a global realization of the very features that led to ancient civilizational "collapses." The narrative of collapse—whether of the Roman Empire, the Greek Dark Age, or the Angkor-Khmer empire—is often used to support the narrative of progress. Civilization barely "survived" these periods. Only with the help of this or that people did culture (i.e., what matters to later humans) survive. Scott strongly critiques these narratives of collapse. What does collapse even mean in anthropologically verifiable ways? It means the dissolution or destruction of the monumental central court, with the consequent loss of social complexity, literacy, monumental building, decline of trade networks, and decline of specialist craft. These losses do not necessarily mean population decline or a decline in general human health and welfare. In fact, they often lead to an improvement in these latter areas. And a collapse does not mean the loss of culture, it means that culture is decentralized.[20]

Collapse actually can lead to an increase in general human welfare. But this is not the story we are told in the myth of civilization, which focuses on the role of management and the managers. When management fails, we deem that the whole has collapsed, even when general welfare improves. However, the more advanced and all-encompassing *technē* becomes, the more disastrous the consequences of its demise. The collapse of modern civilization will lead to massive population decline, given that immense geographical areas are incapable of sustaining themselves without constant inputs of basic necessities like food and water, factors that were less true in the ancient world. That is, because we live in the technical environment, the collapse of technique or management will destroy our environment, reducing the carrying capacity of most regions, not to mention the deskilling and specialization that would render considerable portions of the population incapable of adaptation. This means that the belief in progress is misplaced. On the one hand, management has encompassed far more than previously possible through systemization. On the other hand, this has made all of humanity dependent for survival and wellbeing on a fragile system over which no one exercises any real control. The larger and more complex the system is, the less manageable

20. Scott, *Against the Grain*, 185–86.

the system itself is. This means the progress of management is an inversion of human power. By systematization each individual is relatively disempowered so that the whole, represented as a simplified, projected, and reified "civilization," becomes powerful. Management is not progress, it is the exchange of liberty, as Ellul says,

> The state becomes more tyrannical as it becomes more abstract. Man delegates to the state his responsibility for solving the problems of his society and is trapped thereby in the rigorous and inhuman system. That is the issue, and there is no chance that one day a state will repent and become liberal or personal, the servant of man.[21]

The cost/benefit ratio of this relationship between management and liberty is difficult to consider from any objective point of view, however, because no one occupies such a point of view. Again, outside voices can be used to offer alternatives.

Management is also believed to be *necessary* as part of the structure of cumulative progress. This has been highly present in the so-called "Whig view of history."[22] The view that technology must progress, that humans must grow more intelligent, that we can solve any problem of management that comes our way, is fairly well engrained in popular civilizational understandings. A reified science is able to fix any problem. This necessity is patently absurd, however. It is based on the imaginative creation of a non-human being with will, benevolence, and power that is capable of making progress happen. It is fair to say that the gods of civilization have never disappeared, they have only been depersonalized. God is not dead, god is the projection of the people themselves, as Xenophanes, Feuerbach, Durkheim, and others have noted. Only, modern people are quite easily confused by the depersonalization of a god and the reification of a system, mistaking this as some kind of intellectual progress. The reality behind the old gods and the new is the same—they are all human imaginary constructs. The cosmos is socially constructed and the forces of power within the cosmos are reified and projected. It is simply not plausible within our cosmos to make the gods personal beings with personal stories, though the nature of corporations and nation-states is rather near to this.

21. Ellul, *Autopsy of Revolution*, 270.

22. A term coined by Herbert Butterfield in *The Whig Interpretation of History* (Cambridge: 1931). Whig history is basically a simplistic abridged history that holds that everything is progressing to the present.

Management is only necessary to those who are dependent upon it. Because management is empowered for a purpose, it must be capable of that purpose, or so the thinking goes. And because management is the realm of technique, it is not dependent upon the will of people for its advance. Lost in this broken pattern of thinking, however, is the reality that humans are indeed responsible for all that the system does, and it is collective human faith alone that empowers *techne* and renders it necessary.

Practically speaking, ancient civilization was simply not necessary. For "ninety-five percent of the human experience on earth—we lived in small, mobile, dispersed, relatively egalitarian, hunting-and-gathering bands."[23] So, civilization is obviously not in our DNA. Furthermore, early states were incredibly fragile, so that "it is their rare appearance and even rarer persistence that requires explanation."[24] We have it backwards if we think civilization is normal or necessary. To think otherwise is the classic mistake of a subtraction story. But it is a mistake that thinkers have made for millennia.

Chaos and Civilization: Anarchy and Order

What then, is the opposite of civilization? In the myth of civilization it is barbarism, savagery, "dark ages," and their supposedly attendant form of evil non-governance known as *anarchy*. Recall that in the previous chapter we saw that chaos has no real existence. It is a social projection of that which lies outside of the cosmos. Anarchy has often been endued with the guise of a chaos monster. Theologians like John Calvin, who helped lead a significant social upheaval by his theological leadership, justified submitting the new Reformed church movement to the power of the state because of a fear of anarchy. Calvin expresses this fear and misunderstanding well, and his words speak a very common sentiment,

> It is better to live under the most cruel tyrant than without any government at all. Let us suppose all to be on one equal level, what would such anarchy bring forth? No one would wish to yield to others; every one would try the extent of his powers, and thus all would end in prey and plunder, and in the mere license of fraud and murder, and all the passions of mankind would have full and unbridled sway. Hence I have said, tyranny

23. Scott, *Against the Grain,* 5.
24. Scott, *Against the Grain,* 183.

is better than anarchy, and more easily borne, because where there is no supreme governor there is none to preside and keep the rest in check.[25]

Civilization is endangered by anarchy. This is a given because civilization has its roots as a concept in the idea of governance and management. Any management is better than none. True freedom is evil, liberty that is granted by power is good. According to Calvin, then, lack of liberty is better than radical freedom, which is *obviously* too dangerous to even entertain. Somehow Calvin did not consider that management can exponentially increase evil by unity. As we consider ecology, this means that any "development" or property is better than wildland or wilderness. This is, of course, what chaos has looked like throughout human cosmologies. And by extension of Calvin's reasoning, few today would believe that the undoing of civilization is a reasonable proposal for the sake of saving the environment. Bad management—i.e., what we currently have—is better than no management.

But this understanding of anarchy is a cartoon characterization. Not only does it fail to engage with the thought of anarchist theorists, it also ignores or is ignorant of anthropological history. Obviously this is a rather anachronistic critique for Calvin. As Scott noted, 95 percent of the history of our species has been lived in a "savage" or "barbaric" condition, which was "relatively egalitarian." Civilization requires hierarchy of a wide variety of forms. It requires social hierarchies in which there are at the very least nobility and workers. The nobility's existence is entirely predicated on the production of surpluses by the workers or peasants. That is, peasants have to produce more than is necessary for the propagation and preservation of their own families to feed the court and all of its retinue. When we add to this system a major city, we add a third class of specialist tradespeople and merchants. All of these likewise must be fed by agricultural surpluses. Living in a world of modern industrial agriculture it is often easy to miss this fact. Almost the entirety of human civilization has been made possible by extracted labor by people forcibly resettled into an agricultural core. So, again, "It would be almost impossible to exaggerate the centrality of bondage, in one form or another, in the development of the state until very recently."[26] Tyranny is the basis of civilization, as it forcibly extracts the lives and the livelihoods of many

25. Calvin, *Commentary on Daniel* (4:13).
26. Scott, *Against the Grain*, 155.

people for the sake of a very few. The population of classical Athens, the very home of myths of Western Civilization,[27] was about two-thirds slave. Aristotle, like everyone else in Greek aristocracy, saw certain people as born for slavery, as we saw at the beginning of this chapter. Sparta had an entire people group, the Helots, who were enslaved to them to produce food. Rome captured millions of people in their expansive wars for slavery.[28] The famed Spartan warriors could spend all day training for war precisely because everything else was done for them. Aristotle had the temerity, from our perspective, to talk about virtue when he likely never did a day of manual labor in his life. Indeed, there is a reason hard-work is not a classical virtue—it belongs to slaves. Earlier civilizations, like those of Babylon, Sumer, Assyria, as well as those of Egypt and China, were entirely dependent upon slavery of various kinds.

Modernity would *seem* to fare better. After all, slavery is outlawed in nearly all nations globally. This is a massive achievement in liberty. But it is only rendered feasible by techniques of exploitation that have made slavery economically impractical. As I noted earlier, Adam Smith observed that the economics of slavery were suspect. "It appears, accordingly, from the experience of all ages and nations, I believe, that the work done by freemen comes cheaper in the end than that performed by slaves." Smith's historical knowledge was limited, and that limitation significantly damages the accuracy of his beliefs and opinions in *The Wealth of Nations* (Smith was a master of the genre of "subtraction story"). Though he was probably wrong about the cost of slavery in the ancient world, slaves being relatively cheap in some civilizations, his work reveals that in his world, work done by slaves was indeed "the dearest of any." Emancipation did transform societies by the elimination of a class of people who were legally unable to own property or participate in government. But the alternative, which was often called "wage-slavery," is now simply called "employment." Even Adam Smith, who is not really the economic libertarian he is usually made out to be, understood that the apparent social contract between employer and employee was by no means equal. He understood that employers, which he still calls "masters," can outlast workers in labor disputes, they have reserves, and they are fewer in

27. For a critique of the narrative of "Western Civilization" see Graeber, *The Democracy Project*.

28. Scott, *Against the Grain*, 156.

number and can conspire far more easily. Smith even argues for a living wage to combat this inequality.[29]

It is thus debatable whether modernity represents a superior condition of employment than other systems. Wage-slavery continues the deep inequality upon which civilization is built. Indeed, by globalization and the centralization enabled by technology, wealth inequality has never been greater throughout human history. This is not a matter of moral choice. It is a systematic necessity of civilization.

Modernity has largely escaped enslaving humans because it has, through technology, succeeded in enslaving the natural world to a degree not previously possible. By the power and efficiencies of machinery, human labor became inefficient and expensive. The real liberation of slaves has occurred by turning the creation into a (supposedly) well-tuned machine for the production of products. Of course, the creation is not a machine, and to imagine so is a massive simplification that has had wildly unanticipated and disastrous consequences. Climate change and soil depletion are examples of what happens when you starve and overwork a slave. Human slavery can only cease when creation-slavery is fully achieved. One is exchanged for the other.

Just as human bodies are turned into products or capital for production for business owners, a process called commodification, so too the natural world is commodified by ownership. Early states who turned to settled agricultural production by a slave or peasant population not only commodified the people, but also the land they worked. This problem is not alleviated in modernity, it is exacerbated. By the ownership of all land, private or public, land is transformed into a means for the production of wealth. This perspective, this imaginary, is fundamentally parasitic. The correct conceptual solution is not in a living wage for employees or for the land (i.e., sustainability), but emancipation or liberation.

Anthropological prehistory shows that humans do not need to be managed. The fact that the earth long predates human civilization also shows that human management is not necessary for the creation to thrive. Management, the essence of civilization, is not necessary and it is problematic.

That said, the abandonment of management, called "rewilding," may be an effective way of restoring something of what has been lost in

29. Smith, *The Wealth of Nations*, 96–97.

the nonhuman world. However, rewilding human society would require significant sacrifices. Jacques Ellul put it this way,

> A revolution against the technological society (not against technology) implies decreased efficiency in all areas (total yield, productivity, adaptiveness, integration), a lowered standard of living, the reduction of large-scale public programs, and the erosion of a mass culture. If we are unwilling to pay the combined price of those four reductions, then we are not ready for revolution, the only revolution that is a necessity today.[30]

Rewilding humans is only barely more plausible than sending a chihuahua out into the wild. We are adapted and transformed. We are civilized. Like Enkidu, the wild animals no longer speak with us and we can no longer eat grass. What then is the solution? As I will argue, the most viable solution is actually theological, not primarily practical. Calls for a renewed primitivism based in paleoanthropology, and other intentionally regressive perspectives are not plausible because they are literally unimaginable for the vast majority of well-integrated people. They are perspectives that can only be chosen by an experience of integration into an unmanaged, natural world. No state would consider any such imposition, which would disempower it entirely. Even the best the United Nations can muster is "sustainable development" a completely fantastic belief that "development" is good, and could ever be sustainable.

We can neither live in a futurist utopia, which will inevitably involve ever more management of everything and the increasing transformation of human self-imagination towards computerization and excarnation; nor can we "get back to the garden" of the supposed innocence of primitive hunter-gatherers. As it is, there are relatively few transhumanists, and even fewer anarcho-primitivists, who represent these two logically consistent, if extreme perspectives.

So, we are stuck within a myth of civilization, a myth that necessarily is destroying creation. This is what I have been calling a broken imagination. We are seemingly incapable of thinking our way out of this problem. One of the major reasons for this is simply our inability to manage ourselves. A second reason is our interminable need to mythologize this situation, which provides justification. Until we are capable of realizing that *we are the problem*, we have no reason to expect improvement. Before turning to solutions we will spend the next five short chapters

---

30. Ellul, *Autopsy of Revolution*, 281.

investigating some of the shape of the modern cosmos and see how they all present to us no-exit situations.

These five chapters are representative of some of the most sacred values of our time. They involve material value in economics, human management in politics, material power in technology, self-understanding in notions of identity, and the microcosm of all of these put together in the city. There are other factors that play into our myth of our cosmos, but these are among the most determinative today.

CHAPTER 4

Economic Imaginary

WE BEGIN OUR SHORT chapters on the modern imaginary and its con-
comitant no-exit situation with economics. These five aspects of the
imaginary: economics, politics, technology, identity, and the city, all
work together to form a sum greater than its parts. Of course other areas
than these five could be identified, but these are representative.

Modern economics is formed by two contradictory beliefs. First, we
believe that the earth is a storehouse of limited resources that humans
attempt to rightfully manage and justly distribute according to various
systems. Secondly, we believe that the earth's resources are functionally
infinite and also a nearly bottomless sink for pollutants. This latter belief is now finally being questioned as plastic pollution in the oceans has
reached incredible levels. As the earth runs out of a certain resource, we
believe technology will provide a solution by replacing it with an alternative resource, or finding ways to access more. The problem of "peak oil"
in the early 2000s was solved by the invention of fracking, which will tide
the global economy over until renewables can finally replace fossil fuels.
This instructive example is assumed to be something of a natural law.
Technology will fix it, even if fracking has had demonstrably disastrous
"side-effects."[1]

These two beliefs are contradictory as the first rests on the idea of
value by scarcity and the second on a belief in abundance and harm-
lessness. Somehow we hold these two beliefs and they do not seem to
contradict. We believe in creating value now by maximally efficient

---

1. All effects in a system, technology, or drug, are independent of human intention.
Side-effects are called such by marketing or propaganda, covering for a lack of control.

extractions and that future value is guaranteed by technology's seeming necessary progress opening new avenues of efficiencies, resources, and methods of extraction. All modern economic systems depend on these companion myths. Capitalism and socialism both see the prospect of future growth as necessary, and the source of value for today. This is why we can justify our global debt-economy. A debt is nothing more than a future promise of repayment, and the interest on a debt is a measure of an anticipated growth rate of wealth. If the interest rate exceeds the rate of income growth, then we'll get behind. If our income growth rate exceeds our debt interest rate, we will be able to use debt to capitalize and increase our wealth at a greater rate than not having debt, since we can invest as though we had more money than we actually do. This is true on a personal, corporate, national, and international level. Now, financial debt is merely a social construct. It is a system of trust, enforced with teeth. Again, this is true on all levels, unless you have the biggest military, then you don't ever have to repay your debts because no one can collect, as Graeber has shown.[2]

But if the second of these beliefs (unlimited resources and sink) turns out to be false, which it most certainly is, then the whole economic system becomes a self-deceptive, irrational, and irresponsible race for maximal wealth extraction before the end. Furthermore, if this second belief is false, economics becomes a pseudoscience. Economics is properly understood as materialist religion, with the differing systems merely offering incompatible ways to a very similar utopia or heaven. There are founding prophets in Adam Smith or Karl Marx, both of whom, like the Bible, are seldom read but whose simplified views represent gospel truth. Both capitalism and socialism offer ideal realities accessible by idealized systems of human and resource management. Those ideal realities are actually rather similar—material prosperity for the greatest number of people. They differ primarily on how to get there.

Capitalism rests on the belief that all value is economic. Everything is potentially capital and potentially exploitable for wealth creation. Capitalism sees the creation of wealth and the further means of wealth creation as the source of value. Ecologically speaking this is entirely unjustifiable. It means that nothing has value until it is turned into property or a resource that can be bought, sold, and exploited. Humans are included in this as labor, even if they only sell themselves or their services

2. Graeber, *Debt*.

on a temporary basis. Furthermore, capitalism assigns value to inequalities based in the idea of scarcity. It is important to note that scarcity is a socially constructed reality as well. It is a belief bound to a perspective that chooses to see things as limited and therefore subject to competitive value. Darwinian biology shares this same problematic belief, rooted as it is in economic thinking applied as a theory to historical biological data. Counterintuitively, scarcity is not the source of value, it is the justification of value. That is, scarcity is a chosen perspective that legitimizes competition for resources rather than sharing of resources. Scarcity or abundance are perspectival belief choices, not natural laws. The irony is that each perspective tends to reproduce its perspective on reality in reality. Scarcity legitimizes competition, which encourages competition and a race for rapid exploitation—the so-called "tragedy of the commons." This, in turn, leads to an actual scarcity as a people overexploit local environments. Abundance, by contrast, leads to a relative abundance, because it encourages sharing, which ensures that the carrying capacity of a local environment is rarely reached or exceeded, barring natural disasters.

Capitalism is a very basic form of parasitism. It reduces everything to a constituent material reality, and systematically creates the conditions in which maximal exploitation, which is called "development," is the highest good. If any other parasite or invasive species could develop a worldview, it would be one in which everything were rightly exploited for personal profit, and it would call this "good." That capitalism leads to the common good by using private vice for common virtue is irrational fideism. This faith-statement is only plausible when the common good systematically excludes the entire non-human world, and often a significant portion of the human world. Capitalism may be partly responsible for the increase in an absolute level of wealth across the planet, but in so doing, it must bear much responsibility for ecological devastation.

That said, socialism does not fare much better. Although capitalism is one of the most basic forms of exploitative materialism, socialism is a humanist-materialism. Socialism extracts human needs from the environment and prioritizes human needs above all else. Because socialism shares the belief in value by growth, it too aims to create wealth for all by continual expansion. The dream of Marx was that human wealth would grow to the point at which no one would have to work, then everyone would be equal because there would be such abundance that none would have any need of experiencing scarcity. But in order to get to this dream of communism, we have to go through the necessary stages of wealth-creation in capitalism. This never materialized in history, because Marx, like many others, makes the mistake that absolute wealth is not tied to relative wealth. It does not matter if everyone has enough food, water, and shelter, so long as someone else has something scarce and desirable. Communism cannot be built through resource exploitation. A primitive form of what Graeber calls "baseline communism" seems to have preexisted any intentional form of economic exploitation.[3] Anthropologists suggest that pre-civilized peoples experienced something of an abundance of diverse foods, and had little reason to compete, though not without exception.

The problem is that *all* materialist perspectives are exploitative. Though I do not have space to detail a critique of secularism and religion, I will briefly state the problem with materialist humanism as evidenced in secularism.

Secularism is a form of materialism manifest in the ostensible elimination or bracketing of any notion of transcendence, or determinative non-material reality. Secularism turns human belief into a resource for exploitation. It is the politically savvy perspective that utilizes the beliefs of a people to consolidate power. Religious tolerance is no victory for humanity, it is the victory of states that finally figured out that tolerance leads to an incredible ability to consolidate power by reorienting belief toward the nation. Rather than simply a liberation of humanity from superstition (though it involves some of that), secularism deifies human will. This has the double effect of eliminating a deity to whom we are answerable for our behavior, and separating humanity from the world. Ironically, secularism requires an irrationally idealized humanity, like the great "we" that landed on the moon. It involves a thoroughly religious belief in our species identity that necessarily devalues the rest of the non-human world by turning it into matter. Its terminus is in transhumanism that sees the human will extracted from matter itself. Put simply, secularism is self-idolatry. Ironically, it is not otherworldly religions that are responsible for ecological disaster, it is an all-too-worldly humanist secularism that truly despises matter by making it the sole carrier of value, and the sole object upon which the human will might express itself.

Socialism is the economic model that best fits this collective humanist materialism. Rather than a focus on wealth through competition with other people, socialism focuses on the expression of the human

---

3. Graeber, *Debt*, 98–99.

will over matter. The material world becomes the potentially formless clay upon which we can impress an image of ourselves. This means that socialism turns to godlike collectivities of human will, currently shared between the state, corporations, and NGOs that all seek to do good for humanity. But we also know that help from above creates a paternalism that devalues personal virtue. If indeed we attained the Marxist ideal of such a great surplus of wealth that we all could become aristocrats there would be no incentive toward virtue or will. Because the surplus would be created by a collective, individual virtue would be unnecessary. Such a situation almost begs for a vanguard party to intervene and dominate those who have not developed a will-to-power or personal virtue.

Economics is itself problematic. Our contemporary world is infected with two nearly equally virulent belief systems little different in passion or commitment than the religions of our ancestors. Both of these socially constructed belief systems reinforce ecological devastation. Neither has any resources within them for ecological renewal, because both refuse to place humanity back within the world. The imaginary solution cannot be secular. It cannot involve a materialist perspective. It must be a sublation of older religious and modern materialist perspectives. Neopaganism is insufficient for the task, because it is an attempt of materialist peoples to recreate gods and practices long since made implausible. Nor is a simplistic return to older forms of religions like Christianity, Judaism, Islam, or preaxial religions plausible. We cannot put the genie of materialism back in its bottle. We must go beyond by a new conversion. Christianity can do this, but not by a regressive return to older forms, as we will see. But we cannot imagine that any religion will do; or that all religions offer some helpful resource that a tolerant secular practitioner can use. As noted earlier, this type of secularism turns religion itself into a resource for exploitation, thus adding historical peoples and their beliefs to the list of valuable cultural deposits to be appropriated and repurposed.

Economics attempts to create a *system of valuation* as though valuation lay outside of the collective human will. It is a vast mathematical religion. It is a projection and reification. There is no such thing as the Market, except in the collective imagination. Any ecological future must involve killing this god, and learning to carve new values on new tables. For this to happen, however, requires something that will make modern economics implausible. The only conceivable thing that could do this would be a disaster so great that we finally achieve a level of scarcity so great that feelings of community outweigh desire for competition and we learn to view whatever resources we have as abundant and share them. In other words, the death of the gods of the economy will not be plausible until after it is too late. Economics, as an imaginary, is therefore entirely incapable of solving our ecological problems. It is, rather, one of the root problems of the broken and parasitic human imagination.

CHAPTER 5

Political Imaginary

POLITICS, AS WITH THE other elements of the modern imaginary we are discussing, is only part of a complex. Politics, at is most basic, is the management of people and their competitive values using active methods and systems of control and influence.

In one sense, politics has always been an illusion. It is the illusion of control that is created when things conspire to fit the will of a people. Just as a president or CEO takes credit for the boons a country or company enjoys during their tenure, so also they shift blame when things go badly wrong. Politics is by nature illusory, a nature perfected today. All people live in the greatest emergency humankind has ever faced. All other emergencies our species has faced have resided outside of the influence of intentional human causality or solution. The ecological problems we currently face are human caused and well within the domain of humans to solve. But desperate times call for desperate actions. It is only by incredibly radical changes to the current norms and current projected course of actions that the survival of millions of species and any semblance of our way of life can be ensured.

As with all calls for desperate action, the call will be for a centralized power with an effective police force. Pope Francis sees that nations lack the political will to accomplish what is necessary. Historical attempts at ecological improvement or care have been bold but unenforceable and generally unimplemented. He recognizes that political power has been weakened by the interests of transnational corporations. Short-term politics of party-based systems will continue to be ineffective because they are focused on pleasing the national will for reelection. So Francis suggests that we need enforceable international agreements and states that respect political sovereignty.[1] But Francis offers no indications of how this might work. This is not really a fault of his own, as it probably oversteps his modern boundaries as pope. It is a nice suggestion, but one that cannot be realized. National power respects the sovereignty of others only insofar as it lacks economic and military power to enforce its own will over other nations. Essentially, for Francis' somewhat naïve proposal to work, we would need all nations to be run by genuinely altruistic leadership. The real call, if we were to simply have international cooperation by empowering the United Nations, would be to disempower the superpowers. It would be a call to the Middle East to give up its economic base of power in oil. It would be a call to China to abandon its colonial ambitions of manufacturing domination and resource extraction through its aggressive international investment campaigns. What we would need would be a global international jubilee combined with a strategic disarmament campaign. But that really would lead to a dictatorship of the United Nations with no mechanism for accountability, which is hardly realistic or desirable.

Thus, we see that the political imagination is broken. Political bodies are pure social constructs, with nuclear teeth. This means their existence rests entirely on the collective will of the people. This belief is engrained with deeply held notions of identity, culture, language, and legendary histories. Political entities, as social constructs, are no less and no more real than any ancient goddess. As such, belief and loyalty to these social constructs will continue until they are met with a force of chaos that overwhelms such a deity, or by a generations-long process of decline. Theoretically, only after an international identity has surpassed the national identity in each nation will genuine, peaceful cooperation be feasible. Until then, there must be an emergency government, which has always meant one thing—dictatorship.

In a political crisis, the will of the people must be suspended and action taken based on the necessities of the situation for the preservation of the cosmos. The chaotic monster demands a superhuman hero. A Hitler demands a Churchill. At this point of climate crisis, the ends that will be pursued will be related to the cosmos we inhabit. That is, the primary objective will be the maintenance of the global status quo. The wealthy and powerful nations will have no reason to choose altruism,

---

1. *Laudato Si*, chapter 5.

and will only choose ecological goods if it does not upset the balance of power. It is, after all, those same nations that bear, by far, the responsibility for ecological devastation. This likely means that political solutions to climate change will only reinforce "climate apartheid."

In an emergency, power must be centralized and the inefficiencies of checks and balances must be suspended. The problem is that, once empowered, such systems rarely demobilize. Such a concentration of power will, if ecological disaster is averted (for now), continue a program of enforcement and centralization. Put another way, once we take the step toward the empowerment of a super-national political organization with power superior to any single nation, there is little reason to expect this to end. What we can expect in the face of general political ineptitude is the rise of a vanguard party who, like the Bolsheviks, will demand party loyalty and an extreme of political correctness.

The alternative end of the spectrum of the political imagination is radical libertarianism or anarchism. Nearly all theorists who have spoken about political liberty have understood it to be premised almost entirely on individual virtue. Liberty is a risk to society that relies on a general collective will to détente, respect, and self-control. But everything in our myth of civilization militates against the progress of individual virtue. Humans are now radically specialized and radically isolated. They depend upon countless given structures and technologies for their survival and cooperation. These do not promote *mētis,* but *technē.* The thorough deskilling of the population means that dependence on political solutions is now guaranteed. The only rational political solution to ecological disaster is self-control at all levels. Sustainability at this point in time is less a question of environmental issues, and more an issue of human will. Current ideas for solving climate change revolve around absurd technological panaceas, like artificially refrigerating glaciers, massively polluting the atmosphere to block solar radiation, and colonizing Mars. All of these demonstrate a lack of political will and personal virtue. They are all desperate, totalitarian solutions to maintain some semblance of the status quo without requiring any change to the systems that created the crisis. These represent the pinnacle of the type of vice represented by hyperspecialization and technocracy. This is a situation in which *technē* has entirely replaced *mētis.* There are no significant arguments or proposals for systems of reeducation, life-skills training in food production, water purification, and general neighborliness. At this point, "doing our bit" involves practices that reinforce our systems of ecological exploitation, like recycling. Recycling is, counterintuitively, ecologically problematic. As yet another system of efficiency, it increases the carrying capacity of the environment by enabling high levels of consumption with less immediate impact. Recycling would, of course, be an essential part of a sustainable (not sustainable-growth) situation. But in a world in which our economic and technological imaginations are enslaved to the idea of growth and progress, recycling merely postpones disaster, while soothing the moral conscience. In short, there is obviously no political will for cooperative solutions that empower a diverse people.

The world is as far from ready for self-rule as conceivable, and it is less plausible daily. And this is the broken political imagination. We have made for a no-exit political situation. The true political solution to ecological disaster—the rule of personal virtue and free cooperation of all peoples for a common good—is entirely implausible. Even the mere suggestion of this ideal form of anarchism will sound outrageous, so well-integrated are people into the present cosmos that the supposed chaos of anarchism is a greater evil than the projected ecological disasters themselves.

So, politics will be a necessary part of the solution to ecological disaster, and it must necessarily take the form of a centralized authority with greater power than any single nation or alliance of nations. This will require surveillance, policing, and party loyalty, all with violent consequences for disobedience. This will all be *necessary*. But it will not be good. And, it will not solve ecological problems. For, once such an international authority is empowered, it will have no plausible reason to ever stop the emergency. An institution must seek its own self-preservation, and so once humanity takes the step toward such a global authoritarianism, it is likely a final decision. Indeed, such a situation represents the final end of human imaginary brokenness. Humans will finally achieve godlikeness when they are unified, simplified, made fully legible. But at exactly such point we will have so entirely divested ourselves of responsibility by empowering artificial systems and technologies that it is questionable what human goods or virtues will remain. And as we've seen that the ecological problem rests significantly in the simplification inherent in cosmization, this political act of unification will inevitably demolish meaningful human diversity, and with it, the very cultural values we have enshrined throughout the history of civilization. This diversity is predicated on differences caused by history, adaptations to local conditions, and the vast array of minute determinants that go into smaller, isolated communities. A globally united humanity will share a significant number of determinants and will inhabit the same cosmos. Local adaptations will be superficial and nostalgic.

Politics forms the root of the myth of civilization. Simplification, legibility, and concentration of reluctant populations creating surpluses for a ruling urban elite created the cultures we so prize. It also often created ecological (and epidemiological) problems that led to its own demise. We have not yet learned the lesson that this very process is problematic, and so it will continue to be the myth put forward to solve ecological disasters that it itself created.

CHAPTER 6

Technological Imaginary

OUR THIRD ASPECT TO the modern imaginary is technology. We've already looked at *technē* and its relationship to *mētis*. *Technē* is not, in itself, a problem. The chief problem comes when *mētis* is subjugated to *technē*. In our time, the greatest geniuses are those who are most capable of adapting to a universal system, or to a computer system. Our modern Odysseus is a Steve Jobs or Elon Musk. These are people whose creative knowledge is totally adapted to the logic of serving technique. Rather than seeking to use technique to serve human ends, humans are sought to serve the advancement of technology. This is deeply problematic, because it represents a total no-exit situation. When humans live to serve technical systems, we have created a god to whom we have enslaved ourselves. Not only that, we have created a totalizing and artificial environment to which we adapt more and more. Technology is now an environment.[1] Our very means of expression and imagination have taken on the form of technology. Some instances are fairly obvious, like the ubiquity and invasiveness of the smartphone or social media. More pernicious is our adaptation to the logic of a computer. Computer "intelligence" is entirely *technē*. As such, a computerized imagination is one in which all the world is seen as decomposable into binary logic. The computerized imagination is as simplified as possible. No doubt a computer can create the vaunted "theory of everything." The very idea that there could be a theory of everything belies the subjugation of the human imagination to the computer. Such a theory of everything is only plausible to an imagination that has simplified everything by the creation of the world of the Forms.

1. Ellul, *The Technological System*.

Indeed, the theory of everything has long been known to humans. For Anaximander it was *Apeiron*. For Democritus it was the atom. For Plato it was the Good. For Anselm it was God, the being higher than which none can be conceived. For Hegel it was *Geist*. For the technical imagination it is . . . ? We do not yet have a name for it. In any case, it shares in these previous philosophical constructs. It is entirely depersonalized, of course. It is the projection of the ultimate simplification and reduction. It is what happens when all particularity is removed and all is made to adapt to the universal.

When the universal is a personified god, the demand to believe in and obey that god is total. That might lead to crusades. When that universal is *technē*, it necessitates the submission of all matter to its service. When we make a god out of technology, we necessarily sacrifice everything to this god. Ecologically speaking, this is disastrous colonialism. All creatures become decomposable to their constituent matter. Human embryos are sometimes called a "clump of cells." This type of simplification morally legitimizes anything. By depersonalizing and universalizing an embryo, it is no longer human. This is the same logic applied to industrially farmed chickens or cows. They are just protein products that exist for human consumption. People in the "developing" nations are just "developing" and therefore must be converted to serve *technē*. They must no longer practice their inefficient, isolated, and particular ways of life. They must join in service to the god by becoming "developed" and contributing to the global economy by exploiting their resources.

Technology is often vaunted for its ever-improving efficiency. And this introduces a common error in ecological thinking by disciples of technology, that efficiency is "green." This fails to understand in the very least what efficiency is, as though consuming fewer resources were a good in itself. Every environment has a carrying capacity. The earth has a carrying capacity, with enough resources to support a certain population of certain species. This is never fixed, of course, due to variations. But before human technology, the capacity was rather more stable. Technology raises the carrying capacity of an environment *for humans*, often by *lowering the carrying capacity for other species*. Technology and land-development is the specialization of land for human ends. This often ends up destroying habitat for more diverse creatures. For example, we know that bee populations have been in decline, likely due, in part, to vast tracts of monocrops and lawns, both of which act as deserts for bees who do not have enough variety to feed them throughout the season.

Pesticides likely play a role as well. It is obvious that rainforest deforestation for cattle-grazing land is a massive destruction in habitat for a huge diversity of species for the sake of a highly simplified food chain. grass, cattle, and humans. The consequences of this are globally disastrous and involve climate change, soil depletion, river pollution, species endangerment and destruction, and destruction of indigenous human habitats and ways of life. Efficiencies in fuel economy in automobiles represents a different example. Fuel efficiency reduces the consumer cost of fuel, which often leads to increased use and dependency on cars. Rather than reduce consumption, efficiencies tend to increase consumption to a maximal rate. This has been shown with building larger roads, for example. Larger roads do not reduce traffic, they increase it, because they encourage more usage and more development. As general volume increases, it spills over to side roads too, leading to worsening traffic across the board instead of on just a single road.[2] So, efficiency tends to increase consumption at the same time as it enables higher human populations and consumptions that outcompete other species.

Technology is further parasitic as an environment because it replaces the creation. Those who live in this environment have a *technē*-imagination. They are literally incapable of understanding the natural world or being in an unmediated relationship with it. That means they are systematically incapable of valuing the creation as it is, and as it might impose necessities on a person. Once thoroughly integrated into this imagination, it is nearly impossible to escape it. This means that the creation cannot but be assimilated and transformed into the technical cosmos. Development and growth are deemed necessary. Rivers are dammed for energy and water, with little regard for what is lost in the process. Mountains are torn down by layers for gravel, or seeped with cyanide to extract gold. All of this is justified by people who do not live anywhere near these sites, but demand the resources for wealth and progress. After all, a mountain is nothing more than the composition of gravel. To a mind that sees everything as a computer, this is indeed the case. But for those who have lived near the mountains, the whole is worth far more than the sum of its parts. A mountain is not decomposable without ceasing to be, and to the local person it has value far beyond what is conceivable to *technē*. Indeed, its greatest value lies in remaining untouched by humans.

---

2. Duranton and Turner, "The Fundamental Law of Road Congestion".

A key myth of technology is its ability to continually improve. "Technology doubles" is a phrase I have heard used as a colloquial misquote of Moore's Law, which is not really a law, of course. Moore's Law concerns the doubling of computing power in semiconductors every two years, usually related to the industry timeframe of improving manufacturing methods that miniaturize transistors. This period of progress has now come to the point of diminishing returns based on reaching the functional limits of silicon to resist voltage leaks. Although this was an observation about the speed of progress in manufacturing, colloquially it entered the imagination as a sort of natural law in which technology doubles every two years. This reveals something of how technical knowledge is mythologized into a belief in inevitable progress. This myth is problematic, because it reifies "technology" and makes it into an active agent of its own self-improvement. The reality behind the myth is an incredible continued investment in semiconductor fabrication, and a large amount of research and development. The sources of funding for this investment are rarely questioned, like the source of rare earth minerals used in many computer components. The point is, technology has become reified and self-willing. There is a deep-seated need in the human technical imagination to use technology as a mirror of the projected self-image. Androids and robots in science fiction are some of the most obvious examples. The idea that humans would make humanoid robots is rather comical, in a way. The human form among all the animals is among the least specialized. The main physiological superiority of humans over all other species is the size of our brain, which is related to the smallness of our gut, probably related to the use of fire to externalize digestion.[3] In most other aspects humans are weaker. Now, since a robot has no physiological need of reproduction, digestion, respiration, waste processing and excretion, there is no practical advantage to its being in humanoid form. It can be made faster on wheels. It can be more nimble over terrain by being spider-like. It would be more stable on three or four legs. It would be stronger with a thicker base. But there is some deep desire to create a mechanical mirror, like a child playing with a doll.

While all of that is entertaining enough in science fiction it shows that the imagination is never confined to the mind, but is externalized through construction. The fact that we desperately desire to create human-like machines demonstrates how we have already merged into

3. Scott, *Against the Grain*, 40–41.

a technology-shaped cosmos. We have already integrated ourselves into a world in which we, trying to be like gods, end up acting like children and turning the creation into an elaborate doll house in which we would prefer our own creations to act out a virtual reality. We would rather see our constructed creations fill a dying world than see a healthy world filled with more highly complex and varied creatures entirely outside of our ability to manage. That does not bode well for the future of the earth. And this speaks again to an important feature of our parasitism—it is not intentional. It is that we have a broken imagination. We are stuck in the mirror state of Lacanian psychoanalysis staring at a self-alienated vision of ourselves in order to try and find some stable notion of ourselves. Thus, technology creates a no-exit situation because its entire *raison d'être* is predicated on alienating humans from the natural world. Technology cannot solve ecological problems because it is itself the antithesis of ecology.

CHAPTER 7

Imagination of Identity

THE CONCEPT OF IDENTITY is a curious one that has become particularly relevant in recent modernity through identity politics. Until the near total domination of secular ideology, identities were understood as given and relational, as we saw previously with our brief discussion on names. Only in rare circumstances could identities emerge as something of a personal choice. Now, however, secularism has liberated a diversity of self-definitions by uniting people under the banner of an all-encompassing universal human species identity. These subdivisions of identity are therefore able to be chosen because they do not generally affect the legal status or safety of the individual. This freedom to be whatever we want to be has led to new divisions within society that are less ideological and more related to the relationship of a social construct and the biological realities of the human species. The source of unity that enables superficial diversities is the massive simplification that comes by being politically, economically, and technologically managed. Whatever does not impact our ability to contribute to and be ruled by these systems is a free area of diversity.

Identity is one of the most obvious examples of a social construct, the purpose of which is to increase power in numbers by decreasing personal risk and responsibility. But in order to have an identity, whether given or chosen, one must sacrifice particularities and freedoms. An identity limits options, because for any identity to have meaning it must be set over against a competitive identity. In order to have an identity, then, one must accept limitations and be absorbed or assimilated, to some extent in the group identity. This is all the more true when an identity is engaged in a defensive or offensive campaign against a rival identity. This is most obvious when it comes to national identity during time of war. Neither side allows for neutrality.

The identity of universal humanity is now realizable in a way that had been prevented by national, religious, or other older group identities. While this may seem a great victory for humanity, it generates problematic results for the non-human world. To see oneself primarily as human requires that this identity exclude all else that is not human for it to have meaning. Depending on which moral philosopher one follows, this may not even involve those who have not yet reached a certain level of intelligence, or those who have fallen below a certain level of intelligence—embryos, infants, the disabled, and the elderly. Most certainly it will not include any non-humans within it. This is ecologically problematic because it makes our primary self-understanding set off from the environments we inhabit. We see ourselves as separate beings who only happen to live and move through an environment accidentally. This necessarily produces a hierarchy of value that places humanity above all else. Universal humanity becomes plausible only when technologies and normal lived experiences make local environments superficial for self-understanding. As we will see in the next chapter, this is a vital aspect of urbanism. So, universal humanity, by definition, devalues the non-human world and makes it other. It categorically excludes the environment from self-understanding. In this way we can imagine ourselves as trans-planetary beings who could inhabit space-stations, moons, and other planets, without loss to our identity. Universal humanity cannot be earthlings. Hence, most science fiction now involves space travel as an essential narrative device for revealing the ideology of humanity that the authors wish to illustrate.

Technology is essential to this identity creation. It reframes what is plausible by creating an environment in which the creation is accidental rather than essential. By inhabiting an artificial cosmos, we are now able to refashion ourselves. This is perhaps now evident in the militant demand by transgender ideology to separate the social construct of gender from the biological determinant of sex, and consciously prioritize the social construct. While gender is a social construct with some range of difference throughout human history, those differences have been inextricably linked to a group's environment. No previous peoples believed in gender fluidity or believed in a free choice of gender identity. This perspective is only plausible in a situation in which biological and (identifiable) environmental determinants are deemed morally wrong and consciously rejected. This decoupling of biology and natural environment from self-identity is symptomatic of a technological environment in which human sexuality has already been decoupled from reproduction as its primary purpose. Bernard Charbonneau, one of the early founders of the ecology movement, rhetorically asked in 1980,

> By negating difference [between male and female]—I am not saying inequality since we are talking about incomparable qualities—are we obeying a passion for freedom and equality or, on the contrary, are we being fooled by the development of a society that is becoming a vast factory for the production of standardized substitutes?[1]

Gender fluidity is only plausible when gender and sex are no longer important for social, political, or economic purposes, and identity can be swapped like a consumer good. This is merely one stage of the excarnation of human identity which represents a deep alienation from the natural and non-human world. It further represents a conscious and purposeful devaluation of any necessary link between humanity and the creation. Any such link should be chosen, as though we were all free spirits who chose our form of incarnation, like avatars on social media or the internet. The natural end of this way of thinking is not merely trans*gender*-*ism*, but trans*humanism*. The ideal of a humanity that is able to define itself without regard for natural determinants would be the freedom to never incarnate, to never take on material form. Storage of consciousness in electronic form seems the nearest approximation of this. Here is not the place to evaluate transgenderism or transhumanism, though they represent similar logic. It is important to point out, however, that any self-definition that purposefully excludes biological or natural determinants will *necessarily be ecologically devastating*. Ecological care on a transhumanist perspective is subject to the mere whim of a *supposedly* unconditioned will. All value is supposedly given by choice, which makes all other beings entirely dependent for life upon the will of a transhuman god—an ostensible god who has acquired that status by reduction, isolation, and alienation, rather than reconciliation and responsible relationship. Such is a figure of resentment, not benevolence, and is therefore untrustworthy from the perspective of non-human creatures.

---

1. Charbonneau, *The Green Light*, 87.

The supposedly free will of the transhumanist, and to a lesser extent, the transgenderist, is a will radically conditioned by adaption to a technical environment that has not been consciously chosen as one option among many by some neutral excarnate being. It is no less determined than the previous natural and local environmental situations. Thus, it is a bad-faith assertion to claim that this is some new freedom in distinction from historical determinations. It is merely a modern form of adaptation that legitimates its adaptation by condemning previous adaptations and requiring those former adaptations to comply with anachronistic demands.

The need to identify oneself by group identity is alienation and a reduction of character by creating a "self." The assumption of a universal species identity as primary is the ultimate reduction. This reduction leads to necessary alienation from the nonhuman world, which means the nonhuman world is necessarily devalued, since it is evaluated from an excarnate and isolated perspective. In other words, it is impossible for a universal human species to love the created world. It is highly plausible, on the other hand, for a universal human species to exploit and even exterminate the nonhuman world under the guise of creating a neutral situation in which free choice is possible.

And yet, for any sufficient ecological change, there will need to be a transcendence of local and national identities that pursue their own goods in competition with others. We need global solutions to global problems. But to take on a global identity will necessarily devalue the local and unique environments in which peoples live. Thus, identity represents a no-exit situation. Its solution recreates and intensifies the very problem it might seek to solve.

CHAPTER 8

Urban Imaginary

THE STORY OF CIVILIZATION is the story of the development of settled artificial environments. The first cities were centers of elites, specialist craftspeople, and merchants, all of whom had to be fed by external inputs by a nearby settled and generally unfree rural labor force. The surpluses they extracted were made possible by the efficiencies of environmental modification by draining swamps and irrigating arid plains, making it suitable for grain agriculture. This basic structure of human civilization remained fundamentally unaltered throughout most of human history. And, as the industrial conversion started to transform agriculture, enabling the massive rural exodus to the city of the nineteenth and twentieth centuries, the built environment took on an even more central role in the myth of civilization.

It is therefore easy to say that the built environment is a microcosm of the socially constructed cosmos. The city is the concretized form of the human imagination in all of its aspects. The city is the great mirror of human belief about the shape of the world, as it increasingly became the world of humanity. The city represents beliefs about economics. How are the neighborhoods segregated? What kind of industries are present? It represents beliefs about politics. What type of building lies at the all-important mythical center: a temple, a palace, a business district, a forum? The city reveals beliefs about technology in its layout, its industries, and its infrastructure. The city reveals the self-identity of a people as it takes on a mythical identity of its own that becomes a stand-in for its residents.

As the urban population significantly grew, so too did the imagination of the population urbanize. Roger Caillois, in 1938, explored how the city had become the heroic and mythical stage for literature in the nineteenth century in a way that it had not for previous literature. The city became the fabric of reality as revealed by its mythical qualities, into which novelists integrated people through the imagination,[1] a transformation G. K. Chesterton also noted in 1901.[2] As the built environment increasingly determined imaginary possibilities, so did it change the general perspective on the creation. The sense of the romantic and gothic moved into the city with the people. Art of this period reflected a growing fascination with urban and industrial environments, as it also began to treat the countryside as a place of retreat.

The Urban Imagination

The city has become the dominant environment for the vast majority of humanity. As such, it has radically transformed humanity's ability to imagine the world. To put it as simply as possible—urban people live in an artificial world, see an artificial world, and project artificiality onto the world. Urban people are *systematically incapable of ecological life*, because their imaginative capacity has been made artificial. Of course, there are rare exceptions to this. Only in a non-urban environment is one able to engage with the nonhuman world without the mediation of artifice. Urban people are generally incapable of understanding the natural world, and thus far more prone to invasive and disastrous interventions done out of ignorance. When they do understand the natural world, it is as an object of inquiry, curiosity, or research for potential commodification. The assemblage of technologies and power represented in the urban cosmos creates a thick lens that distorts and shrinks the forces of the nonhuman world, leading to a hierarchical perspective that cannot engage in ecology without visions of management. As we've seen, human management is at the heart of both civilization and ecological disaster, and the city is the concrete representation of this.

A simple anecdote will suffice to show the level to which artificial and technological mediation transforms the imaginative ability. Once, when sitting outside of a pub in the UK with fellow students, the sun was obscured by clouds, the wind came up, and it got mildly cold. The conversation instantly turned toward moving indoors. I looked to the

1. Caillois, "Paris, a Modern Myth."
2. Chesterton, "A Defence of Detective Stories."

sky, saw the size of the cloud, its general direction and speed of movement, and saw that we would only need to wait about 30 seconds before the sun would return with its warmth. The fellow students were utterly amazed by my predictive capabilities. None of them considered looking at the sky to take the most basic of meteorological readings. The basic *mētis* I had learned from my father and experience in the wilderness was almost like magic to those who had only experienced weather predictions through the *technē* of meteorologists.[3] This simple example carries over into reading soil health, understanding plants and their needs, understanding animals and their needs, being able to tell the health of a local ecosystem by years of observation. These skills are inherent to those who have farmed an area for generations. For average urbanites all of this is completely illegible, and the most reasonable course of action is to simplify the external world to make it legible, rather than learning how to read local conditions.

Urbanites have no ability to integrate into a complex natural world. Their default tendency is to simplify and transform. When they go camping, they level and clear a site, rather than adapting to the conditions they find. Leaving no trace to an urbanite initially means not letting the environment leave a trace of impact on the human body, or the paint of a car. And this is all fully reasonable based on the normal experience of living in an entirely artificial world. Projected to the whole ecosystem, the idea is the same. Urbanites want the environment to leave no trace upon them. Thus, the line of thinking of the ecomodernists seeks a continued decoupling of the human from the environment as a way to pursue environmental health. The thought is that environmental problems have occurred because humanity is too dependent on natural resources. If we could continue to urbanize and promote technologies that lessen our dependence on nature, we would be free of it, and therefore it be free of us. This is a line of thinking only plausible within an urban environment that seeks to justify its existence based on the faulty notion that we are *almost there* in the myth of civilization. As Norman Wirzba notes, however, this way of thinking rests on two mistakes. It assumes that the earth will respond to intensified technological development and urbanization in ways in line with historically observable trends. But the scale of human impact on the environment is out of all proportion with any historical data. The second mistake is conceptual, that humans are non-ecological beings.

3. Tristan Gooley is a wealth of this kind of *mētis*.

"This assumption . . . rests on the peculiar, and utterly false, idea that the power of life is internal to us, and that we do not need others to live."[4] The problem with attempting to combat such a view is that everything about the urban experience offers a confirmation bias to it. The city is incredibly simple compared to the natural ecosystem. We can live, day to day, with the myth of self-sufficiency. I wrote elsewhere that the aristocratic myth is to believe that one is self-sufficient when in reality an aristocrat owns a plethora of slaves who do everything for the aristocrat. The irony of the aristocratic ideology is that the aristocrat is really the only one who could likely not be truly self-sufficient, possessing only specialist skills and little knowledge of practical survival skills. The same is true of the urbanite. Just because the sources of life are hidden within a system does not mean that a person is self-sufficient. The city is the only place in which we can preserve and promote the myth that we are gods who need nothing, who can exist *a se*. In short, the city is necessary for human self-deification, which will inevitably be conceptual and actual suicide. In order to become what we are not—an isolated and self-sufficient consciousness—we must biologically die.

Urban Ecology

Cities are necessarily anti-ecological. They are not compatible with their situations. They are built on top of the land. They are centers into which *resources* flow, but generally only *products* leave. They are great factories for turning human and natural resources into products that only serve human ends. Cities colonize the earth. This is not simply true in the ancient world of slavery. Ellen Davis notes that in modern America about one quarter of the population lives in a colony. She further says,

> North American farmland functions in most places almost exclusively as a source of wealth flowing *out* of local communities. . . . Today most small towns in America's grain belt are severely underpopulated. Many are virtually ghost towns. . . . Most farmers who have managed to stay on the land do so as renters or low-paid employees of the multinational corporations; the term "bioserf" has been coined to describe their situation.[5]

4. Wirzba, *Food and Faith*, 297–98.

5. Davis, *Scripture, Culture, and Agriculture*, 105.

While modernity has certainly exacerbated this colonization of rural life, it is not a factor unique to modernity or the modern city. It is inherent in the structure of civilization, in which the notion of development requires this form of colonization. This means that cities have always and everywhere altered the landscape in ways that work for the benefit of the city at the cost of ecological imbalances outside. Obvious and extreme examples are the local extinctions of species by the Roman Empire for gladiatorial games. But as recent anthropology has shown, it is not simply the city itself that transformed its local ecology, the very existence of settled agrarianism radically altered the landscape in ways that significantly reduced species diversity. Again, what the ancients did in a small measure, modernity has taken beyond the limit with industrial agriculture's monocrops of hybrids and clones focused almost exclusively on maximizing annual yield.[6] Thus, the very existence of a city transforms the countryside. This is not even to begin talking about the notion of territory, the building of roads to enable centralized control and facilitate trade, and the building of walls, or immigration law, to prevent the flight of mostly unfree labor as much as keeping invaders out.

The world's population has grown based on the transformation of a richly diverse world into an agricultural-industrial complex that is not sustainable. It has depleted the soil, as has urbanization and suburban sprawl. Modern population levels are entirely unsustainable, even if we could solve climate change tomorrow. This is a factor few seem willing to recognize or discuss. This unsustainability is not a problem of efficiencies. It is a foundational problem with the urban system itself.

Although the city is ecologically problematic in its very nature, it is obviously impossible to now do away with it. It is nearly impossible to even question the *goodness* of the city. As cities continue to grow, humans are ever more alienated from the creation, and therefore cannot understand the creation on anything approaching a relational level. The natural world will always be a potential resource to the urban world. Any amount of preservation or conservation is based on maintaining an ability to exploit these resources later. Thus, the city is inherently parasitic. It produces a parasitic imaginary. It alienates people from the creation. It turns ecology into an optional moral cause among many others. The good of the non-human world only becomes important as it threatens the stability of the global system of development.

6. Scott, *Against the Grain*, 75.

But the city is not just the source of environmental injustices, it is a major source of human injustices. Because it rests on exploitation of colonial labor, the city is no solution to global poverty, for poverty is endemic to it. It is not simply for lack of will, or a corrupt system of distribution that leads to urban inequalities. The very notion of property only has meaning where its value, desirability, and access are unequal. Any value only has value when it is unevenly distributed, creating desire and scarcity in the economic imaginary. Cities, as built environments, significantly amplify value inequality by the quality of development, location, density, and desirability. Cities also have the possibility of amplifying poverty by disenfranchising people of any property and confining them to slums with little hope of escape. Thus, we must reject those, such as Pope Francis, who call for the improvement of living conditions within the city as though it represented a real strategy toward ecological improvement.[7] While the goods he seeks are desirable, the ability of the poor to adapt and make the best of their lives in slums and tenements only serves to reinforce radical inequalities. Their improvement rests entirely upon a system of patronizing philanthropy, which serves to transform economic hierarchy into a moral hierarchy. A broken system must be allowed to fail in order that it may be replaced. The rich, powerful, and technologically advanced are not saviors, they are oppressors who cannot be allowed glory for moderating their oppression. Change only comes to a cosmos invaded by an unstoppable force of chaos. The increasing number of the poor and disenfranchised represent a great force of potential system-ruining chaos that could possibly lead to a necessary revaluation and cosmic reconstitution. Discovering means of making their misery mildly less miserable by beautification of the built environment is neither ecology nor justice. Likewise, Francis's call to increase "our sense of belonging, rootedness, of 'feeling at home' within a city which includes us and draws us together"[8] by means of protecting common areas and visual landmarks, again is a call for making injustice slightly more tolerable. Disenfranchisement is a vital force of chaos that needs to be fostered rather than ameliorated. Cities are irredeemable from the perspective of Christian economic or ecological justice, as redemption requires the property to have been God's in the first place. We cannot solve an ecological crisis with significant roots in the urban imagination without

7. Francis, *Laudato Si*, chapter 3.

8. Francis, *Laudato Si*, 151.

rethinking the urban imagination itself, and growing discontent within urban environments will necessarily fuel the motive for doing this.

Thus, we come again to a no-exit situation. Cities are necessary for housing and giving work to the billions of humans on the planet. More efficient cities are often put forward as an aspect to solving climate change. Densification and the elimination of suburbia would be obviously beneficial ecological moves by increasing agricultural space, reducing water wasted on ornamental lawns, reducing or even eliminating most automobile drives, and taking advantage of efficiencies of scale. These are all feasible changes that can help alleviate some aspects of ecological disaster. But none of these things address the fundamentally broken imagination that views the city as good or necessary. Cities cannot be ecological because their entire *raison d'être* is predicated on eliminating natural determinants. Their purpose is to construct an alternative, simplified, and fully manageable environment in which human will is ostensibly the only real determinant. The city represents an early but profound form of human excarnation. It represents the sum of the imaginative brokenness evident in economics, politics, technology, and identity. In this way, the city is the microcosm of human excarnation.

Part III

A Subversive Theology of Creation

The solution to ecological problems must begin in the imagination and thus help transform both the socially constructed cosmos and the imaginations that exist in a dialectical relationship with it. As we've seen, the imaginary based in the myth of civilization is toxic, especially as it reaches its great concretization in the totalizing artificial environment we know as the city. I will now make the case for a Christian theology that offers an imaginary based on revelation from outside of the human cosmos. Over the next three chapters we will create a brief overview of a theology that can offer a serious alternative to all human cosmoi. Space constrains the outline of this theology, but I have given a similar and more detailed account of this "theology of relationship" in *Plundering Egypt*.

Much ecological work done by Christian theologians can be characterized as an attempt to apply biblical principles to the problems we face. While excellent work has been done by many authors whose books can be found in the bibliography, I want to offer a challenge and friendly critique to these. The problem with what we might call "principlization," or the extraction of principles from the Bible that are applicable to modern situations, is that it makes the Bible, God, and tradition into a resource that aids us in the direction we desire to go. I think this is a fundamental genre mistake, and it reveals the depths of the broken imagination. If the Bible is the word of God, his own self-revelation, it cannot be a resource for human ends. As we will see, it is a force of chaos invading the self-enclosed world of sinful human cosmos. The Bible contains a fundamental invitation to full and total conversion and the renewal of the mind. Anything short of death and resurrection is a subversion of the self-proclaimed message of Jesus Christ. Hence, as we will see, there can be no Christian ethic easily applicable to those who refuse to repent and submit to the kingship of Christ. We must not use God as a means to moderate the effects of human sin.

CHAPTER 9

Creation

Biblical Sources for a Theology of Creation

As WE BEGIN TO outline an alternative imaginary based on the Bible, we have to consider what the sources are and how they are to be used. Genesis 1–2 is most obvious and most commonly used. But it is not alone in the Bible as a source of reflection on creation. Job, some of the Psalms, the prophets, and both the Johannine and Pauline texts consider creation, though an entire survey of the biblical literature is outside of the scope of this book. Each of these texts needs to be read in their own contexts and within the narrative of the whole. Although it is tempting to extract specific texts as data points for the formation of a systematic theology, this is a technique of simplification and reduction that gives us power over Scripture by turning it into formulas. While some degree of this is inevitable, if we are aware of it we can resist the temptation for systematization that cosmizes or domesticates the word of God.

Our chief text about creation in Genesis 1–2 should not be read as scientific or as a systematic theology. Neither genre existed at the time of its authorship. Genesis is clearly a genealogy, a story of the origin of the people of God. It is not primarily a story about the origin of creation. No text of the Bible was written to provide a fulsome theology of creation or the origins of the universe. The creation is not the topic of the Bible. It is the setting of the narrative, and sometimes a *character*. The creation is always in relationship to the Creator. The idea that we can address the creation without considering its relationship to the Creator is, as we will see in the next chapter, precisely the origin of sin. Because of that, when it comes to New Testament texts that speak about the creation, we must be aware that its authors are reinterpreting and revising the relationship of God to the creation through Christ. As we will see, there can be no ethic of creation for the Christian that does not have Christ at its center. That is to say, there can be no ethic or theology of creation that does not have sin, rescue, and reconciliation at its core. To do otherwise is to shortcut the whole story, attempting to compress a narrative into a system of behavioral modification to achieve an ideal state of being. This is to cosmize the Bible, and such methods must be roundly rejected. Any theology of creation that is not grounded in the living relationship of each individual creature to the Creator, but instead seeks to make objective claims about "reality," has not understood the first thing about what creation means. It should go without saying, then, that to read any of the Bible with scientific questions, including ecological ones, is to violate any of its various genres and purposes.

For many scholars, the Bible is a resource to be used for the sake of reinforcing a belief, convincing others of a different opinion, or simply mustering a culturally valued source for one's side. This is often the case within a secular space in which people of various religious perspectives are attempting to communicate based on some common ground. The problem with this approach is that it submits the Bible as a source to be mined as a resource. This is exactly the heart of the ecological problem made manifest in politics—secularism attempts to manage human beliefs and traditions as resources for the production of peaceful human prosperity. In the process of this management, secularism must kill religious belief by submitting the gods to the state, reversing the very basis of all premodern religions in which the gods have authority over humanity. In order for the Bible to be what it claims to be, revelation of God, it *must not* be used as a *resource*. It must rather be a conversation partner, read in dialogue. Secularism is the ultimate and final form of cultural and religious appropriation or colonialism. One must enter into the living tradition of the family of faith that has submitted to the Scriptures in order to read them rightly. This involves a fundamental choice from the beginning. If one does not submit to the authority of the Creator, one is thereby rendered systematically incapable of rightly reading Scripture and engaging with it ecologically.

Creator

We cannot know God *in himself*. We can only know God-*as*. That is, we can only know God by the kind of relationship we have with him and he with us. God's self-revelation is always in a kind of relationship, which shows the character of God, rather than aspects or attributes of his being. This means we can only know God as Creator by entering into a relationship with God as a creature and part of the creation. In the next chapter we will see that this is entirely impossible in sin, and all the more so in the highly developed modern cosmos. This means we can only have access to knowledge of God as Creator through the word about God as Creator. Put another way, there is no room for "natural theology." Natural theology is the most basic and ignorant form of projection, creating a picture of a deity by interaction with one's environment. The modern cosmos has rendered natural theology almost impossible, which is really the origin of Nietzsche's famous "death of God" statements. As Ellul has it, "It is only in an urban civilization that man has the metaphysical possibility of saying, 'I killed God.'"[1] That said, we quickly move to talk about the creation, and so come to know something of the Creator's character by the relationship of the Creator to the creation.

Creation

Perhaps the most obvious thing to say is that the creation is *God's*. God is the Creator. He is fully and totally responsible for the initial shaping of all things. His creation in reality matches exactly his intention. That's what Genesis means when it says that God saw that it was "very good." It doesn't mean it was morally excellent. It means that it was well-formed. The creation's value does not rest in itself, but in God's declaration that it is good. That is, the creation has value *because the Creator values the creation*. It is only in this relationship that the creation remains good and well-formed. God thus bears full responsibility for the creation, and he has full power to create and uncreate it. This union of full power and full responsibility is what is particularly and only characteristic of the one God of the Bible. In comparison with pagan gods of the ancient world, or those of modern creation, who have limited power and limited

---

1. Ellul, *Meaning of the City*, 16.

responsibility, God's character glories in the full expression of this equivalent power and responsibility.

Creation is God's. It derives its identity as creation from God. There can be no such thing as "creation" without a creator. That is why people now speak of "universe" rather than "creation," because "universe" does not require a creator. If the relationship between God and his creation is broken, then the creation will cease to have its right identity, and will instead lose focus. A major misconception of human historical belief is that things can have meaning and purpose in themselves and that this meaning is communicable. That is the imaginational error of projection and reification. Meaning and purpose only comes through relationships.

Ex Nihilo

Creation is by the Word of God out of nothing. This is not a concept explicitly stated in Genesis. Then again, at the time Genesis was written (and/or compiled) there was no conceptual framework for metaphysics,[2] and therefore no concept of nothingness. By the time of the New Testament, creatio ex nihilo solidified in John 1:3 and Hebrews 11:3. This means there was no chaos-cosmos structure to the creation. Genesis specifically avoids any description of Chaoskampf. This is vital, because the Bible reframes the common narrative of human mythology and meaning. God is understood to create in a fundamentally different way to humans. There is specifically nothing in common between God's creation and human creation. Chaos, as we'll see in the next chapter, is a human invention. Thus, Genesis is operating on a different narrative track than the human method of rationality. It is not solely a human narrative, nor one that is the result of projection.

Creation Finished

Creation, as an act, is finished. This is a vital point that numerous theologians, including the current pope,[3] do not seem to grasp. Many of these theologians wrongly merge the action of creation with the product of that action, which is also called creation. The creation (product) is full of life and change, but it is not thereby an ongoing operation. Creation

2. Wagenfuhr, *Plundering Egypt*.

3. Francis briefly advances a theology of co-creationism in *Laudato Si*, 80.

is a finished event, but the creation as a community lives. God's action of sustaining the creation is not the same as continual creation. Humans, therefore, are set firmly within that creation as creatures who participate in the life of creation, but not in its establishment, and thus can be co-sustainers rather than co-creators.

It is a common theme of ancient pagan religions that humans participate in the annual re-creation of the cosmos on New Year's Day. The Bible purposefully does not have a New Year's celebration, although such holy days were common among their surrounding cultures. Also, because Genesis 1 specifically avoids speaking about the creation of the sun and moon by name, it implies that they are not gods, and that their daily, monthly, and yearly "deaths" are not cosmically relevant events. The sun and moon are not personified characters of the story, they are impersonal "lights." This was radically opposed to the ancient societies in which Genesis was written. Every year the whole cosmos reverted to chaos, and it was the responsibility of their religious structures to help the gods triumph anew over the forces of darkness and chaos through right rituals.[4]

Creation was neither perfect, nor in need of development. In the ancient world there was no concept of perfection in the sense we usually mean it today. In the pre-philosophical world "perfection" just meant completion, or fullness.[5] Creation was finished, fulfilled. It is not the "best of all possible worlds." That's just a thought-game of philosophers that ancient people did not play. The finished-ness of creation means that there is no further work to do. It doesn't need to be improved upon. There is no hint in the Bible of such a theology of humans improving or developing God's creation. It is common to believe that God created a world of potentiality that humans were meant to bring to perfection. This is nothing but a Christianization of the myth of civilization, and it has no biblical support. But it is hard to overstate how pernicious this co-creation theology is, as it justifies human exploitations and a purposeful ignorance about the real human and creational costs of civilization. Humans are creatures who, like other creatures, engage in "niche construction." This does not make them special or godlike.

---

4. Eliade, *The Sacred and the Profane*, 76–78.
5. Wagenfuhr, *Unfortunate Words of the Bible*, chapter 4.

Purpose of Creation

God rested on the seventh day. God's Sabbath rest means that God entered a new relationship with the creation that was finished. No longer is God simply the Creator, but is now the ruler of a functioning creation who peacefully sits on his throne. This isn't inactive rest—it is a relationship of peace as God lets his creation flourish under his care, for it is only under God's care that creation can flourish. Sabbath or rest in the Bible does not mean inactivity, it means the state of right relationships flourishing together, rather than working by the sweat of one's brow to eke out a living. Sabbath is actually the *telos* or perfection of creation. The end of the story of God's people in the Bible is the great Sabbath rest[6] in the fullness of God's kingdom rule over all things, a rule that reconciles all things to God himself. The Bible consistently sees creation as made right when it is subject to the peaceful reign of God. But we must distinguish the Sabbath of creation's seventh day from the commands to the Sabbaths of the week, seven years, and fifty years found in the rest of the Pentateuch. The Sabbath commands are methods of protecting and reconciling the creation. The Sabbath commands create a living symbol from which the people of God learn how to rightly be the image of God. The Sabbath is about care for the creation, including the parts of human society and wider creation that we don't normally want to look after, like widows, orphans, strangers, and wild animals, as well as the soil. The regular Sabbaths are a means of educating the people of God into the knowledge of God's reconciliation that will result in the return of God's peaceful kingdom rule and the eschatological Sabbath.

God's Creatures

The creatures that God created are not simply tame livestock for the purpose of human control and benefit. God created the wild things with all of their wild ways. God loves all of his creatures, even the supposedly monstrous. There are no monsters for a hero to slay in the Bible.[7] God created both predators and prey. God created animals that thrive on the

6. Heb 4:9.

7. Some would say Goliath is something of a monster/old-god analogue that the hero David slays to end the chaos and establish the kingdom. That is something of a stretch and it is certainly not portrayed thus in the Bible. Goliath is fully humanized—though large he is not endued with magical abilities or a monstrous appearance.

often grisly death of others. They were not created as his representatives. We hyper-urbanized moderns with our tender tummies are unable to stomach the behavior of the natural world, and many Christians wrongly attribute this to the fallenness of the creation. God, in the book of Job, explains that he has made the raven, lion, hawk, and vulture with their predatory ways (38–39).[8] He gets joy from the wildness of his creatures, even if humans are unable to understand or tame them. God knows when a sparrow dies, and he values it.[9] But there is no indication in Scripture that God is shocked or outraged at natural death or biological lifecycles, nor that God is specially caring toward the cute and cuddly. This raises the question of passages like Isaiah 11 in which the whole earth is filled with the knowledge of God with the result that predator and prey will dwell together without eating each other. Indeed, Isaiah 11 has bears grazing with cows and lions eating straw. All become vegetarians. This is a portrayal of reconciliation rather than of creation, and as such it speaks less to an ideal situation and more to the reign of justice and peace. That it is using animals symbolically should be clear from context in which God deforests Lebanon in Isaiah 10 as a symbol of destroying that nation. God's intent for reconciliation is not the same as it is for creation. Reconciliation is not restoration of creation, but a new creation.

Under God's peaceful rule the variety of creatures interact by their own ways that are not the same as human ways. God's creatures have meaning by relationship to God, not by their relationship or usefulness, or even cuteness to humans. The image of baby vultures (or eagles) drinking blood[10] is not cute. But God made it so and values it, even if humans do not.

God's creatures are his and are valued because of his relationship with them, regardless of humanity. The source of meaning is not within us, but within God's relationship with the animals. This helps us understand that Genesis 1 does not conclude with humanity because humanity is somehow the meaning or purpose of creation itself, or that all the creatures exist for the sake of humanity, but that humans are themselves one among many creatures God created. It also means that our value is not given by our relationship to the animals, to our ability to conquer them, or to conquer the whole of creation, but by God himself and our

8. Bauckham, *Bible and Ecology*, 51.

9. Matt 10:31; Luke 12:6.

10. Job 39:30.

relationship to him. As biblical scholar Richard Bauckham details very well, humans are part of the community of creation, not its crown, nor its center. The sixth day, the creation of humanity, is not the climax of creation, the seventh day, the peaceful flourishing of the whole is. Thus Bauckham reflects on the Genesis command to be fruitful and multiply. This is not given to humanity alone, but to other creatures as well, such that when human multiplication and activity threatens the ability for other species to freely multiply, that is a serious violation of the intention of God's creation.[11] Longman and Walton argue that this is not a command, but a blessing.[12] Human over-abundance thus removes the blessing God gave to other creatures, and makes humanity a curse to them. Bauckham likewise says, "The Hebrew Bible does not suppose that all parts of the world are for human use or habitation."[13] And yet, as we've seen, the development of civilization is entirely predicated on the modification of environments for human use, which necessarily destroys habitat for others.

God's Image or Representatives

The image of God is one of the most used and abused themes of the Bible. It is not a guiding theme of much in the Bible, in spite of its centrality in modern popular theology. Nonetheless, it is an important theme in the first chapters of Genesis and in Pauline theology. Its meaning is fairly clear, if we endeavor to understand what it meant in its original context. Humans are created to be God's image, which means they are God's idols. They are to be symbolic representatives of God himself. In the ancient Near Eastern world in which Genesis was written, the image of God was a fairly well developed concept for human kings, who represented the authority and will of the gods to their people. Many of them had religious rituals and myths that legitimized their kingship. In the Bible, however, *all* humans are given this representational role. And it is just that—a *role*.[14] The image of God cannot have meant something about human being, essence, or metaphysics in the ancient Near East. Being the image of God is a *job* that God has given to humanity, specifically Adam and Eve in Genesis 1–2.

---

11. Bauckham, *Bible and Ecology*, 17.
12. Longman and Walton, *Lost World of the Flood*, 131.
13. Bauckham, *Bible and Ecology*, 114.
14. See Walton, *Old Testament Theology for Christians*, 85.

Being a representative means that a person conveys authority given to them on behalf of another. A representative is not a replacement, as though humans were to take God's place as Creator and Sustainer of all things. Though humans are participants in the work of sustaining creation, God is not thereby absent from that job. Representatives also only have symbolic authority. That is, their authority only works by pointing to or referencing the real authority, which they represent. We often forget that representation is symbolism. Thus, humans as the image of God are to *symbolize* God, to be a living revelation of God in his *character*, though not in all of his functions. In Genesis, this is described as "dominion." This rule or dominion first and foremost must convey the character of God's own rule. That doesn't mean the domestication of all plants and animals, or the building of cities in any and every possible location. It means, at the very least, that humans: value all of creation; understand that responsibility is linked directly to power, and vice-versa; pursue the good and flourishing of all species; and have a personal relationship with each creature, as possible. Let's explore each of these.

Value All of Creation

For God, the creation is not understood as a resource to be harvested for the purpose of further creation, or further refinement. As representative rulers, humans are to value things through God's own valuation, not by their own. Creation has no use-value. Creation is an act of judgment, an act of valuation. The point of God speaking the creation into existence is not simply a demonstration of his ultimate power, it is the image of a king whose word becomes law merely by its speaking. God rules over all things in such a way that they obey the word of his command almost of their own accord. This type of action by a king is always an act of judgment, a decision for one thing and not for another. Human creations, by contrast, develop only by blood, sweat, and tears. We have to tear something down, refashion it, repurpose it, kill it, mine it, grind it, strip it, weld it. All of our creative actions come by violent effort, a fact enshrined in the projected myths of many ancient cosmogonies.

God did not create resources for human exploitation. Oil was not created for automobiles, nor granite for countertops, nor gold for rings and coins. There is no textual or cultural evidence that would suggest that the biblical term "subdue" in Genesis 1:28 constitutes a divine legitimation of the resourcification of the earth. Turning things into resources is to repurpose them for one's own sake, to take them out of their natural contexts and use them for artificial purposes by artificers. This is true of people who are turned into human resources or employees by removal from their families and homes. It is true of trees cut down, and of animals tamed. Subduing the earth should be tied to the similar command (or blessing) of fruitful multiplication. The reign of God through human representatives should be extended throughout the earth, so that God's dominion is shared with humans. It should not be tied to civilizational advances or even landscape specialization through agriculture. One of the great mistakes of interpretation of Genesis has been to assume that Mesopotamia was an arid landscape in need of technologies of irrigation and other agricultural techniques. Archaeology has found that Mesopotamia in that time was a wetland or alluvial floodplain, as has been true of other great centers of early civilizations.[15] So, in Genesis 2:15, the command to "serve and protect" the land should not be rightly understood as the intensive agriculture required of irrigating cereal crops in arid lands. They were not re-forming chaotic or formless thickets or barren tracts of wasteland into neat rows of crops to feed God their landlord.

So, we should also not see Adam and Eve as farmers. There is ample evidence that cereal crops have been cultivated primarily in imperial contexts to serve the needs of taxation, land ownership, and population control. Settled farmers have generally been relatively unfree peoples who produce at least a portion for others. Rather, the fruit trees God had planted in the garden of Eden were to be the food supply of Adam and Eve (2:9, 16). Thus, Adam and Eve were gatherers, like the 95 percent of the history of homo sapiens. They lived off an abundant land that fed them, as even Jesus seems to suggest we ought to do.[16] *The human task in Eden was not agriculture, but land care.* Agriculture is the modification of the land for the purpose of food production using developed techniques. Agriculture is about the production of a resource, and thus the creation of a relationship in which value is given to a thing because of its usefulness to humans. It is ultimately an anthropocentric enterprise. Land care, by contrast, prioritizes the good of the whole, the commonwealth of all creation. It may allow for modification, like erosion control and pruning. But its primary purpose is not the production of a crop. Its purpose is not

---

15. Scott, *Against the Grain*, 47.

16. Matt 6:25–26; Luke 12:24.

determined by humanity, but by the Creator, and thus its value comes from the Creator, not from humanity. This is a type of management, but a management for the sake of the commonwealth, done according to the character of the Creator. This land care is the imitation of God's sustaining work, rather than an imitation of creation, as in co-creationist theologies. So it's also not gardening as we understand it today. Adam and Eve would have been gardeners of a divine palace garden, that as we'll see, is more of an orchard-forest-wilderness than it is an English, Italian, or vegetable garden.

Human Responsibility and Power

The representative image of God would be keenly aware that power must be matched with equivalent or greater responsibility. True godlikeness is, as I would partly define it, the meeting point of all-capability (omnipotence) with all-responsibility. YHWH is revealed in the Hebrew Scriptures as able to save and consistent in his promises. That is, he is *all-capable*, but also *fully responsible*. (That does not mean he is portrayed as all-causing!) Godlikeness for other ancient peoples is expressed in different terms. Achilles, for example, is godlike in his rage and might. He is personally vindictive, demonstrating overflowing power by not being responsible for its consequences. Prometheus ennobles humanity by giving them secret powers and knowledge of the gods without humans becoming responsible for those powers. Prometheus then becomes the great scapegoat, the one who raises up humanity by taking the consequences of his gift upon himself, thus having no power and all responsibility. Of course Prometheus did not intend to get caught, so it was not truly a mission of self-sacrifice.

Adam and Eve, as God's representatives, would have to act with responsibility equivalent to their power. As their power was not great, their responsibility would likewise not be incredibly great. But this also limits human capability and capacity for influence. The great dictators of the twentieth century, like Mao and Stalin, threw away millions of human lives for their often harebrained schemes of modernization. They had an absolute level of power and suffered only small political consequences for their behavior. This parasitism is the inverse of the image of God. Such parasitism is present in owners of major transnational corporations who have insulated themselves from personal responsibility while amassing incredible global power by exploiting resources and people. But this is evident in much smaller ways among relatively powerless people: shopping carts abandoned here and there by people too lazy to take them a few extra steps to return them in a parking lot, single-use plastics, and domestic violence in which a partner abuses the other and blames the victim. These are opportunities to exercise a tiny modicum of power without responsibility, and for many this is too great a temptation to pass by. These acts of irresponsibility reveal the heart of parasitism, though. It is this idea of exercising power at someone else's cost of responsibility that is the inversion of the image of God. This is also the basis of modern economics, politics, technology, identity, and the city.

Flourishing of All Creation and Personal Relationships

Adam and Eve would not deal with creatures as species. As God's image, they would represent God's own character in this regard. Jesus says that God cares for individual sparrows,[17] and the Psalmist notes that the temple of Jerusalem is home to sparrows and swallows in a welcome manner.[18] For those who have lived in any sort of rural, local, and emplaced context, many things are not treated as species but as individuals. Upon observation one may come to know specific birds that return to a similar nesting site each year. Specific trees are known, observed, studied. Nearly everything has a name. And this is what God gives Adam to do, to name the creatures in Genesis 2:19–20. It is normally understood by modern readers that Adam said his language-equivalent of cow, horse, raven, eagle, salmon, and spider. However, given the incredibly small world of pre-mechanical peoples, and especially those who did not sail or ride horseback, such a man would be presented with a relatively small number of creatures. This is not simply an exercise of Adam's dominion in naming these creatures. That's what scientists do with biological taxonomy. Adam's dominion would be exercised as God's—in the value of each individual creature who have their own characters. Adam would have given *personal* names to the creatures rather than species identifiers. This makes them characters in Adam's storied existence, not simply resources for his use. This may sound funny and far-fetched, but bear in mind that nearly everything in ancient literature was named and storied—from

17. Matt 10:31; Luke 12:6.

18. Ps 84:3.

weapons, armor, beasts to slay, gods, even the different directions that the wind blew. Adam (אָדָם, Man) himself is a named individual who represents the father of the family of humanity, with Eve (חַוָּה, Life) his wife. We would think it strange for a pet owner to simply refer to her dog as "dog." Even when meeting other people and their pets we ask for their names and refer to them by their names rather than breeds. This is the more basic and relational stance that only becomes implausible when the sheer breadth of knowledge and experience grows beyond relational capacity.

In such a personal relationship, a person acting in God's character would pursue the flourishing of all the creatures, not individual desires. The command to fruitful multiplication is thus a command to create more people who can live in these relationships with more creatures. As noted, the command to be fruitful and multiply is given to other creatures beyond humans. That means multiplication and fruitfulness is not part of the definition of the image of God. It also means that human flourishing must not come at the cost of the other creatures. God's command (or blessing) to other creatures and to humans is not competitive. It is not as though humans could not flourish if lions or wolves did as well, though later humans acted like this was true. People who talk to their plants are highly attentive to the needs of the plants and care for them appropriately. A gardener knows the disappointment when a single plant dies before its time. To the industrial farmer, this is merely a statistic, an infinitesimal dent in profit. The same is true of people and their pets. But those who run puppy-mills or industrial farms care for profits, not for individual creatures and their welfare. There is no relationship with individual cows at a modern slaughterhouse, they are only products to kill, drain, skin, and butcher, known by its more sanitized term "processing." Such would not have been the case with small-holding farmers whose prized cows may be part of their family for years, and in much of biblical history would have even shared a house with the human family. Animal slaughter was a community event. Furthermore, the Bible clearly speaks against such practices of industrial slaughter and resourcification of animals. In Leviticus 17:3-4, God explains that anyone who kills an ox, lamb, or goat inside or outside of the camp without first offering it to God is guilty of bloodguilt, and must be exiled. *All* life belongs to God, even if it is owned livestock.[19] Note well, the Bible does not command veganism

---

19. See Davis, *Scripture, Culture, and Agriculture*, 97–99.

or vegetarianism. It is not providing a diet plan nor a moral requirement based on species types. Rather, it reveals the relationship God has with his creatures, and his desire for humans in their interaction with the animals. The image of God does not own land or animal. Neither crop nor stock are the fruit of human labor, nor are they a possession. Humans are part of the creation and must be intimately involved with it revealing God's character in all activities, for that is what the image of God means.

What the Image Is Not

Now that we've seen some of the basic traits of the image of God, it is worth noting what it cannot mean. The image of God is *not a priestly role*. There are no priests or priesthood mentioned in Genesis 1–11. Professional priests are a later development to the time period Genesis 1–11 is discussing within the purview of Genesis. Not only that, there is no religion of any kind in Genesis 1–3. There are no prayers, sacrifices, temples,[20] vestments, ceremonies, or any form of mediation through rites or rituals. There are no angry gods to appease, or hungry ones to feed. The first act of religious worship in the Bible, which is neither commanded nor desired, leads to murder. That is significant. Genesis 1–11 has a perspective echoed in many places throughout the Bible, that *religious mediation is not the solution to a problem, it is a false solution that reveals a problem*. God does not demand sacrifices, festivals, or holy days.[21] Even the temple itself is something of an accommodation on God's behalf.[22] Thus, the image of God does not mediate the creation to God. It does not gather the praises of creation and deliver them to God, as Bauckham rightly recognizes, in contrast to the Orthodox tradition.[23] The image of God symbolizes God's presence, and in that way, is a blessing to the whole creation. This is an ambassadorial or political rather than a religious or priestly role.

The image of God is also *not a steward of creation*. A steward is a manager of a large estate or property, appointed by the landlord. In that

---

20. As I've written elsewhere, I strongly disagree with the notion of Eden as a "cosmic temple" for conceptual, theological, and anthropological reasons. In short, Eden is a palace, as discussed below. Temples are conceptual extensions of palaces.

21. Isa 1:11–17; Ps 51:16–17.

22. 2 Sam 7.

23. Bauckham, *Bible and Ecology*, 83–86.

sense, stewardship is a delegated task. In terms of creation it implies that God is somewhat of an absentee landlord. It is not coincidental that deism begins to rise at a similar time to this theological notion, in the seventeenth century.[24] Creation is not entrusted to humanity, and humans are not made its managers.[25] This view has only become possible as techniques and technologies have empowered humans far over the other animals. The dominion of the image of God is, again, the revelation of the character of God. The conclusion of the creation is the rest of God, not his constant work of management. For God did not establish a creation in need of improvement or modification, but a creation in which each creature functioned according to its kind and thrived. To put it in political terms, God created a divine anarchy, a divine non-rule in which no hierarchy or exercise of authority was necessary for the continued well-functioning of the creation. God, as revealed in Jesus Christ, is the one who does not seek to impose his power, but humbles himself. Bauckham points out a number of critiques of the stewardship idea in the Bible: it is hubris, it excludes God's continued action in creation, it lacks specific content, it sets humans over creation, and it prioritizes one text over many others.[26] Stewardship is anachronistic and self-justificatory, and must be rejected.

Epistemology of the Image of God

The image of God is not an ontological category. As I argued at length in *Plundering Egypt*, it is anachronistic to read metaphysics into the Hebrew Scriptures. This is important because the image of God is not thereby understood as something innate to human nature or human *being*. The image of God is a relationship, and as such, *it can only exist within a right relationship*. There is a precise shape to that rightness of relationship, and it is fully oriented toward God.

Although Genesis would not use the word "epistemology" nor would it have understood this as a category of reasonable inquiry, Genesis 2–3 provides a rich account of the method of human rationality and the

24. Attfield, *Environmental Ethics*, 21.

25. Ps 8:6–8 should be understood as hyperbolic. No one would reasonably claim at that time that humans had dominion over sea creatures. It does show, however, that Ps 8 has a theology entirely separated from the *Chaoskampf* imaginary.

26. Bauckham, *Bible and Ecology*, 2–12.

consequences of its perversion. When humans are in a right relationship with God, they mediate their relationships with all creation through God. They understand their function of revealing the character of God to the creation, and thus continually seek to embody the character of God. This character can only be known by knowing God. God names individual creatures, including the stars.[27] He knows intricate details, like numbers of hairs on one's head.[28] The knowledge God has is not objective. That is, God does not know things *as things*. He knows creatures as his creatures. This is *relational* knowledge. This is the difference between claiming "I know theology" and "I know my mother." Of course I know things about my mother, but I cannot but know all of those things through the lens of a lifetime of relationship. I can learn theology by reading a book. I can only know *about* a person by reading a biography. Until you "get to know" someone you don't truly know them. God truly knows his creation. The Hebrew understanding of knowledge, *ydh* (עדי), like other ancient perspectives, has its roots in relational familiarity rather than factual assertions. Where knowing-God is lacking through covenant unfaithfulness, there will be human moral breakdown that itself causes ecological disaster.[29]

Thus, all of God's knowledge is relational. We are not as capable of that kind of knowledge. We all have a relational limit, and for introverts like myself, that relational limit is rather low. That is why I quickly turn to categorical knowledge, and love it. I love the ivory tower, from where I can look down on others with their petty and limited relational knowledge. I can gain the power of knowledge by simplifying those who dwell below. From a distance all things are beautiful, orderly, small, and manageable. But the greatest mistake of theology is to believe that God is a distant, objective observer who sees us as small. The God of the Bible is intimately related to every creature in creation—from the smallest ant to the grandest galaxy. This seems to me the best definition of what godhood must mean: infinite capacity for individual relationships actualized in love. Though it is a conceptual misstep to move from this to the creation, as though *relationality* were, in and of itself, some participation in divinity. This, ironically, is the complete inversion of true relationships by the creation of a conceptual category of relationality.

---

27. Ps 147:4; Isa 40:26.

28. Matt 10:30.

29. Hos 4:1–3.

As the image of God, our knowledge of creation should reveal this kind of relational knowledge. In order to know an animal, for example, we must relate to it through the Creator. This animal is known by God, named by God, and loved by God. When the mind of the image of God functions correctly, it has a divine imagination. That is, it sees all things through the lens of God's relationship with it. Only the image of God can imagine the world rightly, and thus image God to the world.

Truth takes on a different meaning in such a situation. Truth is not a list of objective facts about a thing. Truth is not the correct identification of categories to which a thing belongs. Truth is not the correct description of reality. Truth is not about "reality" at all. For God and for the image of God, *truth is a relationship of faithfulness or constancy.* This is the more ancient or basic meaning of the word "truth" in Hebrew, Greek, and English. They all refer to constancy of character, which, by extension, means accurate representation. Truth for the image of God can only mean accurate representation of the character of God by relating to all things through their relationship with God.

This point is of the utmost importance to understand for the argument of this book. Human imagination, as understood through the lens of the image of God, is shaped entirely by mediating all things through this relationship. Thus, knowledge apart from relationship will have to be mediated by some other relationship, whether through the serpent of Genesis 3, scientific categorization, or identity politics. It is only through relationship with God that any stable concept of truth can be established, because truth is constancy of character. When truth is based on the flux of nature or the universe, truth itself must fluctuate, and the human imagination of reality along with it.

Eden

Before we move on to examine the epistemological transformation given in Genesis 3 in more detail, we must first look at the imagination of Genesis as it pertains to Eden. Eden, which probably means "delight," is a theological vision of what right relationship with God looks like prior to corruption. I hesitate to call it a utopia or "paradise" in the normal sense of that word. Genesis is more nuanced than typical utopias in which all experiences of evil are reversed in a fantastic manner. Bonhoeffer is wrong when he sees the garden as a fairy tale because it is a lush land in the middle of a desert.[30] It makes sense that people assume modern aridity back thousands of years, but it is not accurate.[31]

First of all, Eden is not simply a garden, but a larger space. I think it is plausible to argue that Eden is the name of the kingdom of God in Genesis. It is physical territory that is larger than the garden within it. We know this because Gen 2:8 says that God planted a garden *"in* Eden," thus indicating that Eden was a wider area within which the garden was placed. Furthermore, there are two exile events in Genesis 3 and 4, Adam and Eve *from the garden,* Cain *from Eden* to Nod. Cain is sent away from a suitable and fruitful home in Delight to wander aimlessly in a dangerous and hard territory called Wandering.

Secondly, the garden of Eden is best understood as a palace garden, or perhaps a palace forest-orchard-wilderness. Much literature has lately spoken of the garden of Eden as a cosmic temple, and though there is some merit to these arguments, I have elsewhere argued in detail that the palatial idea is far superior. Palaces have gardens. Gardens are managed natural land that symbolically display the power of the king to order the natural world to his will. God's garden may thus rightly be understood as wilderness. Human gardens are highly simplified and orderly. We cut hedges into square shapes, trees into rounded shapes. We make clear and paved paths, arrange plants in places most pleasing to us, and perhaps even create peaceful water features. A palace garden is part of the microcosm of the palace complex in which the ordered gardens represent the civilization of the natural world by bringing it under the king's control.

But creation is *God's* garden. It is ordered according to *his* design and desire, as explained in Genesis 1. The natural order *is* the order of God, and as such, land unmanaged by humans is precisely what God's garden would look like. This is suggested in places like Ezekiel 31 in which Eden is not a garden like we normally understand it, with vegetables, fruit trees, and flowers, but a great forest. Thus, the garden of Eden is the choicest of God's forests, at the very least. It is also a place to walk in the cool of the day. The image of a king walking with his advisors in a land that most suitably demonstrates the restful, peaceful reign of his kingdom is not hard to understand. It is in that sense a "paradise," or palace garden.[32]

---

30. Bonhoeffer, *Creation and Fall*, 53.

31. Scott, *Against the Grain*, 47–55.

32. Paradise is a Persian loanword used by the Greek translators of Genesis in the Septuagint, thus indicating that these Second Temple Jews understood the garden of

Thirdly, Eden is not the whole world. It has boundaries. The whole creation is not part of God's kingdom in Genesis 2–4. Does that mean that outside chaos still reigns? Is there chaos that humans must venture to quell at some point? Certainly this is a common theme in ancient cosmogonies. Because this myth is so prevalent, many scholars assume that the presence of chaotic imagery in Scripture means that the Bible retains this perspective. I would suggest that Genesis 2–4 is a story about creation from a later perspective that anticipates the need of reconciliation. This is why we can easily ask unanswerable questions like, who does Cain fear if not Adam? Whom do Cain and Seth marry, sisters only? Why is the land outside of Eden portrayed as the wild east? Genesis 2–4 is not interested in creating an airtight story about creation that works out its logical consistencies in detail. It is interested in setting up the great contrast that will occur throughout the rest of Genesis 1–11, and really through the rest of Scripture. There is a people of God and a kingdom of God who are set up *against and for* the rebellious kingdoms of the world. Thus, the forces of evil in the Bible are not a remnant of chaos, but the active rebellion of human civilizations that are responsible for the corruption of creation. Human groups are often personified into chaos beasts, just as Ezekiel 31 both personified Assyria as a nation, and then turned it into a great world-tree that set itself up against the trees of Eden. Human orders of great empires set themselves up against God and his people. Rather than *Chaoskampf*, God laughs at the hubris of humanity.[33] Thus, the mission of Adam and Eve as the image of God is not to pacify a chaos through their dominion. Their mission was to represent the peaceful rule of the kingdom of God. Reconciliation is anticipated in the very narration of Genesis 2.

This is a vital point, and one upon which a deep disagreement will emerge between myself and other ecotheologians. What is the human task? For many it is a task of management, stewardship, or care for creation. I will argue in the next chapter that creation, as God created it, is irretrievably lost to the human ability of perception. Thus, the human task is not to keep and maintain a creation no longer perceptible. It is certainly not a mission of "development," or the myth of civilization. The task is reconciliation.

Eden as such a palace garden.

33. Pss 2:4; 37:13; 59:8.

Adam was created out of the soil to care for and protect the soil. This Hebrew word-play is often missed when Adam is created out of "dust." I always imagined some kind of dry clay or silty soil, like we have in Colorado, which turns into a fine dust when very dry. Adam is created out of the fertile and wild soil of the garden. Given that Mesopotamia in the ancient Near East was an alluvial plain, the soil from which Adam was made would have been very fertile, not the dust of the arid desert. His role was to care for this soil. But Genesis 2:15 cannot be read without the remainder of the narrative, which continues through Genesis 4, as indicated by the dividing phrase "these are the generations of . . ." found in Genesis 2:4 and then again in 5:1. Adam's role *was* to serve and protect the soil from which he was taken. This fertile soil is not simply the soil, it is symbolic of the creation itself. It is the source of life for all living things, including of the man himself. It is never personified as a "mother" and to do so reintroduces a lot of ideas Genesis is specifically avoiding, like the deification of the earth and creation by sexual reproduction. Some ancient Near Eastern cosmologies have the copulation of a primordial male sky god with a female earth/soil goddess, as is also the case in Hesiod's *Theogony*. But in the Bible, soil symbolizes the rule of the Creator over the creation, and the soil itself will provide something of a litmus test for the state of creation thereafter. This is why the soil cried out when Cain killed Abel. Human crime is reflected in the soil itself. This will then explain the flood and why God enacted the great uncreation. The link between the health of the soil and human sin is also seen especially in Leviticus 18.

Eden is local. It is emplaced. It reveals God as God-with-us, empowering us to work with him. Eden's boundaries imply that the world outside has need of the image of God, but that it must be continually local. Christ has no *universal* reign, in the sense of ruling over the universe as *pantocrator*.[34] His reign will consist in putting all things under his feet and the submission of all rebel forces.[35] That is, his reign is incarnate and relational, and is the result of reconciliation not domination. It is not the impersonal, aloof dominion of an emperor. This shows that the image of God must be emplaced and local to accomplish its task. The moment it systematizes it engages in the type of simplification that leads to centralization, power, and rejection of responsibility.

---

34. See Ellul, *False Presence of the Kingdom*, 69.

35. 1 Cor 15:25; Heb 2:8; Phil 2:10–11.

No Creation Ethic

But we cannot shortcut the process of the Bible and systematize it. This is the problem that leads to ecological disaster applied to the Bible itself. As Christians, we can only engage in the story of Eden from long after this story, and after Christ's earthly ministry. This means that we cannot properly know what the image of God is, what the human task is, what creation is, or even who God is, through the story of Adam and Eve in Eden alone. Genesis 1–2 cannot serve alone as the basis for any ecological ethic based on abstracted principles. It must be read as the introduction to the story of sin, rescue, and reconciliation. In that sense, Eden is not a utopia that we should aim to rebuild or recover. Eden is like a great-grandmother in the genealogy of the people of God. It cannot be recovered, and we must learn who we are through the stories of our ancestry. This is exactly the function it plays in the book of Genesis as a whole. Utopianism must be thoroughly rejected.

CHAPTER 10

Temptation and Sin

THE ACTION OF CREATION occupies, by volume, a very minor place in the Bible. That God is the Creator is assumed throughout the Bible, but it is not often the main point. Rather, God is far more regularly characterized as the Rescuer, Liberator, Savior. This is true for both the Old and New Testaments. But Genesis 1–3 is given pride of place in the Bible as a proper introduction. Creation is only the introduction of the Bible. God is not continually in the act of creating. Maintaining a created order is not the same as speaking all things into being. This does not mean that God is no longer the Creator. Again, we must not confuse the act of creation for the product, the creation itself. While God does not change, the creation does. God's role shifts from Creator to Rescuer in the face of the big problem. But what is the big problem, according to the Bible? Rebellious humans.

Theologians have traditionally labelled this problem as *sin*, with its basis in Greek *hamartia* (ἁμαρτία). Genesis does not call the actions of Adam and Eve in Genesis 3 sin, however. Their actions are not given a specific label. Instead, their actions are described in a variety of ways. It is the apostle Paul who describes the notion of original sin, linking the actions of Adam to a fault that lies within every human thenceforth. It is therefore useful to listen to the text of Genesis 3 on its own terms before integrating it with the rest of Scripture and Paul's theological commentary.

Temptation to Cosmos

There are two primary temptation narratives in the Bible, Genesis 3 and the temptation of Jesus in the Synoptic Gospels. The temptation of Jesus is a recapitulation of the temptation of Adam and Eve, combined with an experience similar to Israel's wilderness wandering. They are designed to prove the man, to test his purpose and his faithfulness. What we find in the temptation of Jesus is that the Spirit of God brings Jesus into the wilderness for the purpose of being tempted. That is, God leads Jesus into the place where he will be tempted. Why would the same not be true of Adam and Eve? God created the serpent and placed it in the garden for the same purpose—to test whether the image of God can rightly represent God in the field. Of course we know the story of their failure, and though I love commenting on the text of Genesis 3, I have done so in depth elsewhere.[1] So, let's get to the heart of the matter.

The serpent is said to be more "crafty" than all of the other creatures. This is worth dwelling on for a moment, as scholars have recently revised some traditional thinking about how we understand this concept in Greek literature. Odysseus in Homer is often called crafty, sly, cunning. James C. Scott considers that the Greek word *mētis* should not carry the negative connotations we associate with it. *Mētis* is better understood as the local, applied knowledge one gains from experience. It is the skill of a *craftsman*.[2] Even in English the link between craftsmanship, craftiness, and craft is clear. The serpent is wise and intelligent, not simply a trickster. He seems to have the right kind of wisdom and seems trustworthy. This is a strong link to tricksters of old as found in blacksmith gods of Hephaestus/Vulcan, Ptah, or Wayland. The knowledge of those who are specialists in their crafts, who seem to be able to come up with the right answer at the right time through alternative ways of thinking, was often perceived as dangerous, though useful.[3] Notably, all of the gods I just mentioned, as with the serpent in Genesis 3, are physically lame or made lame as something of a restriction on their power. It is possible that the serpent in Genesis is accessing similar mythical backgrounds and ideas. But what links these disparate cultures and their different crafty tricksters? Ancient peoples recognized both the attraction and danger of specialization and

---

1. Wagenfuhr, *Plundering Egypt*, chapter 4.

2. As far as I am aware, the sly god of crafts is always masculine in ancient literature.

3. The Hebrew עָרְם is similarly ambiguous, referring both to craftiness, wisdom, and prudence. The positive sense is seen in Prov 15:5; 19:25.

secret knowledge. Trade secrets were kept very close by medieval guilds, and consequently such guilds could wield incredible political influence, as modern corporations do today.

The temptation that Adam and Eve faced, put into this context, is for a secret specialist knowledge, a kind of initiation into a secret club from which God was ostensibly excluding them. The serpent's temptation was that they would have the knowledge of good and evil. This is where the deception of the serpent occurs. The knowledge of good and evil is not a trade secret of divine beings. It is knowledge that belongs to the one Ruler alone. This is because in an era long before Magna Carta, all law was the personal judgment of an authority; there was no notion of an objective law code to which even a king must submit. The king is the law, and his judgment is law. The king could pass on instruction or his counsel, and this is likely what *torah* means.[4]

The temptation to be like God, then, is a temptation to become judges or creators of value. This is what Friedrich Nietzsche realized in his philosophy. For him, the *Übermensch* was made superior by the will to power and the transvaluation of value. He realized that willing power is to not submit to judgment or evaluation, but to create value. God's judgments formed the creation. Recall that judgment is definition, and definition is precisely how all creation takes place. Thus, the temptation is to become fellow creators. Again Nietzsche understood this when he, through his character Zarathustra, says, "Companions the creator seeks and not corpses, nor herds or believers either. Fellow creators the creator seeks, those who inscribe new values on new tables."[5] And this is precisely the temptation of the serpent, to become co-creators with God, to move from creature to creator, to move from community to individuality by isolation. At this point it is important to note that the temptation is not to something inherently evil. As Paul will later say, "Do you not know that the saints will judge the *cosmos*? . . . Do you not know that we will judge angels?"[6] This godlikeness of judgment is not inherently out of the reach of humanity. Human striving, creativity, transgression of boundaries, is not the problem that the serpent raises. The problem is *method*. The method by which humans go about attempting to be godlike is illegitimate, irrational, and parasitic.

---

4. Walton and Walton, *The Lost World of the Israelite Conquest*, 90.

5. Nietzsche, *Thus Spoke Zarathustra*, 21.

6. 1 Cor 6:2–3.

Eve "saw" that the fruit was good for food and pleasing to the eye. This "seeing" is the irrational deception. One cannot simply "see" value, one must judge value. As I said in the previous chapter, Adam and Eve as the image of God would have to have a living and active relationship with God in order to properly perceive creation and its value, and thus interact with it rightly. The serpent's temptation is cunning in that human loyalty to God is challenged at its heart, but without a direct line of assault on God himself. God is indicted as untrustworthy because the value of the creation should be obvious without relational mediation.

Now, the fruit of the tree was not magic and it did not communicate the knowledge of good and evil. Eating the fruit merely symbolized the betrayal that had occurred. Adam and Eve chose to become like God by being judges of value. But in so doing they cut themselves off from the source of their knowledge. No longer was knowledge mediated through their relationship with God, it was mediated through a projection. No longer did they perceive creation, they saw Nature. Other peoples would see gods and goddesses. People of the Enlightenment would see atomistic matter. In all of these cases the source of knowledge by which people make evaluations is no longer the Creator, but the creation and their own evaluations of it. The apostle Paul speaks of this as a darkening of the human mind and a consequent exchange of the glory of God for imitation of creatures.

Because they have decided to judge for themselves what is good and evil, they no longer submit to God. The absurdity of the situation becomes clear in that, whereas God can be confident of his judgment or evaluation, humans require projections. This is never more evident than in online interactions on social media in which people, with the cover of anonymity, are far bolder in their evaluations. This is the opposite of godlikeness. The action of judgment is godlike; the cowardice is all-too-human and shameful. The irony is that the shame lies not in nakedness, but in our clumsy self-covering and projections. It is precisely in attempting to be godlike that humans reveal their greatest weakness, and in that weakness become destroyers, parasites, and chaos monsters.

Sabbath Disrupted

But Genesis 3 continues where Genesis 2 ended. Adam and Eve were previously naked and unashamed. After eating the fruit their eyes were opened and they perceived their nakedness. Now nakedness is not a concept of which they would have otherwise been aware. No other creatures clothe themselves. They desire the covering of mediation. They must now project an image upon the world and all other relationships. Their identities now have to be constructed in a crafty manner. To do this, they must turn aspects of the creation into resources for repurposing, by turning leaves into clothes. Such an innocuous act betrays the underlying transformation in their imagination. No longer do the leaves belong to the trees for photosynthesis, or to the ground for rot and soil replenishment, they now belong to them for their purposes. Creation is turned into resources, and this re-confirms the establishment of the false authority of humanity in attempting to become godlike.

The Sabbath rest of God's creation is disrupted by these actions. Not only are Adam and Eve exiled from the garden of Eden, they are given curses. Adam is cursed with toil in food production, Eve with toil in human reproduction. Obviously both will share in both processes, so this shouldn't be taken as some tacit admission of the assignation of gender roles. Rather, it is an active curse by God upon his rebellious people as a consequence from which they may learn. This is not vindictiveness, but punishment for education, correction, and protection of the creation.[7] Humans may yet again act as the image of God, provided they submit to God's authority and are reconciled. God's kingdom reign can and will return, as is hinted at by the promise of the crushing of the serpent. Indeed, as we will see, Jesus is the one who inaugurates God's kingdom reign by defeating the power of rebellion and freeing humans of God's curse through discipleship and union with Christ.

The curse on labor in food production is not the intensification of Adam's normal agricultural labor, it is the creation of agriculture.[8] Note that "cursed" in 3:17 is passive. God is not actively cursing the ground or transforming creation into something bad. The soil is now cursed because of the agricultural labor of humans. It is cursed by the commodified relationship the man has with the soil. Adam ate from the trees of the garden of Eden. He gathered what creation produced and ate from a great abundance. Now there is scarcity, which demands hard labor, and for this some form of gardening or farming is required. But this is no easy task.

7. God's discipline is a theme in much of the Bible: e.g., Lev 26; Jer 31:18; 1 Cor 11:32; Heb 12; Rev 3:19; and throughout the Proverbs.

8. Many read this as a metaphorical recording of the anthropological transition from hunter-gatherer to settled agriculture. Scott, *Against the Grain*, 72.

Instead of God's Sabbath rest, humans are given hard labor. Certainly there is good that may come of this labor. Those who work hard generally grow in physical and mental strength and endurance. Labor is often the grounds upon which community and character are formed in us. Writers like Wendell Berry or Norman Wirzba show the benefits of the deep connection to the land that the hard labor of agrarian life brings. But we must be clear *agrarian life is disciplinary, not telic.* That means that city building despises the discipline of God, as Cain does.

The soil is cursed because humans will now repurpose it, and it will produce thorns and thistles. These are not evil plants or weeds in creation. God is not now introducing weeds. There is no such thing as a weed in God's creation. Human agriculture will now transform the landscape and the soil will fight this transformation. It will continue producing native plants that are best suited for a location, even if these are of no food benefit for humans. These will become weeds to the human mind set on producing a surplus of food for an empire out of a workable plot of land.

Eve's curse of labor in childbearing is similar to Adam's in food production. Instead of Sabbath peace between male and female, where each is a suitable helper for the other, now the woman will submit. There are challenges in translating 3:16, with various English translations entirely contradicting others. Is the woman's desire for her husband who will rule over her? Or is her desire set against his, and he will rule over her? Either the woman lovingly submits, or does so unwillingly. The hint at the correct answer comes from the curse of the ground. Adam is at enmity with the ground, and the woman with the man. The submission is unwilling and violent. Recall that pre-agrarian peoples were "relatively egalitarian."[9] It is within the context of settled agricultural life that gender hierarchy becomes far more prevalent. Ancient peoples who understood themselves as embedded within the natural world and its cycles, often compared women to the earth, and their wombs to the soil. The connection should be fairly obvious—the womb is the place where the human seed develops, implanted by the man within the woman to bear fruit in due season. Enmity of the man with the soil is akin to the enmity between the woman and the man.

With this connection in mind, we see that just as humans will now fight with the earth for food, so now man and woman will not be at peace. The enmity between human and soil, male and female, and humans and

---

9. Scott, *Against the Grain*, 5.

the serpent is the running theme. Sabbath is lost because God is rejected. The curse of increased pain in birth again puts humans in their place as part of the creation, not as masters over it. How can humans claim to be gods when they age, die, and cannot easily reproduce themselves?

Sabbath is broken even more clearly in the enmity between humans and the serpent. Their rivalry shouldn't simply be understood as Satan vs. humanity. This is the birth of chaos. Now that there is enmity between the creation and humans there is fear. What is chaos but the experience of fear and powerlessness, and its reification? The serpent will now become, for humans, the chaos monster who seems to be at fault for every bad thing that happens. Slaying it will fix every problem. This is the beginning of the human act of cosmogony through which all of creation is re-read as a history of conflict of civilization vs. chaos and disorder.

After this great confrontation, God exiles Adam and Eve from the garden of Eden. From this point in Genesis, God is the adversary of human ambition. In their desire to be godlike, God prevents them from seizing immortality by eating of the tree of life, which may itself be one of the two columns of the throne of God from which the river of life flows.[10] They are not to have access to God's throne if they have made themselves rivals of God. Let's just pause for a moment to reflect again on this idea that the garden of Eden was an orchard-forest-wilderness. If that is the case, as Ezekiel seems to suggest, God is enthroned upon his wild creation, as in Psalm 29. As the God of the wild, he is going to be understood thenceforth as a force of chaos. The enmity between God and humans means that humans will perceive the acts of this God as inimical to their desires. This is what Cain does, and we see this chaos imagery in the flood of Noah and again in God's confusion of the people of Babel.

Craft and Violence

Genesis 4–11 continues the story of humanity and it traces the development of techniques and technologies. In response to the curses of the God who now seems like the author of chaos, humans create ways of overcoming chaos. As a result of estranging himself from God, who brings Cain to account, Cain builds a city. Cain also makes a name for himself as he makes a lineage for himself. His son and his city share the same name. He is craftily imposing himself upon the world by developing an artificial

10. See Rev 22:1–2.

environment. Rather than the garden, humans choose to live in cities. The built environment is the full extension of the development of clothing—the creation of a mediated and projected identity used as a covering or mask. It is notable that Cain's motive for building the city resides in his rejection of God's protection. Cain will accept nothing from God, but will do it himself. He will construct and evaluate his own creation, which like Adam and Eve's clothing made of leaves, is shameful and ridiculous. Nevertheless, God does not openly oppose it.

Other people in Cain's lineage are responsible for the development of other techniques and technologies. They are the crafty ones, who invent the best of human culture—the urbanites, musicians, smiths, the herdsmen. No such attributions are given to the line of Seth who are treated in a different manner in Genesis 5. Note that Genesis 4, which contains the line of Cain through Lamech, is the conclusion of the creation narrative that began in chapter 2. The story goes from Eden through temptation, exile, murder, exile, civilization, and finally vengeful violence. Lamech, the seventh generation of Cain, is the completion or perfection of Cain's line. There is an inescapable link here, then, between violence and craftiness.

What is it about creativity and violence, then? Why does Genesis have such a problem with human creativity and civilization? Creation is unique to God. Human creativity is an entirely different category of action. It involves a different subject (God the Creator vs. human creatures), a different object (nothingness vs. God's creation), and a different behavior (speaking/judging vs. reshaping). Thus, the error comes in how we imagine creativity as though it were an imitation of God, as though we become godlike through these actions. We use creaturely methods to try and transcend God's creation. This only comes by violent transformations of God's creation.

Among those who recognize the antiurban and anti-technological elements of Genesis, many scholars confidently state that technology itself isn't evil, only that it was misused for violence by Cain's line.[11] That answer is not satisfactory. Why does Genesis even mention Cain's line as crafty people, if it believed that Seth's line did similar things but in nonviolent or nondestructive ways? I think the answer must take us back to the ancient mind and its suspicion of specialist knowledge.

---

11. E.g., Bauckham, *Bible and Ecology*, 34–35.

Specialists are good at what they do, but they often stereotypically lack what we might call practical wisdom or political savvy. Specialists, by definition, do not work for the common good but for private and special interests. They are a political force that must be managed, not empowered. When specialist knowledge (*techne*) takes over, violence is often the result. Why? When someone who values the development of a specific project more than the common good is met with resistance, they will act according to their values and will sacrifice the common good for their private interest. Thus the "mad scientist" archetype that we saw in its ancient form in blacksmithing gods, and in the wile of the trickster figure (e.g., Loki). Such figures are stock villains in modern comic book mythologies as well. Now, I am not claiming this is precisely what Genesis is intending by linking Cain's line with civilizational development. More likely would be the prevalent theme in the Hebrew Scriptures of suspicion of power centers like Egypt, Assyria, Babylon, and later Greece and Rome. What is often not told in narratives of civilizational progress is its human cost. We must remember that the Bible was not written by the "winners" of civilizational progress, but by the victims of civilization. It is a collection of books written by escaped slaves, backwater prophets, minor kingdom officials, fishermen, and farmers. Even its kings David and Solomon are minor figures on the imperial scale. That is to say, the Bible opposes the myth of civilization, and an essential part of that myth is the linking of human skill in craft and the necessity of civilizing the savage, or creating cosmos out of ostensible chaos. The Hebrews were savages civilized by slavery in Egypt. Moses, the civilized royal "goes native" by his long exile in the Midian wilderness. He returns as the liberator. It is not hard to see that such a story would not well-dispose a people toward civilization. In early Genesis, then, Cain's line represents the cosmic line and Genesis recognizes that development requires destruction.

Another simple way to think of this is simply in the requirements of building a city. Civilizations may have collapsed due to deforestation. The economic necessities and realities of maintaining a large ancient city could easily overtax its miniscule transportation capacity, meaning the capital city could starve itself as a victim of its own success. Without destruction of forestland there can be no farming, and without centralized control, expropriation or taxation, and the creation of hierarchies, development is not possible.[12] If the whole creation were perceived *as*

12. See Scott, *Against the Grain*, 195–200.

creation, the destruction of forestland for the type of intensive agriculture that states demand for taxation purposes would be literally unimaginable. Those who live in isolation from the land and who spend their time in artifice or craft, cannot help but see the land as a resource for their own ends. They are not part of the community of creation, they are masters who seek growth, profit, development. Once people are unable to perceive the creation as creation they must live in a world they can create, control, and manage. The creation becomes Nature—a reified other. Genesis presents Cain's line as descent into human parasitism through the lens of craft, civilization, and violence.

God's curses given to Eve and Adam in Genesis 3 have presented themselves as key points in human "development." The reduction of the danger of childbearing and the easy production of a superfluity of food have been major tasks for modern peoples. Like Cain with his city, those who reject God turn to alternative means of achieving good. However, the rejection of God leads to unanticipated consequences. Ecologically speaking, we have created a vicious cycle of soil depletion, climate change, agricultural industrialization, habitat destruction, and forest clearances in order to produce more food to feed the world. This, combined with lower infant mortality and mortality in general, has led to a rapidly growing global population since the Industrial Conversion. As population grows, so too do new means of food production, many of which are now proving deeply unsustainable. Morally, we believe that averting human hunger is superior to decimating the soil and global forestland. But this prioritization of human need and the resourcification of the earth, i.e., parasitism, will lead to major harvest shortfalls within a few decades, according to the UN soil report. If this comes to pass, we will have done little more than pass off our starvation to our (more numerous) grandchildren.

The Flood

The culmination of human parasitism is seen by rampant violence and continual evil intent. This gives context for the flood, which otherwise seems to be the greatest act of violence in the Bible. The order of creation is corrupted by the commingling of the "sons of God" and the "daughters of men." By the loss of the people of God, there remains no further hope for the creation or for human justice. The flood is the primordial act of near uncreation. It is here that God is revealed to be the God of chaos in ancient cosmogonies.

Genesis rewrites the common cosmogony of the ancient Near East, appropriating its imagery to reveal something about God. The flood serves the great purpose of denying the existence of other deities, as well as revealing that God will most certainly not destroy the creation (again). The great flood is not the victory of the good high god over the monster of chaos. It is the justice of God revealed in wrath against the corruption of creation by humanity and its evil. From the human perspective, the God of chaos wages war against human order. The flood also sets the stage for God's acting though a new line of specially chosen people. At first it was Adam, then Abel, then Seth, then Noah, and then Abraham, Isaac, and Jacob. These are the patriarchs of the line of God's people in Genesis. Each of these lines is threatened or destroyed in some way, and most of these have branching lineages, not all of which continue in the character of God's people. Genesis could be called a genealogy of God's creation and people with the challenges they faced and God's rescuing activity on display. So, the irony is that the flood is God's *salvation* for the creation by preserving its integrity through a great purge. But the Bible is also clear that, although God will do anything for his creation, he will not again destroy it. That dubious honor apparently falls to us.

Babel

The conclusion of the flood sees the immediate return of sin. The story of Babel is vital to understand as the culmination and completion of the Bible's narrative of prehistory, or its introduction. Genesis is about the people of God as descended from Abraham, Isaac, and Jacob. This is why it ends with Joseph in Egypt as the prelude to Exodus. Genesis is the story about how the people of God found their way into Egyptian bondage and how they forged a unified identity. Babel, as the conclusion of the prehistory of Abraham, continues the theme we saw clearly in Cain's lineage. At Babel, humans have built an artificial environment for themselves, a city and a tower-temple. At Babel, humanity is united in spirit and in language. God opposes the construction of their built environment, and he opposes their unity. The unity is not an evil in and of itself, of course, except that this unity comes from self-creation through construction. That is, through projection and reification.

Humans do not gain or create value by construction, but we imagine that we do, because we refuse to take responsibility equal to our power. When we build something, we identify ourselves by it and thus establish a reality by which we can judge our experiences. We create something objective and real, redeploying it in the task of valuation as our point of reference and objectivity. This is the grounds of truth for a people. God does not oppose the building project of Babel itself, but human unity of purpose in self-construction. God opposes the sin of Adam and Eve, particularly when it is expressed in the multiplication of power through cooperation.

Babel is, like all cities, a microcosm both of human reality and human sin. The two become the same in the city, because the objective of the city is to create a reality that may form the basis of valuations that do not rest upon the knowledge of personal judgment. The city creates an environment in which humans are able to live by "natural law," offloading the responsibility for judgment on the mere act of adaptation to environmental necessities. The natural law of the city, however, is entirely different to the natural law of non-human environments. Furthermore, the identity of a people becomes concretized by construction. It is the literal microcosm, built to correspond to the human imagination. It is concealed from conscious thought so that it removes the burden of responsibility for judgment. This is the structure of human sin, and the city of Babel is human sin made into a fully built cosmos.

God's opposition results in disunity. Here the theme of diversity and *saming* that I introduced earlier comes into play. Human cooperation works through the construction of common identity. This identity is a projection, of course. Identity is a pure social construct. As such, identity works by integration and saming, by reducing a time-bound and ever-changing complex individual with complex spatiotemporal relationships into a single timeless, objective identity. The people at Babel worked to be unified. The cost of this kind of unity is the end of diversity. While it is currently popular to "celebrate diversity" this sacred secularist task is actually a totalitarian repression of *meaningful* diversity.[13] Our celebration of differences is actually a root metaphysical claim that race, gender, sexuality, and religion are all categories of diversity that must be submitted to a higher categorical unity. That is, whatever diversity we celebrate is a barely masked form of saming and integration. True

---

13. Wagenfuhr, "Jacques Ellul and Charles Taylor."

diversity is irreconcilable, because it cannot be submitted to a higher value or identity. True diversity requires relationality and a refusal of categorical similarity. Ecologically speaking, the human process of saming is cosmization, and it leads to the destruction of true ecological diversity. Saming is domestication. This is why those who do not conform to this celebration of diversity are called names fairly synonymous with savage or barbarian, like *racist, bigot, homophobe, xenophobe*, people who *fear* the truth rather than *hate* a different group identity. It is not accidental that people who are susceptible to receive this name-calling tend to be from poorer and less urban areas, as all savages are. This is not uniquely modern, of course, nor actually related to the symptomatic issues involved like race or sexuality. It is easy to spot historically by those who are given pejorative and highly simplified titles, like pagan (hill-person), heathen (from the heathland), or hillbilly (a hill-person).

The Babel story thus reveals God's rejection of the human practice of saming seen in making a name for ourselves, because the consequence of the myth of civilization is that humans become out-of-control parasites. "This is the beginning of their work and now nothing that they propose to do will be impossible."[14] It isn't that God is afraid that humans will take over heaven, it's that their unity spells doom for diversity. This is why the consequence of confusing the language makes sense. God, once again as the author of ostensible chaos to human civilization, introduces an inability for people to understand one another, which ensures a fair level of diversity and disunity. It is hard to overstate the importance of disunion for diversity, if the proposed union is categorical rather than relational. Categorical union, or saming, destroys diversity, though this simple logical fact rooted in categorical and logical hierarchy is politically impossible to speak now.

Creation Lost: Social Construction and Epistemology

Now that we have surveyed the Genesis account of human sin, the background narrative for the story of reconciliation through the people of Israel, we turn to the Pauline perspective. In Romans 1, Paul outlines an imaginative inversion that lies at the heart of sin. For Paul, sin clearly follows a pattern of rebellion—the mind being darkened, with the result that people do irrational and immoral things. This order of operations is

14. Gen 11:6.

crucial. Sin does not consist in sexual deviancy, in murder, in greed, or in exploitation. Those are symptomatic. Injustice is not the root issue; it is the dark blossom of the corrupt tree. The root issue is *relational rebellion and the darkening of the mind.* In Ephesians 4:17–24 Paul speaks about sin both as a darkening of the mind and a hardness of heart (i.e., rebellion against God), which result in reprehensible practices.

For Paul, and I would argue for Genesis, sin is *a broken relationship that leads to an epistemological problem.* By estrangement from the Creator, creation is lost. It is fundamentally impossible to perceive *as creation.* This is the basis of the social construction of reality. The very concept of reality, as an objective existence of fully independent matter, is problematic. It is categorically impossible to know, even for God, that there could be such a thing as a *thing-in-itself,* let alone reality independent of the participant. I say "participant" because reality contains the myth of the observer. For many moderns the idea of God is like a great scientist who is an independent observer of reality, the projected truly-removed-one who is capable of full neutrality. God is not an independent observer, but is always and only known by the relationships he has with the creation. God is the incarnate Christ. God is the one with a personal relationship with every creature. God is not neutral and cannot be neutral. This is an intrinsically ecological concept because it demands all things be connected by their relationship with God.

Neutrality is a false myth because it removes the subject from the object in a relationship. Just as Heisenberg came to learn from quantum mechanics, observation is a type of interference. There is no such thing as passive observance. Even God is always in some kind of interested relationship with his creation. Also, when we remember that creation came by judgment, it becomes impossible to believe that God created neutral fact or reality that is independent of value. What God created was declared good. The very act of God's creation made his creation good, because of the character of God and the character of his relationship with the creation.

The effect of sin on this situation is not to obscure reality, it is to *construct reality.* Sin is based on the idea of independent judgment and evaluation, as we saw. Once humans do this, they come to believe that their projection of a concept of neutral reality exists and that they can be independent or neutral observers of it. Thus, sin results in the social construction of reality. The more people agree with the social construct, the more "neutral" and "real" it becomes.

This also means that creation is irretrievably lost to the human mind. Creation is never neutral, but always exists in the presence of God. Creation can never be understood as a resource for exploitation then, because that would require theft in the very presence of God. Instead, we destroy the notion of creation by estranging ourselves from the Creator. This enables us to believe that the "outside" world is a conglomeration of living and dead resources that can and should be exploited for human use. Anthropocentrism is inherent in the idea of reality, and modern materialistic humanism is the apex of this self-deception. It is not, however, new.

Ecologically speaking, the result is that human parasitism is inherent in the structure of human consciousness. The human mind is darkened, and it bears fruit that evinces this darkness. Although modernity reveals this darkness in sharper relief, it long preexists modernity and any notion humans have had of ecological degradation. In sin, *creation becomes chaos*. The created order becomes random disorder, chance, luck, fate. Natural spaces become wild, savage, out of bounds, and undefined. Humans begin to perceive their task as spreading civilization, as though their highly simplified methods of creating cosmos out of ostensible chaos were a benefit to everything. From the perspective of creation, however, human attempts to cosmize chaos are actually the introduction of a great horde of chaos monsters to an otherwise healthy set of relationships.

Conclusion

Humans act as parasites because of sin. Sin begins with a desire for godlikeness, a desire to create for oneself by the task of judgment and valuation. This necessitates a broken relationship with God the Creator. Estrangement from the Creator leads to an inability to perceive creation. Human minds are darkened by rebellion, and this leads to parasitic and self- or species-centered behaviors and beliefs. Injustice is symptomatic of this broken imagination. In this situation, humans project a false-reality, a socially constructed reality that is based on a flawed premise of reality. This situation is the root of ecological problems that are now coming to their conclusion and fullness.

Two other traditions of understanding sin compete with what I have laid out here: sin as metaphysical and sin as moral.

Those who see sin as a corruption of human nature tend to provide solutions through sacramentalism and worship practices. They tend to highlight participation in the divine nature, whether through the Eucharist, through church membership, or through more Eastern Orthodox notions of *theosis*. As I argued in *Plundering Egypt*, such a metaphysical perspective would not have been historically possible in much of the time of authorship of the Bible. Ecologically speaking this perspective, partially represented by Pope Francis in *Laudato Si*, has a potentially large problem. It upholds the human desire for godlikeness and gives it spiritual and mystical tasks to attain this. While many of these practices can be ecologically beneficial for the individual, it remains an individualist's escape from the human cosmos. The ascent to heaven is precisely the opposite of the good news I will narrate later. At its worst, this perspective promotes an escapist attitude. At its best, it sees humanity as playing some mediatory or priestly role for the creation, a view which is itself unbiblical and ecologically problematic in itself.

Those who view sin as moral corruption are probably the much larger contingent, and it is with them that I mostly contend. On this perspective, sin is lawbreaking or immorality. Through the power of the Holy Spirit, or asking Jesus into your heart, the Christian is able to act in accord with the law of God and be a good, moral person. This perspective misrepresents the concept of *torah*. Simply put, *torah* is the personal wise instruction of an authority figure who is treated as an authority because of his wisdom. *Torah* is not "law" if by that we mean it is an impersonal force to which even kings (like God) must submit.[15] Ecologically speaking, however, this perspective is deeply pernicious, because it turns sin into specific actions or personal behaviors that can be fixed. On this perspective, ecological disaster is akin to alcoholism. It is an addiction to fossil fuels and to consumerism. But like many addictions, through alternative habituation and therapy, we can break the bonds of this slavery. This is disastrous because many authors and leaders provide entirely *achievable* aims of moral transformation. Walking instead of driving, recycling, conserving, buying less stuff are all good as far as they go, but they do not even begin to approach a real solution to widespread and immanent ecological disaster. Now more than ever, sin is revealed in its corporate and structural nature. Baptizing practices that make only minor impacts on an ironclad system of injustice, and no effect on the imaginational

---

15. Wagenfuhr, *Unfotunate Words*, chapter 6.

substructure, provide people with satisfaction for guilt that they are on the side of the good guys. But personal moral transformation, which fits perfectly well into the agenda and bottom line of major corporations and states, will do little more than assuage guilt. It is a vision of sin that is far too small, and so its vision of reconciliation is likewise far too small. This too small reconciliation with God is no reconciliation at all, and thus also will not reconcile humans with creation. It will continue to minimize real problems because it is incapable of grasping that sin can be larger than one's personal behavior.

The message of the Bible on sin is that *everything* must change. "Creation earnestly waits for the revealing of the children of God."[16] These children of God are those who have had their ways of thinking entirely transformed by the renewal of the mind.[17] The whole of creation groans because it has been enslaved to corruption, subjected to futility.[18] Humans are the enemies of God and his creation. All of our achievements, everything we call "good" is corrupt[19] and corrupts the whole of creation. Until our minds are transformed by their return to the correct point of reference, God the Creator, there can be no true ecology. This mental transformation can only come by relational reconciliation, not by any independent personal moral, intellectual, spiritual, or religious effort.

16. Rom 8:19.
17. Rom 12:2.
18. Rom 8:20–22.
19. Mark 10:18; Luke 18:19.

CHAPTER 11

Reconciliation

THE SOLUTION TO SIN in the Bible is *reconciliation*, not salvation, nor forgiveness. The Bible is not about going to heaven when we die, or what is often meant by "salvation" in popular religion.[1] Salvation and forgiveness are means to reconciliation, not ends in themselves. Recall that the root problem of sin is relational brokenness in rebellion. Injustice and evil are the symptomatic results of sin. This means that rescue from injustice, while vitally important, is not the end in itself. Therefore, sin cannot be fixed as though it represented a malfunction in a machine. Christianity in a modern technological, urban, economic, and political environment has understood sin in ways fitting to its cosmos. Sin has been *translated* into modern language, which means that the solution to sin has also been translated. But in a wholly constructed environment, this translation has completely obscured the meaning of sin, and thus its solution. We think that the solution must be something constructive. We cannot allow it to challenge the very order of the cosmos. And yet, that is the very message about sin in the Bible. It is foundational and it means that *everything must change*. Heaven and earth will pass away, but the word of God endures forever.[2] That is, the cosmos as we know it will be destroyed. It is temporary and fleeting. Our environmentally bound broken imaginations are systematically incapable of solving our own problems, because the problem is endemic to the way that we think. We're stuck in a vicious feedback loop where the more we create and integrate into a totalizing cosmos, the less capable we are of imagining alternatives. The revelation of God from

1. For more on this see Wright, *Surprised By Hope*.
2. Matt 24:35; Mark 13:31; Luke 21:33.

the outside must then be the basis for any real solution, because it has to intervene in the feedback loop and break its cycle.

This is reconciliation in the Bible. It is the repeated story of God's intervention in human death-spirals to rescue people, and the creation from people. But reconciliation is perceived as chaos by a fully enclosed and self-absorbed cosmos. From the wilderness wandering of forty years, to Jonah's sojourn in the deep and in a sea monster, to God's joyful description of Behemoth and Leviathan in his self-revelation at the end of Job, to the Babylonian exile, to Jesus's wilderness temptation, and many more similar events, God is the one who breaks into an orderly cosmos to disrupt it for the sake of reconciliation by means of the renewal of the mind.

Reconciliation in the Hebrew Scriptures

While we do not have space to describe all of the acts of rescue and reconciliation in the Hebrew Scriptures, as they are many and have very similar shapes, we can focus on the formative event of the exodus for the people of God. The story begins in Genesis 12 with the call of Abraham, as a counterpoint to the narrative of Genesis 11, Babel. God calls Abram out of Ur, out of civilization. He brings him into a period of wandering in a largely unsettled land, a wilderness. He makes a covenant with him, that he and his descendants will be a blessing *for the purpose of blessing everyone else*. God gives Abraham guidance, *torah*, by which Abraham will be formed into a faithful representative of God's task of reconciliation. He is tested, fails, succeeds, and his lineage continues in this pattern. Joseph, his great-grandson, ends up in Egypt, second in command, apparently blessing the peoples of the world through his wisdom, but with the result that the people of God end up as slaves in a great empire. This is a classic pattern.

God similarly calls Moses out of Egypt after he murdered an Egyptian man who was beating a Hebrew slave. God rescues Moses, brings him to wander for a time in the wilderness, establishes a covenantal relationship with him, guides and empowers him, and commissions him with the task of rescue. Then Moses goes to set about on the project of liberating the people of God from Egyptian bondage.

The people are rescued or liberated from Egypt. God moves on their behalf against the structures of human power and civilization. God destroys the economy of Egypt, the very economy that Joseph had helped to save through his foresight of drought. God becomes the very agent of chaos to the precise imperial order of Egypt, decimating their systems of livelihood and their inheritors. Indeed, the miraculous murder of the firstborn sons of Egypt needs to be understood in this light: God systematically destroys the structures of Egyptian civilization and value, as he did in Babel, in ways foundational to their civilizational order. Linguistic unity is disrupted in Babel, systems of property and power inheritance are disrupted in Egypt. Egypt was a highly centralized grain economy. Nearly all of its property and up to half of its crop yields belonged to the Pharaoh, which were then disbursed in a centralized fashion.[3] The death of the firstborn sons, on top of the destruction of all the agricultural products, is all directly linked to liberation of the slaves and destruction of the system that enslaved them. As we'll see shortly, God's *torah* for the Israelites is opposed to Egyptian-style imperial rule.

God leads his people into the wilderness. They must remain in the wilderness for the span of an entire generation. The wilderness is a place where God intentionally crafts a people to have the kind of character needed for the task to which he has called them. Living for four hundred years in bondage produced an imaginary that needed to be deeply transformed. The place for this is wilderness. It is a harsh place, usually symbolized in the ancient Near East as chaos. But God provided daily bread, reeducating the people to understand that dependence upon God is the basis of a reconciled relationship, and the basis of a peaceful life in the land.

In the wilderness God established a covenant with the people. This covenant is rather unfortunately called "law." Again, it is not law in the modern sense of an impersonal system, it is *torah*, or instruction. It is the wise, personal guidance of an authority. This covenant is not for the purpose of pleasing God or for forming obedience, as though these were the primary ends in themselves. This *torah* is for the sake of forming a people who are worthy and capable of bearing God's mission of reconciliation with the same character. While breaking this law is sin, sin is not simply lawbreaking. That is, we tend to think of sin as violating legal commands, when the real sin is *disloyalty* and *rebellion*. As Jesus clarifies, however, sin is in the intention long before it becomes action, which is only the

---

3. Davis, *Scripture, Culture, and Agriculture*, 71.

fruit.[4] By rebellion one acts as though God had not rescued his people from bondage. Thus, we see that the problems throughout the wilderness generation are more related to the rebellious attitude of "stiff-necked people" than specific minutiae of legal violations.

God brings the people to the promised land and gives them tenancy of it. Throughout the Bible there is no notion of personal, private property as we now know it. The covenant of God with Israel is a longterm lease agreement whereby they are allowed use of the land for their livelihood and flourishing, provided that they do what God has required them. What does God require? To use the flourishing of the land to bless *all* peoples, including even foreigners. God does not bless the people because they are good, or for any reason concerning the people themselves. God blesses them with material blessings so that they can demonstrate reconciliation to the world. If they misuse the land—for profit, by hoarding it, by despoiling it, by not allowing it rest, God will evict them.

God does not give the land to the people as a gift. The earth is not a gift of God to humans. The creation is always God's and God's alone. While many agrarians argue for seeing the land as a gift, the problem with this is that a gift implies some kind of ownership transfer, which depends on many cultural factors. But God does not transfer rights of ownership or management to humans at any point in Scripture. The use of land is entirely conditional in the Bible. Rather than a gift, then, the land is entrusted within a covenant to the covenant people of God.[5] What that will ultimately mean for us today is that, not being in the Mosaic covenant, *we have no claim to any land whatsoever*, and no divine legitimation for the possession of any land whatsoever. All nations, all landlords, all corporations, are land-thieves from God, or squatters.

The mission of God's people, then, is to be agents of reconciliation between God and humans, between humans and other humans, but also between humans and the land itself. Let's take a look at some of the ways in which reconciliation applies to the land in the imagination, with consequences in practice.

4. See Matt 5:22, 28.

5. God is often spoken of *giving* the land to Israel (e.g., Exod 20:12), which might imply it is as a gift. However, gifts in the premonetary world were not understood as a total transfer of ownership, like a quit claim deed in modern real estate. A gift for premonetary peoples became an heirloom or an "inheritance" in the language of the Bible, which may even return in honor to its original possessor who imbued it with value. Thus, Israel is a tenet-farmer, rather than the farmer-owner, according to many parables of Jesus.

Reconciliation with the Land

Reconciliation with the land means seeing the land's produce as a blessing and a gift. God, not human labor, nor the state, is to be seen as the provider. This tears down the connection between work and reward, which forms the basis of motive for acquisition. In the wilderness God is shown to be a generous giver of manna that cannot be stored up. All the excesses immediately rot. The manna story reveals an inversion of the economy of Egypt, as Davis argues.[6] No one can get rich off of storage, nor will hard work lead to wealth. Again, God's people should simply gather the abundance God has provided and share it. This is seen again in the narrative of the spies who enter the promised land and return with a symbolic amount of the fruit of the land.[7] The Shema itself is given precisely so that God's people would remember that God has provided an abundance of produce for which they did not labor.[8]

God brings his people to a pre-prepared land. Thus, they are not participants in the formation of cosmos. They cannot make a name for themselves, as at Babel, by construction and projecting their self-image onto a built environment. The conquest of the land is presented in the text as denying the potential for the people to credit their own strength or ability for it.[9] There is a liturgical requirement for the Israelites to regularly integrate themselves into the story of the exodus, not only through Passover, but also through the first-fruits tithe.[10] This is a continual injection of an alternative narrative to the daily lives of Israelites who would otherwise be tempted to integrate into their environment and observe themselves as rightful owners of all that they have. Similarly, this is the grounds of the many prescriptions against mingling with foreigners. They are to be a holy people, a people set apart, a people who live by a different way with a different imaginary than their neighbors. If they achieve this, they become a city on a hill that cannot be hidden, and the peoples surrounding them would come to them to learn of their success, discover God and his *torah* by the witness of his people, and bring their own people to reconciliation with God. This is presented as nearly

---

6. Davis, *Scripture, Culture, and Agriculture*, 72–74.

7. Num 13–14.

8. Deut 6:10–11.

9. Josh 24.

10. Deut 26.

happening with the Queen of Sheba in Solomon's reign, and of course symbolized in the visit of the Magi to Jesus as a child.

Other unique practices and imaginaries of reconciliation with the land in the Hebrew Scriptures are found in Jubilee, Sabbath(s), and throughout regular agrarian practices described in the Torah. Jubilee is not entirely unique to Israel or the Bible. Debt forgiveness was a somewhat common practice in the ancient world as a political tool for realigning fealty.[11] But the Bible is unique in calling for regular redistribution of land and forgiveness of debts that prevents any human authority from benefitting from this. This is important to understand for ecological purposes because the regular redistribution of land reduces the plausibility of centralized control in a command economy. Israel would, if it kept this command, be systematically incapable of developing a strong urban center with a powerful elite who have significantly more wealth than others. The regular liberation of slaves and elimination of debts every seventh year undermines the possibility of generational poverty and a stratified social organization. Because land was tribal and had to be redistributed, each extended family unit would have extremely high levels of land care for the sake of their own heritage (נַחֲלָה).[12] Their investment in their tribal land would be maximal, as opposed to centralized command economies in which a peasant class would be required to grow grain and deliver as much of it to the urban palace center as demanded by the monarch. Thus, the economic system established by the Mosaic covenant had a high level of land care built into it.

The land is a blessing, not a resource. It has the strong potential to be abundant for the needs of the people themselves, and with a surplus that is to be saved for the widow, orphan, sojourner, and priest—people who were not able to possess land or inheritance.[13] Reconciliation with God requires living at peace with the land and treating the land as a beneficiary of God reign. The required Sabbath year fallowing of the land is not only for the benefit of soil fertility in a time before knowledge of crop rotation, it is explicitly said to be for the benefit of wild animals.[14] In Deuteronomy 15 there is a curious and seeming contradiction that reveals the purpose

---

11. See Wagenfuhr, *Plundering Egypt*, 156–58.

12. See Davis, *Scripture, Culture, and Agriculture*, 106–10.

13. The Israelites are often said to possess the land (e.g. Exod 20:24). Possession here is like the gift. This kind of possession is the long-term, though ultimately limited, inheritance, as the Hebrew (יָרֵשׁ) itself indicates.

14. Lev 25:7.

of the land and the realities of life—"There shall be no poor among you" (15:4) and "There will not cease to be poor in the land" (15:11). God will provide such an abundance that the surplus may be lent to other peoples. But there should never be poor among God's people. *Surpluses exist for sharing, not for profit.* The poor must be fed. This opportunity to share with the poor will always exist because there will always be life circumstances that lead to situational poverty. Israel must take care that situational poverty never becomes generational poverty. The land is not a tool for enslaving, for developing social or economic hierarchies. The land is, therefore, not a tool for wealth-creation, because ultimately all claims to ownership of land is theft from God.

The Israelites do not keep the covenant of God. They are vomited out by the land, exiled, allowed to be conquered by imperial forces who do not respect the land. In these situations of rampant injustice all around, the prophets of Israel imagine what the healing and reconciliation of all creation looks like. Richard Bauckham reviews these scenes, which he labels "ecotopias," as a way to envision what the prophets believed about what reconciliation looks like. These ecotopias show features of the orchard-forest-wilderness of Eden, an absence of predation, flourishing and verdant plant life, peace between competitive animals, peace between humans, friendship with wild creatures.[15] In short, this vision of *shalom* is the peace of God's kingdom reign.

Notably, the Bible is full of attestations of the parasitism of the human imagination in an agrarian world. The *torah* of God—full as it is of wisdom applied to the context of its hearers to establish a just life of peace with God, each other, and the land—does not seem to have been effective in creating such a world. It seems that the narrative histories of the Bible portray the continual failures of the Israelites to live up to this *torah*, something that Moses and Joshua see as inevitable.[16] God seems to have established an ideal for a people in a place and time. But the people are continually corrupted by integration with their neighbors, as we saw with the merging or confusion of the lines of Cain and Seth in early Genesis. The demand for holiness must be seen as integral to any biblical ecology. Holiness and a quality of separation must be maintained. The human imagination is incapable of willing itself to the good. It is subject to a profound number of determinants and influences. The influence of

---

15. Bauckham, *Bible and Ecology*, 115–29.

16. Deut 31:29; Josh 24:14–27.

wealth and power is too great to resist. In this vein, the people of God demand a king in order that they be like the other nations. They want to be a competitive empire, even at the cost of taxation, conscription, and corvée labor.

God has called his people to a type of freedom-in-wilderness, to a thriving in relative poverty, to a sharing of surpluses and the systematic undermining of structures of wealth-creation. Whether it is the wilderness generation wishing to return to Egyptian slavery,[17] or the generation of Samuel who demand a king,[18] the people refuse to be part of a community of creation, and demand to be lords of the world, even if this means individual subjection.

Reconciliation in Christ

Jesus came proclaiming the good news of the reign of the kingdom of God. The cosmos is the realm where God is not king. The cosmos is rebellious territory where God does not reign, not because he cannot, but because he will not. Jesus proclaimed that the reign of God was breaking into the cosmos in himself, that God would be revealed as the rightful king of a rebellious empire. Certainly his followers and enemies understood this very clearly. Jesus claimed to be king so that Pilate, Herod, and Caesar were wrongful kings. Jesus was crucified as the king of the Jews. Understandably, this deflated his followers who were expecting the redemption of Israel.[19] That is, they were expecting him to establish a sovereign nation with territorial demarcations, and its own code of law derived from the Torah.[20]

The expectations were not entirely off, but they misunderstood the work of God in history and in their own lifetimes. Jesus proved himself to be the rightful king of all things, the representative of two warring factions: heaven and earth. In his death he made peace between these by reconciliation. Without going into the deep debates of atonement theory, Jesus understood his own purpose as to go to his death at the hands of empire, wrongfully tried, convicted, and killed. He also said that he would be raised from the dead. In the ancient world the king was the

17. Exod 16–17; Num 11; 14; 21.
18. 1 Sam 8.
19. Luke 24:21.
20. See Wright, *How God Became King.*

representative of the people to their gods and their gods to their people. The king was able to symbolically enact something that had real effect for the people as a whole. Ancient peoples did not have the distinction we have of something being "only" symbolic. We tend to believe symbols exist only in the mind. In the ancient imagination, symbolic actions were always effective for something. Thus, if Jesus was God incarnate, his death represented the death of God at the hands of humanity. In the great battle between heaven and earth, God chose to lose rather than to fight. This is fully consistent with what we saw with the flood narrative. God would not pour out his wrath in such a destructive way. Instead he drank down the cup of his own wrath, sacrificing himself and allowing evil to win, apparently. God was victorious in his defeat, however, not simply because Jesus was raised from the dead, but because in Jesus God provided a way to break the power of sin.

The message of the Bible about sin is simple—everything is broken and everything must change. Jesus, as Paul understands him, did just that. He triumphed over the rulers and authorities by putting them to shame, and this disarms them.[21] In Christ, all are able to die to their rebellion and be raised up anew with Christ as a new creation.

Jesus established the kingdom of God, and by his temptation, ministry, and faithful life and death, he proved himself the worthy image of God. He is the one who can rightly represent the character of God. He accomplished reconciliation between God and his people and began the reconciliation of all things, which is the goal.

Salvation and the Image of God

Just as Christian theology has tended to overcomplicate the kingdom of God, so too has it become widely confused about salvation. The common view of salvation, that humans have immortal souls that leave the body at death and go to either bliss in heaven or eternal conscious torment in hell is a creative syncretistic blend of biblical, Greek, and Norse imaginations. Salvation, as the New Testament has it, is exodus. Just as in the Hebrew Bible, God engages in the same pattern of rescue, covenant, wilderness formation, promised land, and mission. Salvation is the first step of this process. For predictable reasons (i.e., submission to and legitimization of structures of power in the name of God), much theology has made

21. Col 2:15.

salvation the goal for the afterlife. An escapist faith *can* legitimize ecological exploitation. But although many Christians have held this position, it is certainly not the position of the Bible.

Paul makes clear in many places that the purpose of God's rescue (salvation) is ultimately for the reconciliation of all things.[22] The notion that God sent his Son to die so that we could be saved really inverts the whole thing, because it makes the good news about what God can and has done for the individual. This contributes to a cosmos in which the individual is preeminent and the whole of creation exists to serve and satisfy the individual's desires and needs. This is probably partly why Evangelicals have been late to the ecology movement. Even the famous John 3:16 explains this point correctly. God's love is demonstrated for the world of sinful humans, not to extricate individuals from it, but to rescue the whole thing.

This rescue then, requires the formation of a people who are prepared and worthy of the task of representing God on the mission of reconciliation. For Paul, God chose people from before the beginning to take on this task of reconciliation by *becoming* the image of God in Christ. The image of God is something that must be attained, not through moral effort, but through the work of God in making his people coheirs and children with Christ by having the character of Christ. In Romans 8:29, Paul is making a larger argument about the rescue of the whole creation, which suffers and groans together as it awaits the revelation of God's children. That is, creation suffers until the people of God attain the character of God in Christ. This God has predestined to happen. So, "Those he foreknew, he chose ahead of time to become the likeness of the image of his Son . . . ."[23] Elsewhere Paul explains that Jesus is the image of God[24] and that we must become mature as we grow into the stature of Christ.[25] This all implies that something about the image of God is mangled beyond recognition because of sin. Humans are incapable of representing God rightly based on anything in their nature, especially if they live according to the flesh in the pejorative sense the New Testament uses. In order to rightly represent God and do his will, his people must become like Christ, with the mind of Christ.

22. 2 Cor 5:18–20; Col 1:20.

23. Rom 8:29.

24. Col 1:15.

25. Eph 4:13.

This is perhaps one of the most vital points of this book. *There is nothing within humanity that makes it capable of doing what God has purposed for people to do* to reconcile all things to himself. There are no resources within our nature, within our civilization (which is rebellion), or within our normal capabilities for reconciliation. That means that ecologically speaking, Scripture holds out absolutely no hope for the world. The whole creation has been subjected to futility, to death, and corruption against its will. God allowed the creation to be subjected in this way in hope that the whole creation will be set free from its slavery to corruption and gain the freedom of the children of God.[26] Paul understands that the rescue of the whole of creation is predicated on the revelation of the children of God. God's people must become the image of God in Christ. Then the creation may be freed from its bondage to decay, a bondage to which God allowed it to be subjected by human evil. Ecotheology must, then, be based on the rescue of the people of God and their being equipped to be the image of God in Christ to rescue the creation from the futility of the powers that rule the world. But how then do we become the image of God in Christ? Once again, the imagination or mind plays a central role.

The Mind of Christ: Reconciliation and Epistemology

In order to become the image of God in Christ, we must have the mind of Christ within us. This is described by Paul in Philippians 2. Jesus was in the form or likeness[27] of God, but he did not consider this something of value by which he would identify himself. He emptied himself, taking the form of a servant, becoming like a human. As a human he humbled himself. He became obedient to death, the death of the cross.[28] This hymn of Christ expresses the root of the reconciled imagination. It has long been the subject of controversy for what it may or may not claim about the ontological realities of Christ incarnate. This passage is not primarily about the being or essence of Christ, and whether his incarnation was ontologically real. The point that Paul is making by using this poem is to explain the divine imaginary or way of thinking.

---

26. Rom 8:19–21.

27. Greek μορφῇ. This is closely related to Rom 8:29's συμμόρφους.

28. Phil 2:5–8.

The mind of Christ begins with self-denial, rather than self-affirmation. Jesus denied his privilege. Rather than coming as the obvious king, he served. But, after placing himself in a position of weakness by emptying himself (kenosis), he revealed his great obedience to God by humbling himself further to death by crucifixion. Rather than trying to become godlike, as Adam and Eve, God became humanlike. The Creator became a creature. Rather than pursuing power without responsibility, like Adam and Eve, and all nations, corporations, and structures of human sin, Jesus emptied himself of his privilege of power, but took on responsibility that was not his. Jesus inverted the power-responsibility relationship. In the next chapters we will apply this to ecology.

In order to become mature, then, we must have this as the heart of our imagination. Paul elsewhere entreats believers to not be conformed to the age/world (αἰών), but to be transformed by the renewal of the mind.[29] The renewal of the mind in Christ means an epistemological resurrection. If we are reconciled to God, that means we once again have access to the concept of creation. Then our relationship to the world can again be mediated through God. But things have changed. There is no recovery of the mind of Adam and Eve, but of Christ. We can never know God as Adam and Eve did, as creator only. This is a good thing, and is part of the plan of God from before the foundations of the earth. We can know God as Creator-Reconciler. That is, we now know creation as creation-lost, Eden as Eden-plundered, but also as crying out for rescue. Knowledge of God in Christ is inherently ecological in that sense. It can never be the ignorant knowledge of the garden of Eden. It must be the mature knowledge that can feel the deep loss, and that can learn to see and suffer the injustices with the creation, as indeed with human injustices against each other.

Previously I rejected the idea of humans as a priesthood of all creation. Here we see the folly of such an idea, as though creation currently could give much glory to God. In the face of the potential for humans to cause the extinction of over one million species, we are silencing the praise that we have been unable to hear. Rather than a priesthood, for humanity to have the mind of Christ we would need to become the ones who suffer with and suffer for the creation. Rather than bringing praises to God, the creation brings its lament to us. The mind of Christ opens our ears to the vocal cries of agony of destitute people, and to the non-human cries of the creation. God has been listening to this lament for

29. Rom 12:2.

millennia. The epistemological reconciliation with God leads us to finally hear the creation's groans as it is subjected to futility under the heel of human civilization. Like the saints under the altar of God in heaven, we will hear the cry and repeat it, "How long until you judge and get justice for our blood from those who live on the earth?"[30] Surely the groaning of creation would say something similar, if we had ears to hear.

The mind of Christ means that we can now perceive the world again mediated through a relationship with God in Christ. But the relations have all changed. God has not changed, but the creation has, and so too have humans and our socially constructed realities. We can only know God as a reconciled enemy. This means we must see how humans need to be reconciled to one another and to the creation. It is impossible to hear the cries that God hears and not be moved with compassion as he is himself.

The renewal of the mind leads us into the wilderness to be formed and equipped. The experience of reconciliation and its liberation from enslavement to the cosmos is joyful, at first. But this release is to the hard life of wilderness. The mind of Christ is heavy. The blood that cries out from the soil[31] has now become a deafening roar. The injustices we can finally see with the love of God seem so great that the temptation will be to return to slavery in Egypt, to blissful, destructive ignorance. Indeed, this has been my personal experience, with each successive year revealing more and more the depth and power of the cosmos, aided in no small part by living in and near a part of a "colony" on American soil and coming to know systems of injustice and corruption. The more our minds are enlightened by Christ, the darker the cosmos becomes,[32] and the more alien. "In order to be prepared to hope in what does not deceive, we must first lose hope in everything that deceives."[33]

Renewal of All Creation

The hope of all the Bible is the reconciliation of all things. This is not understood as a do-over, a restart, an eternal recurrence, or a clean slate. History matters and nothing is lost from the sight of God. In reconciliation

30. Rev 6:10.

31. See Gen 4:10–12.

32. See John 3:19–21.

33. From Georges Bernanos as quoted in Ellul, *The Reason for Being*, 47.

with God, we are enabled to return divine meaning to history as well.[34] We are able to see the importance of all things as in the presence of God.

The goal of creation is resurrection. Christ is the first among all his adopted co-heirs of his kingdom. But resurrection requires death. Christ went through death, and so must all of his people. I am grateful for Wendell Berry's novels, which have allowed death its place in the course of life. As a creature that is part of the community of creation, there is a time to die.[35] We moderns need to learn to accept our deaths as rightful. Not only that, part of resurrection is suffering together with Christ,[36] as he suffered the pain of sin and death on behalf of all.

Will all the creation die as well? Theologians are deeply divided on this. Some are fearful of a type of conservative fundamentalism that believes that everything will be destroyed by God with fire—so why bother caring for the creation? This is a lamentable theology that has an entirely inverted gospel of personal salvation. But this false theology should not lead to denying the real potential that the creation may suffer death in order to be created anew. Certainly the imagery of Revelation suggests this, however dramatic it is. And we may need to ask whether God, having submitted himself to death at the hands of humanity will not also submit the whole of creation to destruction by humanity—provided the revelation of the children of God is too long in coming to fruition. Such a theology has never been conceivable, before the Second World War. For over seventy years now the fate of the whole earth has been in the hands of a relatively few number of people with nuclear responsibility. Now the fate of the whole earth rests with the shared responsibility of all the people to radically change our parasitic ways. Though we must note that the richest corporations, individuals, and governments bear the brunt of responsibility for ecological disaster, their existence depends on the continued will of the people. Will all things be submitted to humanity, as in Psalm 8, with the effect that we destroy God and the creation? Perhaps. Or perhaps our destruction of the creation will only be, as in the murder of God in the crucifixion, a false-victory that actually proves a victory for God. Perhaps God will go to the ultimate limit to allow us to prove to ourselves our incapability of doing what Adam and Eve desired, to be like God.

---

34. Ellul, *Subversion of Christianity,* 147.

35. Eccl 3:2.

36. Rom 8:17.

In any case, the hope of the Bible is not for fixing broken systems, or even for solving injustice on its own. It is impossible to decouple idolatry or rebellion from injustice in the Bible. The Bible has no profound resource for secular nations to exploit for the sake of fixing what is broken. One cannot have the mind of Christ without reconciliation with God in Christ. This means we cannot, in good faith, *construct* a theology for saving the planet that the nations will honestly implement. Any real biblical theology must call for kenosis. No nation can divest itself of power. That is suicide, the very denial of the concept of the nation. Thus, the hope of resurrection must be extended to the whole of creation. Just as God will raise up all humans, including those peoples now made extinct by genocide, so too can God raise up species that have disappeared, including those for which we are responsible. Perhaps we will not be able to ever clean our oceans of microplastics. But God can. That does not mean we do not try. But it means our hope is in resurrection, not repair. Our focus on repair should be a symbolic anticipation of the restoration God will bring. But we have to come to grips with death and loss. That is part of God's story of creation, reconciliation, and resurrection.

Nothing is lost from God's story. Nothing is forgotten. The same will be true for us. We will be raised up from the dead. We will retain the character development and growth we have gained by the work of God in our wilderness journey. Our hope is the land of promise, the great sabbath rest for the people of God in the land God is preparing for us, a land of reconciliation.

Biblical Imagery

A very brief excursus is necessary here before we discuss the visions of the fullness of the kingdom in the Bible. Imagery in the Bible is not photographic or a representation of "literal" reality. We should not be surprised that literature of the biblical periods would do what the visual arts did not. The Bible does not portray reality photographically. Biblical imagery is symbolic and evocative. This is somewhat obvious in the Song of Solomon. But in Jesus's apocalyptic sayings and the book of Revelation there is confusion about this. When we consider the city of God in Revelation, the heavenly Jerusalem, it is important to not immediately assume it is like a person describing a photograph. The imagery is highly symbolic.

The City of God

"The Bible begins in a garden and ends in a city." With this trite phrase many assume a biblical theology that synthesizes human rebellion and divine intention. That is oversimplified. We already saw that the garden of Eden is probably best understood as something of a great orchard-forest-wilderness. We also saw that the garden of Eden is probably best understood as the gardens of a palace. God would walk in the cool of the day with his advisors within the walled garden. The gardens are outside of the palace, and Adam and Eve were not welcome into the throne room. We also played with the possibility that the two trees of life and judgment represent the twin columns of the throne of God, making the wilderness itself the throne room of God (and there is no built environment). Adam and Eve were not welcome to partake of the tree of judgment (knowledge of good and evil), thereby prohibiting them from enthronement.[37]

Perhaps the greatest change when we consider the heavenly Jerusalem image in Revelation is that the people of God are now at the very throne of God, and that there is no temple. The measurements of the city imply that it likely has the same cubic ratios as the holy of holies in the temple,[38] i.e., God's throne room. This means the people of God have received a promotion, which shouldn't surprise us. Paul, after all, says that we will judge angels.[39] Jesus's Parable of the Talents implies that the reward for faithfulness in the kingdom is related to some level of authority. The people of God are now rulers with God of his kingdom. They are rightly exercising the dominion of God, with the character of God. They are partaking of the tree of knowledge of good and evil by exercising judgment.

We do not need to go into most of the imagery of the heavenly Jerusalem here. The main point is that God lives with humanity in a reconciled heaven-earth. The people of God inhabit a shared space with God. There is no need for a socially constructed reality here, because in full

37. Textually, this comes from the idea that the two trees are in the middle of the garden and thenceforth flow the four rivers. This is imagery that will later be used of the rival tree of Assyria in Ezek 31, which parts river waters into streams that water the agricultural fields. Other world-tree imagery, the *axis mundi*, is useful to consider here. Likewise, the two cherubim that spread their wings over the lid of the ark of the covenant, the footstool representing the throne of God in the holy of holies. This throne is later in Rev 22:1 that from which the river of the water of life flows.

38. Rev 21:16.

39. 1 Cor 6:3.

communion with God, the creation lies open for interpretation mediated through God himself. Again, this isn't objectivity or knowing a thing-in-itself. It is knowing God and God's perspective though still as humans. God's people live in the same environment as God, and their imaginaries would thereby be filled with the freedom and possibility that entails. This is the beatific vision. But it is not a passive observance that divinizes the being of a human, this vision is the face-to-face experience Paul describes in 1 Corinthians 13:12. Indeed, Paul again connects vision with epistemology. Now, through love, we see God as though he were a reflection in a tarnished mirror, but in the fullness, face to face, which means that we will know God as we are known by him. Here is the very renewal of the mind found in a relational knowledge of God. Reconciliation means that the mind, once again, is able to have knowledge mediated through God. But this is a relational knowledge, not a factual or ontological knowledge. It is a knowing-in-love. As such, our knowledge remains perspectival. Only now, our very environment is that of God's palace itself.

Of great importance is that the incarnation is eternal. God's choice to be incarnate in Jesus does not cease. This reveals God's eternal commitment to his creation. He will not abandon it but has taken it upon himself to be a creature with his creation forever. There is great hope here, that Christ cannot allow creation to eternally perish, because he is an enduring part of it. He is the first-fruits of its new creation.

Other biblical images are important too as they fill out the picture of this fullness of God's reconciled reign. The book of Hebrews describes the city of God as the great Sabbath rest of the people of God. This should reveal to us not just the rich meaning of the seventh day rest of God's peaceful kingdom, but also the Sabbath years and jubilee. All slaves are released. All debts are canceled. Sins are forgiven. People are reconciled. This is the hope that motivated saints to suffer martyrdom.[40] But importantly, this is not a city built by human hands. As with the promised land of Joshua,[41] the people of God in Hebrews do not participate in the construction of the kingdom. This means that none of the work we do for ecological justice is *building* the kingdom. The kingdom is not a construction project. It is not a built environment.

This raises some excellent questions. Does the Bible ultimately support the myth of civilization? Does God make the myth of civilization

---

40. Heb 11.
41. See Deut 6:11; Josh 24:13.

come true finally by the heavenly Jerusalem? There is little reason to think this beyond the superficial fact that, for modern people, "garden" and "city" are somewhat opposed. The Bible is a story of progression. But it is a story of the progression of the people of God and the *transcending* of the cosmos. Babylon the Great of Revelation is far more developed or civilized a place than the Babel of Genesis 12. It is far more evil than Sodom and Gomorrah of Genesis 18–19. Babylon the Great represents the human cosmos, as ruled by those in rebellion against God. It is the final city of the line of Cain and its perfection. The message of Revelation is not that God affirms human progress, God's wrath on Babylon shows this. Rather, this ancient tale of two cities—Babylon and Jerusalem—is a literary method by which John continues the contrast begun in Genesis between the line of Cain and Seth. The people of God do not *build* their homes, they don't *own* them. They are dependent upon God. The city of God is not full of human inventiveness, and we have no participation in its construction, as with the promised land. But Babylon is wealthy, sexually liberal, full of trade and commerce. It is the *cosmopolis*, the cosmos-city.

We return to Ezekiel 31 to the contrast of Assyria portrayed as a great tree. It is a tree so big, so beautiful, that even the trees of Eden envy it. The description of Assyria is similar to that of Babylon in Revelation. It is big and beautiful, the best of its kind. It even seems to make the corresponding garden or city of God jealous. In Ezekiel 31, the tree of Assyria is cut down and made desolate. The tree then morphs into the armies of Assyria and the trees of Eden into the armies of Israel, who all go down to Sheol together.[42] This contrast between the forest of Eden and the tree of Assyria is reminiscent of Revelation's two cities. And it is within this vein of imagery that we need to understand the picture of a great city in Revelation. The point of the imagery is not the urban setting. The city itself is the symbol. Babylon is obviously metaphorical for an entire empire, and by extension, an entire imperial way of life. Jerusalem is the only suitable image to represent the promised land, rest, and the presence of God. Considering it theologically however, I think we can make a good case against understanding that the eternal future of humanity is urban, and that we should work towards a just urban future.

---

42. The Hebrew Bible knows no distinction between the destination after death of the righteous and the wicked. See my chapter on hell in Wagenfuhr, *Unfortunate Words*.

Revelation uses the city to highlight themes of reconciliation and a new heavens and new earth. When God comes to live on earth from heaven, he brings his palace with him. This is the most glorious palace conceivable (hence the gold/gems). For its size it is practically world-encompassing, at least as would have been understood in John's time. It clearly represents God's throne room. There is a stream that flows from the throne that gives life and is for the healing of all the peoples. This stream is a common ancient Near Eastern symbol of life-giving power having its source with the god. The city has walls, but so too did Eden. The important trees of Eden are present in the city. And a city was often the place of refuge for people displaced by the decimation of imperial practices. The heavenly Jerusalem is a home for the homeless and wandering people of God, a final promised land to inhabit. Jerusalem is a stand-in for the whole of the promised land. If the resurrection presents a final reconciliation, the people of God rule with God, at his side, and gather the abundant natural produce of a reconciled creation without worry, without storage, and without accumulation. The city of God has no granary—God supplies its daily bread.

I'm not sure any real theology about what the resurrection of creation will be like can be found *directly* from the imagery of Revelation. What we can say is that God will judge human civilization. Its progress and wealth are merely masks for oppression and injustice. God is preparing a home for his people. Their task is not to build it, but to inherit it, and to be worthy of such an inheritance. This inheritance involves the reign of God on earth. The question, then, isn't how humans get to participate in creating the eschaton, but what character will they have when it comes. This is, after all, Jesus's exact portrayal of the eschaton in Matthew 24–25. The far bigger question the Bible has is, "Whose side are you on?" and "When the Son of Man comes will he find faithfulness on earth?"[43] In all this, there is no real discussion of what kind of life people will live in the resurrection. That is, will they farm, live in cities, have technology, etc.? All of that is speculative when it comes to what the Bible has to offer. But given that nothing of history is lost, at the very least a memory of the world as it has been under all sorts of human constructed environments will remain. Given that all of them involve significant injustices and ecological costs, and that the whole purpose of urban living is to construct an artificial environment amenable to human systemic control,

---

43. Luke 18:8.

it does not seem that there is any purpose in an urban environment in the kingdom. But, at the same time, I would not be convinced that agrarianism holds the answer either. Agriculture is clearly understood in Genesis to be part of the consequences of sin.

It is curious that the Western mind focuses so intently on the fulfilment of personal desire in the resurrection, when the Bible offers almost no indications to aid in such idle dreaming. The Bible is concerned primarily for the full reign of God over all things, and the place of God's people as part of this. It is a radical statement that there is no temple in the heavenly Jerusalem. God lives with his creation, and God judges his creation, setting it free from bondage to death, decay, and human exploitation. *God's judgment of creation is new creation.* This is why God's judgment is delayed until the end/beginning. His judgment symbolically falls upon Babylon the Great, on the cosmopolis, the microcosm of human sin. There is no redemption for human urban structures or agrarian practices, because God is not their author. Instead, the people of God are redeemed or rescued in an exodus from the great city.

How to Be Reconciled with Creation

Reconciliation with creation does not mean minor modifications to our way of life. It means repentance. It first means acknowledging our individual and corporate participation in structures of exploitation. After realizing the depth of our evil, we have to consciously choose to work against the incredible pressure to justify ourselves or to shift blame elsewhere. We must take full responsibility for what we have done and what we continue to do. We must seek for knowledge about the depth of our evil, as well. Living in reconciliation means actively seeking to know how we have wronged the other.

When reconciling with God and other people the next step is contrition. We have to viscerally feel our guilt. God desires a broken and contrite heart.[44] Unless our hearts break for *our responsibility* in the state of creation, there will be no reconciliation. We cannot simply mourn its destruction in general, as this is a type of mourning that we subtly use to justify ourselves. We can feel bad for the creation without taking responsibility and initiative to be reconciled.

44. Ps 51:17.

Also, when reconciling with God or a living person, we must seek to right the wrong we have caused. The simplest way is repayment for damages, as Zacchaeus does. When it comes to murder, however, this is obviously out of the question. Murder cannot be undone, nor can genocide, or speciecide. We cannot bring back *that* polar bear, even if we were to somehow raise the population. God demands that every animal must be presented at the tabernacle, otherwise the killer has blood on his or her head![45] That specific animal belongs to God, who allows Israel to eat its meat. Leaving behind questions of obedience to Levitical law codes, the theory behind it is still valid. God views the killing of animals as murder unless done properly. "Whomever kills an animal must make restitution, life for life."[46] This is simple if a neighbor killed a cow. What if no restitution can be made? How can we bring back what is forever lost? And is it not worse that we do it industrially? As Davis says, "Our own culture, especially in North America, certainly operates the most death-dealing meat market that the world has ever known. Considered within the context of creation, it epitomizes our ingratitude for what God has done."[47] Our ignorance of this is no defense, it is part of our culpability that we have offloaded the gruesome task of industrial slaughter. The Bible does not command veganism, and that's not the point here. The point is that God cares for his creatures and *they are not ours* to do with as we please. We have turned living things (נֶפֶשׁ חַיָּה)—a concept that, in Hebrew, is shared between humans and other animals[48]—into protein products, breaking individual lives God values down into an impersonal and generic commercial product. What does reconciliation look like in this instance?

And what does reconciliation mean when entire mountains have been strip-mined for private corporate profit, and in the case of coal, for one of the most environmentally destructive products? Can mountains be rebuilt? The point is clear, we cannot be reconciled through restitution, or making it good. We cannot even begin to conceive of what making up for our wrong could look like. The same is true with human relationships. What restitution can be made to Native Americans for the

---

45. Lev 17:3–4.

46. Lev 24:18.

47. Davis, *Scripture, Culture, and Agriculture*, 97.

48. Bauckham, *Bible and Ecology*, 21.

genocide that benefits all of the western hemisphere's nations? We cannot repay the dead.

When restitution is not possible often retribution is just. Certainly this is how the Hebrew Bible understands justice, and how nearly every nation does as well. The recompense for murder is often life, either in prison or capital punishment. Most ancient societies that permitted or tolerated murderers, adulterers, or rapists in their presence would have a curse set upon them. The whole people were guilty of the sin until the evil was purged from their midst.[49] Retribution in our circumstance would have to be some modified elimination of our species. That's inconceivable to us, naturally. Few murderers want to die or think that their deaths are warranted, especially for those involved in systematic or industrial processes of murder or destruction, as Hannah Arendt showed well.[50] It is difficult enough to convince people that climate change is real, let alone begin convincing them that we collectively bear bloodguilt for every animal slain in industrial slaughterhouses. Going beyond that to some sort of self-punishment seems preposterous. And yet, if we consider the perspective of the creation as a whole, would it not be *just* for it to "purge the evil that is within it?" Would it not be *just* for the whole of creation to vomit us out like the parasites we have proven to behave as?[51] Then the land would enjoy the Sabbaths we have systematically denied to it.[52] The reaction to such a proposal, biblical though it may be, would invariably be some kind of protest about the unfairness of this.

Convincing the world of the extent of its guilt is nearly impossible *because we do not know the Creator, and thus do not perceive creation.* If we truly perceived creation *as creation*, the knowledge of human evil would overwhelm us, and it should. Until we understand the depth of our guilt, our repentance will be minimal. And in terms of systems of justice or discipline, it often takes a heavy sentence passed upon a criminal, accompanied with therapy, to make them see the crime from a perspective other than their own.

When we understand the depth of our ecological guilt, we have no room for self-justification in the superiority of our species. This only serves to condemn us further by making us all the more responsible. God

---

49. As seen throughout Deuteronomy with the phrase "purge the evil from your midst." Also evident in the Greek story of Oedipus.

50. Arendt, *Eichmann in Jerusalem.*

51. Lev 18:25, 28; 20:22.

52. Lev 26:34–35.

did not create the creation for us. He created us as creatures within the creation for himself, to represent his character to the creation.[53] This is the power-responsibility dynamic at play again. Ancient peoples understood far more the depth of their own relationship to the land and the animals, and had a greater sense of responsibility for it. Modern urbanites eat protein instead of Bessie. They ship out their single-use plastic waste to landfills instead of living near to their rubbish and thus being conscious of it, its size, its constitution, and who lives off of it. Every step forward in power results in a step backwards of our consciousness of responsibility. If this pride can be broken and we can be brought to see the depth of our shared guilt, then we would have to acknowledge that our own deaths are but the smallest token towards fulfilling retribution we could imagine. In any case, Paul explains that all had deserved death for their sin[54] long before there was much knowledge about the extent of human evil in the destruction of creation.

But though justice may demand the destruction of the human species, this is not the course God has taken. God is merciful and forbearing,[55] perhaps even to the point of allowing us to destroy the creation. Perhaps God is so slow to anger that all creation will perish before he acts in judgment. If so, God's forbearance is meant to bring us to repentance and reconciliation. The longer we do not act, the more we store up wrath for ourselves on the day when God's righteous judgment is revealed.[56] But perhaps the human destruction of creation is precisely what God needs to demonstrate the fulfillment of human sinfulness to us. The precise and exact inversion of godlikeness that is revealed in humanity is our desperate drive toward annihilation *as we seek to be creators*. When once we have ended this creation without necessarily intending to do so, the depth of our sin will be revealed to us by our own actions with no other possible narrative choice, no other possible self-justification. When the creation is gone, there is nothing to hide behind, no fig leaves, no automobiles, no internet avatars. All will lay naked and exposed before the great judge.

Thus, justice will come and forgiveness is offered in Christ. God will cancel the record of our trespasses, if we are in Christ. But we still must be reconciled now. And though we cannot work miracles of resurrection

---

53. This is not priesthood, which, in all religions, is founded on a mediatorial role. Humans were not created as go-betweens, but participants.

54. Rom 3.

55. Rom 2:4; 3:25.

56. Rom 2:4–5.

in the creation, we can first and foremost stop our destruction. We can also seek to decrease our impact by strategies of de-growth, decentralization, disempowerment as a species, rewilding, refusal of management, refusal of convenience, refusing to live *off* of the land, *on* the land, or even simply just *indoors,* and choosing to live *in* the land. We can seek to reintroduce predators into our ecosystems and stop resource extraction. We can return to small family organic farms, revitalizing smaller communities, help start soil restoration, and learn how to eat again. Once we see the world as creation-near-death but beloved by the Creator, most of the actions that could possibly move toward reconciliation become fairly obvious. That is, we have to understand the nature of our sin to understand how we can be reconciled.

Part IV

A Christian Ecology

In Part IV we look at the theoretical and practical results of the theology we described in Part III. What can and should Christians do? This is not so much an *ethic*, insofar as ethics is a field of philosophy rooted in establishing rational grounds for action. This poses a problem if humanity has a broken imagination or epistemology. Rational grounds for actions will be based in the environment in which they are plausible, meaning they will inevitably tend to replicate some method of stabilizing a particular environmental situation. In a sense, then, ethics are always integrative. A Christian ecology will need to begin with the opposite—a disorienting or disintegrational movement. But it is not disintegration for its own sake, of course, but as the starting point of a renewed and reconciled imagination that must be first isolated from its patterns of brokenness.

CHAPTER 12

A Subversive Theology of Creation and Ecology

Now that we have surveyed a biblical theology, it is useful to put it together in more systematic and abridged language for the sake of engaging common theological themes. Christian theology, rightly conceived, is inherently ecotheology. It is thus subversive to the myth of civilization. We briefly look at the doctrine of God, humanity, and finally the human imagination as impacted by these doctrines.

Doctrine of God

Theology proper, for the Christian, must begin with the incarnation rather than the Trinity, or even revelation. It is only in Christ that God is fully revealed. Put another way, it is only in Christ that God took on human form and could thus reveal himself in a way suitable to human understanding. Only in the incarnation could God invade the human imagination on its own terms. This has major implications for ecotheology. Christianity, rightly understood, ought to be inherently ecological. This is because it holds that God became human. Inherent within that statement is the fact that the Creator joined creation as a creature.

The incarnation is the mission of God in reconciliation, not in creation. Jesus does not promise new creation until he returns in judgment. Again, judgment is creation for God, thus the return of Christ promises new creation by his act of judgment. The central act of God in Scripture, then, is reconciliation, not creation. Both creation and sin are

149

presupposed by reconciliation, of course, but they are revealed through reconciliation. We can only come to know God as the Creator as we first know him as the Reconciler.

Thus, the incarnation must form the basis of ecotheology, because it is how we come to knowledge of God. Our minds never transcend our human forms. Knowing God is possible as a human in a humanly way. Christianity is a creaturely faith. It is not a way to ascend to the realm of excarnation in heaven. This means that, any who believe God became flesh and remains so now cannot despise the creation of which God himself is part. That this creation will all pass away is clear enough in Scripture, but it holds this only within the context of the second coming of God to dwell with and within his renewed creation forever. Thus, while the incarnation certainly offers a high privilege to humans, it is not exclusively about humanity. Instead, God became flesh for all of creation.

That said, we know that God, as the Creator, created all things out of nothing by speaking. God is not a creature and did not create the creation as a fellow-creature in a creaturely way. There is no ontological familiarity between God and the creation. God is wholly other. It is a false shortcut if we try and form a Christian ecotheology based on forging a more familiar/familial link between God and the creation. This is a re-paganization of God in a way that Genesis and the rest of the Bible carefully avoids. The only hope for creation is the judgment of the wholly other God who loves his creation by giving his unique Son for it. God could not rightly judge the creation if he were himself constrained to it. He must retain his authority which can only happen by separation.

God is only known by his acts of self-revelation. God cannot be known by investigation of the creation. Again, to make the creation reveal God is a tempting shortcut, but this is to confuse the product creation with the completed action of creation. We cannot look at the creation to know anything about the Creator. In any case, as I've already said many times, creation as such is lost.

That God is revealed only in action means that God is always revealed as in a relationship, never in himself. All actions are located in space and time. Thus, all knowledge of God must be knowledge in relationship, not knowledge of God in himself. Revelation must also be a relationship with humans *as humans*. That is, God may reveal himself to other, non-human creatures, but we can never know that. All that is relevant to us is God's revelation to *us*. That means we can only ever have a knowledge of God that is suitable for humans to know. It must fit the capability of our minds.

Because all revelation is an action, in order for any person to have knowledge of God, rather than simply knowledge of theology, it must be revealed by God. This means that Adam and Eve were the only two people who could have known God as the Creator. God is not revealed to us as Creator, but as Reconciler, since knowledge of God must come through confrontation around our rebellion. We first know God only as rebellious peoples who are called to repent and be reconciled. Ecologically this means that we can only know the creation by knowing the Creator, and because God is only revealed to us in his role as reconciler, we cannot know the creation as it was. We can only know the creation as enslaved and subjected to decay and futility. *Our knowledge of the creation is, therefore, knowledge of our sin.* We can only have speculative, subtraction knowledge of the creation as God created it. We can never know creation as creation personally. Thus, we must approach the non-human world mediated through God in Christ as guilty wrongdoers seeking forgiveness and reconciliation. This transforms any notion of creation care or stewardship. Not only are we not tasked with stewardship by God, we have no right to approach the creation as co-creators or even co-sustainers with God. Creation has no need of either from us, and we've proven incapable of both. Thus, we must approach the broken creation with broken and contrite hearts.

God is revealed as God *pro nobis*. But this is not enough. God is also revealed as *pro creatura*. God's for-us-ness is at the very same instant God's for-creation-ness. The two cannot rightly be distinguished, again unless "us" constitutes some excarnate spirit. But this raises a major question. If God is for us and for creation, what happens when these become seemingly competitive? How can God be for humanity, if being human means being or becoming civilized, which always comes at the cost of the creation? The answer is, of course, that God is for us only by reconciling us to the creation. A right relationship of God therefore requires a reconciled relationship with creation.

God is most clearly revealed in Jesus Christ. This means that the Triune nature of God is revealed only in the coming of God as a creature. The only way we can have a glimpse of the inner relationship of God with himself is by God's outer relationship with us as human. Another ecotheological wrong shortcut here is through social trinitarianism. God does not have the property of relationality. God does not communicate his properties to humans.

Thus, we must reject the Eastern Orthodox notion of *theosis*, that God became human so that humans could become divine. God does not divinize creation, or humanity in isolation from creation. We are not brought into the inner life of the Trinity. The inner life of the Trinity is extended to the creation, to be experienced in a creaturely manner. All fellowship with God is in God's self-abasement, not in human exaltation above the limits of creation. This comes through union with Christ, which as we will see in the next chapter, is understood in *embodied* language. Union with Christ is membership in his body, the *ekklesia*, the people of God. The Triune God cannot be accessed directly, nor mediated through creation, but in the *body* of Christ alone.

Doctrine of Humanity

That said, humans are invited into the life of God through the incarnate Son to have fellowship with the Father through him in the power of the Holy Spirit. This is not a spiritual or mystical ascent, but the descent of God to us.

Humans are creatures. As I've emphasized, we cannot be fellow creators with God. The idea that our creative capacities are somehow related to God is false. Just as the Fatherhood of God is related to his eternally begetting the Son and is not related to his relationship with humanity or the creation, so too the role of God as Creator has no relationship to human creativity. As said earlier, God's act of creation differs from human acts in every aspect. The only connection between the two is linguistic, and that only in certain biblical translations. In the Hebrew Bible, every instance of the verb "to create" (*bara*, בָּרָא), has God as the subject. By contrast, humans "make" (*'asah*, עָשָׂה). This linguistic difference is effaced in the Septuagint, in which both God and humans "make" (*poieō*, ποιέω), a confusion that is avoided in the Greek New Testament with "create" from (*ktizō*, κτίζω). The Vulgate, and many English translations keep this distinction. It is curious that some modern English translations miss this distinction as the LXX did.[1] Thus, it seems rather clear from biblical usage that God's creative activity is distinct from human making of things. The Greek *ktisis* (κτίσις) is only used in biblical and later

---

1. E.g., Gen 3:7, ESV.

Christian sources in the sense of creation or creature, i.e., belonging to God alone. This sense is not found outside of Christian literature. Thus the notion of co-creation is not biblical. There is no biblical evidence for such a perspective.

Ecologically speaking, this is crucial, because it establishes that human attempts at creation, as we saw with Cain and his lineage, is specifically a counter-act to God's own. But once humans imagine their making as creating or their craftiness as creativity, the creation itself necessarily suffers violence. For, making is at its most basic form, niche construction. Humans are like bees, termites, beavers, and other animals in modifying an environment to suit their needs. The error is divinizing this making—turning making into something that gives meaning and that thus desires progress. Beavers are content to build their dams and lodges. Humans must learn to do the same without mythologizing; without grand narratives of epochal transformations by the building of cities.

Thus, humans can only be related to God in his role as Reconciler, not Creator. Humans have long rejected God as Creator, instead imagining themselves to be creators. So long as this happens, sin will be glossed over, and no true ecology will be possible. The Hebrew Scriptures do not teach the *imitatio dei*, the imitation of God. They, rather, continually highlight how different God is than all others.[2] God gives humans instruction, *torah*. But *torah* is not the path to godlikeness, nor even true humanity, but to righteousness. The righteous are those who can stand in up in judgment, who are not undone by the just judgments of God that both make heaven and earth pass away and create a new heavens and a new earth.

Representation is not the same as imitation. Imitators attempt to achieve similarity in being. Representatives attempt to rightly represent in their own way the will of their king. Representatives do not try to usurp the throne by surpassing the king, but aim to faithfully do their duty. This is the distinction between the line of Cain and the line of Seth.

Humans are only to represent God the Reconciler to the world, which means bearing the call and revealing the reality of reconciliation. *Humans are not capable, on their own, of achieving reconciliation*, either with other humans, or with God. We attempt to accomplish this by saming—reduction of difference. True reconciliation must preserve whole all

2. E.g., Exod 15:11; Deut 33:20, 26; Job 38; Pss 89; 113; Isa 44:7.

individuality and personality, and this is only possible by the work of God who is capable of an infinite number of personal relationships.

Ecologically this means we need to be circumspect about our ability to solve the problems we have created. This calls for the humility of an ambassador who is faithful to her king. Christians must be entirely clear about this: only God can reconcile. But we can reveal.

Thus, the doctrine of humanity must center around representation—the correct meaning of the image of God—not around a sharing of divine attributes. Humanity has absolutely no ontological connection or sharing with God. Instead, God takes on commonality with humans in reconciliation by the incarnation, which enables humans to rightly represent God *as they represent the human man Jesus Christ.*

Imagination and the Mind of Christ

Throughout this book I have spoken of sin as a broken imagination. Paul believes that, in Christ, there can be a renewal of the mind, seen in having the mind of Christ. Reconciliation thus achieves a form of epistemological renewal. This is described by Paul in Philippians 2:5–8, which we survey here.

In order to be like Christ, we must reject the sin of Adam and Eve. Their sin, recall, was to become like God by deciding or judging what is good and what is evil for themselves. This sin was to reject God and take God's place as the creator of meaning and value. The only reference points they had from then on were themselves and the now ostensibly godless world around them. In such a situation they, and we, have to make up complex systems of projection. We socially construct reality.

Jesus denied the temptation to be counted equal to God, or to take the place of God. Throughout the Gospel of John, Jesus portrays himself and his relationship to his Father as one of strict *obedience and submission.* Jesus and the Gospel writers see him as unique because he is the only one who does the will of God. This is in contrast to later theology that has majored on metaphysical questions, which are a distraction. The problem of sin is not about *being,* but about *behavior* that is rooted in a broken imagination that comes from rebellion against God.

For us to deny godlikeness is to deny our desire for the power to determine value independently of God. Ecologically speaking, that means asking the question about the goodness of the things civilization calls good, like human management, political representation and identity, technology, economics, development, growth, and progress. How might we submit all of these to the evaluation of Scripture and to the God of all creation?

Godlikeness is also about status, about imagining ourselves above our station. Denying godlikeness is to live in creation as creatures. Rediscovering ourselves as creatures is integral to the process of reconciliation in Christ. This has all kinds of implications that Christian ecotheologians so well describe in their theologies of place, land, food/eating, and animals.

Christ's self-emptying is explained as taking the form of a servant and being born in human form. Paul isn't really intending to make a point about the exact nature of the incarnation here. Rather, he (or the poet he quotes) is emphasizing the humiliation of Jesus. The mind of Christ looks like emptying oneself of one's power and privilege for the sake of serving others, specifically those below oneself. If we put this in the context of the creation and ecology, humans need to serve the creation and take on the form of creatures. Of course, we are already creatures, but the structure of our lives is an attempt to escape this reality. Being a creature means living *within* the creation, *for* the creation, rather than outside of it and using it for ourselves. Christ's kenosis is the exact opposite of parasitism. It is pursuing the good of another even at one's own expense. For Christ it is particularly the good of those who are far below him in status according to his true nature. For us it should be the same. We must pursue the good of those who are far below us in status and value. This is obviously true on the human-human level. We must make the good of the poor and destitute far more a focus than pleasing the rich and ensuring they gain profit. It means resisting climate apartheid to the last. But it also means taking up the cause of non-human creation and creatures. We must learn to put ourselves below the things of lesser value, like this sparrow or that raven.

Some practical implications of this will, of course, sound radical. We should call for habitat restoration for many creatures who have lost much of it. This will now inevitably mean the demolition of whole areas of human "development." It will have to mean the removal of dams to restore rivers. It can mean rewilding—restoring areas by simply leaving them be. Conceptually it must mean turning management on its head. Rather than managing "natural resources," we must manage *ourselves*, our desires and demands.

But the most radical thing to suggest as part of taking on the mind of Christ, is that we should humble ourselves to death. We cannot be children and heirs of God in Christ if we do not suffer with him; if we are not crucified with him.[3] Truly being like God means dying to ourselves and submitting to death. Now, of course we are all going to die. It has appointed to us by God. It is one of the curses God has put on us that we have not yet found a way around. Humbling ourselves to death is partly to simply acknowledge the rightness of our deaths. It is humbling ourselves to the curse of God. And if we humble ourselves to accept this curse, perhaps we should humble ourselves to accept the other curses of God that have always been designed for our good in forming us to learn our place and how to balance our power with responsibility. Practically this could mean something as simple as returning to the land in gardening and farming, in organic, local, seasonal, and appropriate ways. It also means pain. Genesis 3 mentions pain in childbearing, which is really about the difficulty and danger of becoming a great people, the great desire of the people in the context of Genesis. Physically it does mean accepting the pain of life. But it also means accepting limits on the size of our ambitions for propagation of ourselves and our names.

It means reducing our desire to make an impact. Making an impact is a violent action that imposes an imprint of ourselves onto the world or onto other people. It is the formation of the world in our image. This is how people feel like life is meaningful, when they can see images of themselves in others or in the wider world. God has made it painful for this to happen. God has hardened the world and softened our bones, so that the creation resists being conformed to our self-image. Technology has replaced our bones with steel, and now the creation models neither itself, nor images of ourselves, but the forms and impressions of machines and machine environments. This fundamental transformation is rarely understood or perceived. *We have not conquered creation. We have been conquered, along with creation, by the powerful but simple and incredibly violent machines of our devising.* We have not become immune to the pain of impressing ourselves, we have instead projected this onto our own creations, as in Babel. This means we have not become stronger. We have not improved our character. Instead, we have devolved in character and stature by externalizing ourselves and our virtue onto creations alienated from us.

3. Rom 8:17; Gal 2:20.

What does it mean to die to ourselves? For generations the Bible has been interpreted as having statements that are obviously not meant to be taken "literally." Dying to ourselves, suffering with Christ, are good examples of texts that are usually spiritualized. Paul did not see it that way. He saw the story of his life within the story of Christ's life. He saw his union with Christ as total. He did not fear bodily death, and would boldly go to bodily death, believing that his bodily death *for and with Christ* was key to his attaining the bodily glory of inheritance with Christ.

The time is coming when being Christlike means giving up livelihoods we have trained for, giving up homes and homelands for the sake of the kingdom. It will mean entry into danger as ambassadors bringing chaos to an orderly and self-enclosed world. And it will have to mean the death of everything we previously valued because we have to die to our entire broken imagination. Once our value systems and identities are put to death, we will no longer pursue making an impact because it will have no meaning or value.

If we want to be glorified with Christ, we must take on his character. This is what we were predestined to do.[4] Should our own humiliation be limited to only becoming slightly lower human beings? No. God became what he was not. We must become what we believe ourselves to be above, both human and non-human. We must deny the great divide between humans and the non-human creation, and serve the least of both of these together. God is the God of the wild animals, the predators, the scary beasts, the cute ones, the large and small, and he loves them all. We must learn to love them enough to restore them to full freedom in their habitats. True rewilding cannot be monitored.

For much of creation, the best way we can love and serve it is by simply removing ourselves and our impacts from it. Instead, we should consider how the creation can impact us and make us more creaturely. For it is only when we are properly creatures that we can understand the heart and character of God. Only then will "the heavens declare the glory of God." Human civilization made its impact on God. Jesus bears the scars of crucifixion, the impact of the hammer, nails, and spear. Shall we shy away from being impacted by the creation as well? Should our hubris not be kept in check by the long process of dying? Shall we not bear the scars of the thorns and thistles as we toil for food when Jesus

---

4. Rom 8:29.

bears the scars of a crown of thorns?[5] These are not spiritual realities that are separate from the physical. To claim that the kingdom, or that our kenosis is merely spiritual is to deny the entire meaning of the incarnation. Christ's incarnation was his self-emptying. So we must also return to the soil from which we came, and dig up the concrete that covers it.

A Subversive Theology

The problem with Jesus is that he is an uncivilized man, a savage. He did not lead a settled life. He did not pursue economic flourishing. He did not contribute to the common good of his city or district like a responsible citizen. He did not work. He mocked and subverted the payment of taxes. He criticized the structures of human authority and hierarchy. He ate and drank with social outcasts. He claimed that he would tear down the temple. He did not seem to own anything at all. Jesus did not contribute to or support the myth of civilization.

The words of Jesus in the Gospels, especially the Synoptics, have been ironically some of the most divisive in the church. They are entirely clear, incredibly radical, and therefore problematic for churches who seek to use Jesus to integrate people into an environment. Examples of this include turning the other cheek, the blessing of the poor and condemnation of the rich, the first place of the humble, the impossibility of serving God and money, or any two masters, that we are not to call any human by a title of authority, that we are not to swear oaths, that we are to love our enemies, and many others. The great shame of the church is that it has not taken its ostensible king at his word. That Jesus is using hyperbole in the Sermon on the Mount is often taken as obvious. But what if Jesus's words were serious? In Matthew 6:25–33 (Luke 12:22–31), Jesus tells his hearers to imitate the birds. They do not practice agriculture. They do not worry. God provides for them and he will provide for us. Within this simple teaching is the condemnation of all civilization, based as it is in agricultural surpluses. Could it be that Jesus is advocating a hunter-gatherer existence, much like birds, or like the Israelites eating manna, or receiving a promised land with harvests they did not plant, or Adam and Eve eating only of the trees of the garden? Jesus says that the gentiles are the ones who worry about the future, about food, water, and shelter. God's

---

5. Both Paul and Peter make bold claims about the filling up and participating in Christ's sufferings, Phil 3:10; Col 1:24; 1 Pet 4:13.

people, if they are reconciled with him, will know that God provides. In this way, Jesus follows many of the civilizational critiques of the Hebrew Scriptures. Reconciliation with God means dependence upon him, rather than upon the works of human hands. Civilization demonstrates "little faith." This is less crazy than it sounds. "There are, even today, large stands of wild wheat in Anatolia from which, as Jack Harlan famously showed, one could gather enough grain with a flint sickle in three weeks to feed a family for a year."[6]

Jesus is the bread of life. He claimed to be more vital than satiating natural needs. When tempted by filling his material needs first, he responds to the devil from Deuteronomy, "Man does not live by bread alone but by every word that comes out of the mouth of God."[7] Rather than having vitality from the earth, Jesus understands that God is the source of life. It is not what goes into the human mouth that is truly important, but what comes out of God's mouth. Thus, in John 6, Jesus again refers to the manna story and links himself with the bread that has come down from heaven. He claims that those who come to him will never be hungry or thirsty. In the Lord's Prayer, Jesus teaches the line "give us this day our daily bread." This request seems to be rather more literal to Jesus than to us. Jesus expects that God is capable of granting to people enough to eat without having to labor hard for it. I do not seriously think Jesus is asking us to pray that God would work through the complexities of global industrial agriculture, and through our work or welfare income to provide enough money to buy food to eat on a regular basis. This is not dependency upon God, but upon the human system, which is full of anxiety. The feeding of the five thousand reveals the kingdom of God by the abundance come through sharing under the authority of Christ.

This is a theology of subverting the whole human project. The Triune, wholly other God invaded his broken creation dominated by a rebellious humanity to bring it to ruin. He did this not by open destruction, not yet. In the incarnation God did not judge the world. But he established a people, united to him in Christ, an embodied, local, ambassadorial people who were tasked with revealing the reconciliation they themselves had tasted to the whole world. They do this not through word only, but through the symbolic actions of healing, like Jesus himself did. But this healing of creation cannot achieve reconciliation fully.

---

6. Scott is here referencing Harlan, *Crops and Man*. Scott, *Against the Grain*, 11.

7. Matt 4:4, from Deut 8:3.

This people of God are to always point to him and reconciliation in him. Outside of this they have no hope in a human or transhuman future. This people is the *ekklesia* (ἐκκλησία), and the subject of our next chapter.

CHAPTER 13

"Come Out of Her"

An Ecclesiological Ecology

THE MISSION OF RECONCILIATION in the Bible always involves a people. In contrast to the flood in which God overwhelmed the world with power in judgment, God works subversively through his people to win the world through reconciliation. The people of God is one. Its only source of unity is God himself.[1] It is constituted solely by the relationship of each individual to God unmediated by any system, structure, or institution. But, by reconciliation with God, his people must be reconciled to one another, and therefore associate as a people with a common identity, an identity that is based solely on God himself. Each individual has an entirely unique relationship to God, with its own story and meaning. Thus, it is God alone who can unify his people, for he alone provides the common ground. In this way, God is both the source of unity and of true individuation. Beyond his people, all of creation is brought into community solely by its relationship to the Creator, which again, allows for total individuation, and thus true liberty.

The mission of God in reconciling all things to himself finds expression in emplaced peoples. In the Hebrew Scriptures, this was the people of Israel, though not all Israel was faithful. In order to work with and through this people God had to speak to them and reveal himself in forms and institutions understandable to them: temple and palace. God did not demand nor desire either, but accommodated to the needs of

---

1. Eph 4:4–6.

the people in establishing structures of religious and political mediation. The Hebrew Scriptures are clear that God does not live in buildings. He does not desire sacrifices. He cannot be contained, nor manipulated by economic deals in votive offerings. God is not a source of power for the people to use for their ends or for their legitimation. God has covenanted with them in a highly conditional manner so that the purpose of reconciliation remains at the forefront. The religion in the Bible is only part of the form, but not the content of revelation or mission. Thus, Jesus claimed that he would tear down the temple and replace it with his people. This was always the purpose.

In the same way, the palace and kingship was clearly an accommodation to the people by God. God does not mediate his power through human power structures, which is to invariably legitimize injustice. God may use these rulers, but he has not brought them to power, and does not legitimize them.[2] Jesus, the godly king, reveals the true character of divine authority, which is a type of anarchy, in the sense of having no hierarchy whatsoever. Those who desire to lead must become the servants of all and humble themselves. No one is to be called "teacher" or "father,"[3] which, in the Roman world, meant that there was no rightful human authority. The emperor portrayed himself as the great father of his people who were his household. In God's household there are only coheirs with Christ, adopted children.

Thus, there is no king but Christ, and no mediator/priest between God and humans but Christ.[4] This means that the good news of the kingdom of God is a radical liberation from all structures and institutions of power. To the cosmos, Jesus is the greatest possible chaos monster. In the New Testament, the institution Jesus establishes is called the *ekklesia*. I hesitate to use the word "church" for all of the complexity of meaning that has culturally.[5] This assembly of people is the body of Christ, the presence of God in the world. In that way, it is the politico-religious representation of God. That is, the *ekklesia* is the assembly of the image of God. For Paul,

---

2. Nebuchadnezzar is the obvious example, see Jer 25. Rom 13:1–7 has been used as the baseline text for a biblical legitimation of human authorities, which runs counter to other texts and themes in the Bible, and within Paul himself. Romans 13 should be seen as the problematic text rather than the starting point. See Ellul, *Anarchy and Christianity*, 77–85.

3. Matt 23:8–12.

4. 1 Tim 2:5.

5. See Wagenfuhr, *Unfortunate Words of the Bible*, 110–15.

it does not seem that individuals are entirely capable of representing God alone, but only together. In this way, the *ekklesia* is the image of God as it reveals the kingdom in the character of Christ.

Therefore, the temple metaphor for the body of Christ has been subverted by the state throughout the history of the church. The historical church was eventually brought back into the role given for religious institutions—providing divine legitimation for structures of power. Put another way, temples exist to legitimize the palace. The church was brought into this role as well. This is not a role that befits the people of God in representing his kingdom. The representation of the kingdom of God cannot be owned by any kingdom, or other human institution. Because of that, it is better to talk about the *ekklesia* as an embassy of the kingdom of God.[6]

Paul explains that all who are in Christ are ambassadors of God's message of reconciliation.[7] If we extend this idea into an institutional framework, we can develop the concept of an embassy of the kingdom of God. An embassy is an outpost of a foreign nation. It represents the policies and interests of its homeland. Ambassadors do not owe or swear allegiance to the rulers of the land in which they live, although they do obey their laws.

As discussed earlier, people live within socially constructed realities that I have been calling a cosmos. We are born into them and are deeply integrated into them. Our perceived freedoms are mostly constrained to the imagined possibilities of this environment. The kingdom of God must be understood as an alternative environment in the fullest sense of the term. We cannot create, bring, or construct the kingdom of God, as Bauckham warns, "To do so would be disastrous, because we are not capable of creating utopia or ecotopia, and attempts to do so have always proven damaging."[8] Thus, the role of an embassy is to *reveal* the kingdom to a foreign land. By this revelation the kingdom of God is able to question the framework of the present cosmos in which it is present as an embassy. This revelation requires providing a suitably coherent alternative environment in which people are able to experience the kingdom as *normal*. As Bouma-Prediger puts it, "If our good news is truly good, then

---

6. Others have written about this, notably Jonathan Leeman, *Political Church*. I developed this thesis independently and have some critical appreciation of Leeman, though arrive at a rather different perspective.

7. 2 Cor 5:20.

8. Bauckham, *Bible and Ecology*, 125.

we who call ourselves Christian must be the community God calls us to be."⁹ This requires four characteristics: plausibility, tangibility, holiness, and invasiveness.

Plausibility and Tangibility

The embassy of the kingdom of God must make the kingdom plausible. This simply means living out the teachings of Jesus about the kingdom in enough space and time that it can be experienced as an environment. It has to be a place where the last are first, the first are last, where no one is called teacher or father, where no one lords it over others, where the meek are valued, the mourners comforted, the hungry fed materially and spiritually, where peace is made.

But in order for the kingdom to be plausible, it must be tangible. It cannot exist in word without flesh. The heart of ecotheology is incarnation, so the community must focus on embodying the body of Christ and his kingdom. Worship events in temples cannot begin to approach the tangibility requirement for an environment. This means that church institutions will be systematically incapable of representing the kingdom until they develop tangible communities that live by an entirely alternative understanding or epistemology. Such a community must also practice intentional ways of being visible to those in the larger nation. For the kingdom to be experienced as reality it must become a constructed reality through intentional human institutions. It is hard to overstate how far from plausibility and tangibility many modern church institutions have become. For quite some time, when Christianity was a native and embedded religion, especially among rural peoples, the church provided many basic social services, and thus was experienced as something integral to the environment. It was a plausible and tangible representation of civic life under the aegis of God. With the victory of secularism, this has largely been rendered unacceptable and in some cases, illegal. While this has had some negative impacts on the wider world, as it has lost a sense of real community, place, and civil maturity for adults, it now demands that the *ekklesia* work in intentionally new and different ways to create an alternative environment. Contemporary church movements have innovated and struggled to find a meaningful niche in a post-Christendom world. Their expressions have turned toward experiential and recreational forms

9. Steven Bouma-Prediger, *For the Beauty of the Earth*, 118.

because these are the only plausible and tangible areas of life left open in a secular space for some kind of divine influence. Furthermore, the simple time commitment of one or two hours per week has led to a need to intensify the experience and expectation of experience so that church will be able to compress the need for the otherness of the kingdom of God into the given timeframe.

This is, of course, not really possible. It has created churches that focus almost entirely on intense worship events in which people are expected to meet with God experientially. This ironically aids in making the kingdom less plausible, because it restricts the kingdom to an intense experience, which is rarely achievable outside of a well-crafted worship event. It hyper-spiritualizes and thus tends to excarnate Christianity. This also has served to eviscerate the church of any great ability to transform the daily lives of its congregants, or of the wider culture. The temple-church is entirely and necessarily complicit in the culture it inhabits for these reasons. This means that it is complicit in ecological devastation, and it is systematically incapable of offering any public critique, which is an overreach in a secular world. A temple-church must remain focused on the transcendent (i.e., unreal for the purposes of governance), and bringing small tastes of transcendental experience.

Holiness and Invasiveness

An *ekklesia* must remain holy—separate from the cosmos. This has been a requirement for the people of God since their beginning.[10] It is the meaning and purpose of salvation, to rescue a people for God. He has rescued a people from bondage to the cosmos and its enclosed imaginary. This was true for Abraham, for Moses and Israel, and for the church of the first two centuries. An embassy cannot be an embassy if it acculturates to its host nation. Christians are called to be radically other,[11] which means they are called to be barbarians in the technical sense of the term of nonstate people who resist assimilation, and who represent the danger of otherness and chaos to the state or cosmos. This is part of the reason God calls a people, a tribe, an *ekklesia* rather than individuals. This must be a living community that can sustain itself and each other in opposition to the state's cultural and imaginational reach.

10. Throughout Leviticus, especially 20:26.

11. Rom 12:2.

At the same time, however, an embassy must be present within a host nation. It cannot be outside of it. Salvation is the first step of the mission of God; the goal is to be ambassadors of reconciliation. This is only possible by a real presence within the cosmos. This presence is an invasiveness. It retains the holiness, the total separation and difference. As such, it represents the seeds of chaos within a cosmos. It exists to sow doubt, to open cracks in an enclosed imaginary. It brings elements of the kingdom of God into the kingdoms of the world.

Combining these four attributes is difficult, both for the *ekklesia* itself, and for those involved within it. Throughout the history of Christianity there have been attempts at some of these very things.[12] But they often have had the idea of creating or bringing in the kingdom of God, or confusing the community with the kingdom itself. The notion of an embassy retains the function of representation. The influence of an embassy may spread, but it will never take over a kingdom of this world. It works, not to take over power, or to provide only a safe haven for victims of power, but to consistently undermine human cosmologies. *The ekklesia exists to make the cosmos implausible.*

Individuals must also be highly trained in order to live within a hostile climate as aliens; while retaining their true allegiance. These are the skills of ambassadors, or spies. As ambassadors, Christians are indeed called to such maturity that they are capable of living as foreign agents. Again, this is not something that most worship-event based churches come near approaching.

The *ekklesia* must be a subversive, revolutionary people but never a party. It can never achieve its ends if its demands are implemented by structures of civilization. This is to recommit the sin of Adam and Eve, by separating the desire for the good from its source in a living and active relationship with God. Both progressive and conservative Christianity are guilty of this collusion by seeking to make structures of sin less bad. But this is a false gospel, a false good news. Any sense of justice implementable by those who do not submit to God is no justice at all. It is the judgment that creates the knowledge of good and evil, leading to further alienation from a God who is seen as unnecessary for justice.

---

12. Including recently, Dreher, *The Benedict Option*. Dreher's coming "dark age" and call for escape has similarities to my argument, but is rather conservative and has little vision for invasive critical engagement. He instrumentalizes the church for the preservation of the West.

But, like any ambassador or spy, tactics must be contextualized. Participation in the world on its terms can be of a tactical advantage, as in the Parable of the Shrewd Steward.[13] But it is vital that we do not thereby confuse success in a political action as a victory for the kingdom of God. Tactics must remain part of a larger strategy, and individual ambassadors must be trained sufficiently to understand this.

Embassy and Ecology

The uniqueness of Christianity is not a resource that can be instrumentalized for ecology. Its core ecological message is inextricably rooted in reconciliation with God in Christ. There can be no ethic without submission and faithfulness. To create such an ethic is to submit already to a secular materialism that views human religion as a potentially expedient resource for moral transformation. The problem with this, although it may sometimes be effective in behavior modification, is that it reinforces structures of power and the wholly enclosed imaginary of the modern cosmos. *If the Bible is a resource for ecological ethics, then it actually has very little to offer.* It upholds some classic agrarian principles as outlined by authors such as Wendell Berry, Ellen Davis, and Norman Wirzba. There is little problematic about the vision for renewal they see in trying to return people to an agrarian, emplaced, and self-limited imaginary, provided this is understood as disciplinary rather than telic. But there is also little about it that is uniquely Christian or biblical. What this means is that, if we develop an ecological ethic that has principles applicable to a secular world without requiring active submission to God in Christ, we have actually subverted the entire self-proclaimed purpose of Jesus Christ. To do that seems to me the essence of antichrist. To put it another way, *Christian ecotheology runs the risk of making God himself a resource for human exploitation as a means to species survival.* This is a submission of God to humanity, or even of God to the creation. This is precisely what happened at the crucifixion, the mentality that Jesus came to expose to open shame on the cross. But, of course, it is difficult to imagine an alternative. Can we not use the Bible's agrarian teachings to help people see the relevance of the biblical message? Certainly. But it must offer something unique, or it ultimately offers nothing. If the reality of the living God and his demand for reconciliation is superfluous to the

13. Luke 16:1–9.

ethic we produce, then it will not lead people to that end, it will be its own witness for the uselessness and meaninglessness of the God of the Bible.

The embassy model of *ekklesia*, however, offers a different way. Building an embassy means offering a plausible and tangible alternate environment that can therapeutically renew the mind in a way that does not require superhuman effort or mental ability. We cannot save the creation by demanding that normal people become saints by an effort of self-willing or by top-down management. Both demands are entirely implausible. As we discussed previously, ethics is a method of integration. It only works by offering plausible alternatives, and thus rarely questions underlying structures of power or imaginational givens. This means an alternative environment is necessary. People must be able to experience an alternative to see it as a possibility.[14] Ethics cannot undermine the imagination upon which it is built. The embassy model can plausibly call for the destruction of all current cosmoi, and all current imaginaries if it is capable of creating alternate environments.

This means that the role of the *ekklesia* is to create environments that make the biblical ecotopias outlined by Bauckham plausible,[15] though obviously not fully realized. In order to remain present and invasive, such an embassy must remain in touch with the surrounding cosmos and know how and where to push the boundaries. Again, it cannot create, build, or bring the kingdom itself. But its role is not simply to exist, but also to bear a prophetic message—the message of Jonah to Nineveh of God's coming wrath poured out on humanity for its destruction of the creation. We will be judged and the call is to repentance and reconciliation. Those in power will not often hear this, but as has happened with the church throughout its history, the victims of civilization (i.e., the vast majority of human population) are those most ready for the good news of the kingdom of God. And now that we are at risk of "climate apartheid" according to the United Nations and the distribution of wealth has never been more uneven in human history, the number of those who would be receptive to the call of God increases daily. The *ekklesia* must not see its role as courting the wealthy or powerful. Jesus only has a message of woe

---

14. As an example, David Graeber believed that the success of the Occupy Wall Street movement was in the opening of the imagination of participants for an alternative way of government. Graeber, *The Democracy Project.*

15. Isa 11; 32; 35; 41; 44; Ezek 34; Mark 1:13; Rev 21. See Bauckham, *Bible and Ecology,* 115–29, 175–78.

to them. The kingdom of God does not belong to those who succeed in civilization.[16]

The Movement of Christianity

Unfortunately, the Christian life and the role of the church has often been understood as something static. This made sense in premodern times when social roles and hierarchies were more or less fixed, and change was hard to notice over generations. Niebuhr's *Christ and Culture* models represent well the unhelpful perspectives on how Christianity has been viewed as a *state of being*, rather than a constant *movement*. Christian traditions have divided into various perspectives on how to engage with the world. But the *ekklesia* is made up of individual people who must all go through a process of exodus, formation, experience of the promised land, and reentry into the world of sin. The *ekklesia,* as embodied in a community, will need to go through this process as well. There is a time for exodus, a time to form communities of the wilderness, a time to try and influence the wider culture, a time to fight against the world. But they must be put into their proper narrative location in a person's and a community's life within a particular context.

This movement is required for the renewal of the mind. Very few people are able to think in ways that are implausible in their environments. Without extricating a person from the daily patterns of life in the modern cosmos, the reality of the kingdom of God will reside in fantasy, groupthink, and apparent miracles only. The renewed desire for the miraculous, and belief in regular miracles found in charismatic movements reveals much about the Christian imagination in the modern age. The daily unreality of the presence of God, the nearly clockwork precision of the highly controlled and managed modern cosmos demands that, if God is real, he must be a highly interventionist figure who works in ways that defy explanation in the self-enclosed modern materialist imaginary. The idea that God lies behind mysterious causalities in the creation becomes more implausible the more scientific knowledge advances, for if God is relegated to working in the "gaps" left by scientific explanations, the closing of those gaps makes God redundant. Thus, in order for God to seem to be real, exceptions and gaps in the enclosed system must be found. Ancient practices of divine communication, through various forms of

16. Luke 6:24–26.

divination, have moved from natural occurrences, like astrology, to the interpretation of apparent coincidences in areas of the built environment. The pernicious difference between these is that the natural world was not actively formed for the sake of control, whereas the modern is, such that integration into it and belief in divine communication through it, plays directly into the hands of the powerful.

Exodus

Babylon the Great in Revelation 17–18 is intended to be symbolic of Rome, and by extension, the human cosmic order. God's judgment upon this representative city/whore is not unique to imperial Rome, for its condemned practices are hardly limited to Rome (as those of Babylon in Jeremiah 51, to which Revelation 17–18 is alluding, are not limited to Babylon). God is bringing his judgment upon these and all centers of human power and wealth. The call to the people of God is to "Come out of her, lest you take part in her sins, lest you share in her plagues."[17] Once again we see the pattern of exodus, a leaving of civilization, both to survive and to avoid participation in sin. While there is little point in arguing for a specific interpretation of complex and contested literature like Revelation, it serves to show that God's judgment lies upon human civilizations, and that the people of God should not share in the consequences of God's wrath upon human civilization. They should, therefore, leave. It is important to consider this call in the Bible. The call of God on his people is to leave civilization, potentially leaving family, friends, and livelihood behind in the process. Noah does this. Abram represents the archetype. Moses had to work for the liberation of God's people from Egypt, as God's judgment fell upon that empire. The same happens with Lot being rescued from Sodom. God's people are not at home in human civilization and they should leave it behind, if at all possible. They have been liberated in an exodus and should not desire to return, as Paul says, "For freedom Christ has set us free. So, stand fast and do not again be subjected to the yoke of slavery."[18]

The call to leave, to escape, is a call to exodus in order to be formed as a people who are capable of representing God's mission of reconciliation. Unless there is a period and process of separation, of learning

17. Rev 18:4.
18. Gal 5:1.

holiness, the call to reconciliation cannot happen. This separation is not permanent, though. There can be no call to reconciliation without a re-entry after attaining a new identity.

If humanity has created an inescapable system of disaster, the call-ing of the *ekklesia* is not to fix minor issues here and there and so pre-serve the parasite to continue its devouring for a few more years. The role of Christians is to leave the world in order to be holy. Like Lot leaving Sodom behind, our role is to allow the judgment of God to fall upon sin and not look back. God's judgment will be revealed. Sometimes the role of God's people is to simply not be there when it happens, and not to lament it as do the kings, merchants, and sea-traders do in the de-struction of Babylon the Great.[19] Rather the role is to "Rejoice over her" destruction.[20] Throughout the Bible, the Day of the Lord is understood as frightful judgment that is best to escape if possible. But, although the day of judgment is darkness and not light,[21] the defeat of injustice is worthy of celebration. Biblically, the costs of civilization so outweigh its benefits, that its destruction by God's judgment is to be welcomed and praised.

At this point, perhaps, physical departure from urban centers is not what is demanded. Although, it may very well be that the time is at hand for an intentional founding of Christian ambassadorial communities in the wilderness where sustainable agrarian lifestyles may be practiced in preparation for the anticipated disasters of climate change. What is needed, though, is an exodus from ecologically disastrous imaginaries, like belief in profit, in hierarchy, in the earth as a resource and property to be owned, in humans as good and rightful managers, not to mention abandoning allegiances to nation-states, to transnational corporations, and other powers that own people and control their lives.

Escape is the first step in the biblical journey. Sometimes the escape begins with a physical departure from a location, like Egypt or Sodom. Other times the escape begins with a strong doubt. The growing move-ment for climate justice is an incredible opportunity for the good news of God's reconciling kingdom as demands for some escape from the current way of the world grows.

19. Rev 18:10, 16, 19.

20. Rev 18:20.

21. Amos 5.

Wilderness Formation

Coming out of Babylon the Great is the first step, but it is an entry into the wilderness. This can be an actual wilderness or a metaphorical one. In either case, it is an experience of disorientation. But the wilderness is an important place biblically. It is the place where God forms people through challenge and difficulty. It is a place where character is formed. It is also the place where a community is able to break down their former identities, their former allegiances and divisions, and be united by God. The wilderness is where the people of God learn dependence upon God.

Practically this means the *ekklesia* has the hugely difficult task of developing into something plausible and tangible. This is and will continue to be a wilderness activity. We have crucial allegiances, identities, and values that need to be broken down. We need to learn to think differently, to think about different options, to discern the false foundations of the thoughts of the world. It is then also learning to farm sustainably and organically on a smaller community level. We need to re-learn actual wilderness skills, and not like television portrays them. Survival is not the primary goal here, the reconciliation of creation is. We need to learn to live *in* the creation *as creation*, rather than *on*, *over*, and *outside* of it. For many urbanites this will be difficult. It means experiencing heat and cold and compensating for these with clothing choices rather than altering a whole environment. It means experiencing seasons, eating things appropriate to the seasons and locales. It means sharing what God has provided, as we rethink notions of work and reward, and of private property. It also means forming relationships for learning local and practical knowledge, like Moses learns leadership and delegation from Jethro, or Elisha learns from Elijah. This form of discipleship is not simply about spiritual skills of accountability or prayer, it is about skills that do not separate physical action from the spiritual. But, an agrarian lifestyle is meaningless unless grounded in and oriented toward the reconciliation of all things in Christ.

Promised Land and Community of Blessing

While the wilderness is important for formation, there is a time for the development of sustainable, long-term, emplaced communities. This should involve sufficient adaptation to the local conditions of the creation, as well as to those of the dominant society of an area, while maintaining holiness. The focus at this stage of formation is in developing common practices of equipping new ambassadors by creating a plausible, tangible, holy, and invasive environment. This type of equipping will certainly involve education, learning about the people of God and its history, learning the word of God, learning about the dominant culture and its values. It should also involve equipping in practical skills of engagement, discussion, and tactics of loving subversion. It must also likewise involve a deepening of community bonds by common work, common life, and mutual accountability.

Ambassadorship

Once a community has a certain level of maturity it is able to finally get to its main mission, which is to be ambassadors. This is a task of entering back into the dominant world for the sake of bringing people out on the journey that begins with an exodus. It is also the proclamation of the prophetic message of judgment and reconciliation. Moses, of course, does just this when he goes to Pharaoh. This is what Jesus did in Jerusalem. Other prophets did this to more and less of an extent. But we see important images of this in the book of Kings where the prophets Elijah and Elisha act independently of either temple or palace to be a blessing even to the enemies of Israel. The story of Naaman is an excellent example of the ambassadorial role that satisfies its intended purpose by the submission of a foreign commander to the God of Israel.[22]

God brought chaos to Egypt through Moses. Jesus preached that he came to bring a sword and to set a fire to the earth, to create human division rather than human unity.[23] God is the author of chaos in Babel, and the one who destroys Babylon the Great. God is the one who brings disasters to cities.[24] God sends the flood, destroys Sodom, Jericho, and many other cities. God is not safe, nor the God of order according to our cosmologies. God does not fit our cosmologies and so neither should the people who represent him. Being an ambassador of *this* God and his kingdom means refusing the order of the world and, like spies, subverting the socially constructed realities of a people.

22. See 2 Kgs 5. Also see Ellul, *Politics of God and the Politics of Man*.
23. Matt 10:34–7; Luke 12:49–53.
24. Amos 3:6.

What the Embassy-Ekklesia Is Not

This basic structure of movement from exodus to reentry as ambassadors is prone to many misunderstandings that fixate on one or more of the movements of Christian faith. Some will inevitably focus almost entirely on holiness, on the formation of isolated communities that attempt to build the kingdom of God. Obvious examples of this are in some Anabaptist and monastic traditions. By far the most will pursue a syncretistic option that legitimizes structures of brokenness by merging the kingdom of God with the kingdoms of the world. This option, modelled well by Pope Francis in *Laudato Si*, attempts to use Christian tradition to influence the world to more just structures. The motive is fine, and many of the ends are laudable, but it continues the counterproductivity of social engagement that has characterized the church since the birth of secularism in the Reformation. One could easily characterize most mainline Protestantism in the same category, as well as Evangelicalism. It is syncretism because it merges the concept of the kingdom of God with human civilization. The result of this is the problem that inevitably plagues theological liberalism—it joins social movements after they have sufficient mass, with almost nothing new to contribute. This has the effect of disempowering the church by seeking to make it relevant to social causes, a wholly servile perspective. This submits the reality of God/Jesus/the kingdom to ideas of justice that do not require belief in God. This means God is an optional extra who only exists for the purpose of blessing wider cultural movements. This is true of politically progressive or conservative movements. In all of these cases, Christians often invalidate their ambassadorial role by allying God to human causes. It has also been useful to structures of power, because it appropriates a prophetic message and is able to use the blessing of important figures to gain power, perhaps never more evident than in the role of particular Evangelical American Christians who were willing to sacrifice almost all previous work of justice and family values for the sake of gaining power and using government authority to legitimize a supposedly Christian "worldview."

The third area of potential error is in certain versions of the "redemption" option. This option, popular through Dutch Reformed theology, is something of a merging between the two traditional options of separation and syncretism. The idea is that the world is full of broken structures and the gospel is the solution to these structures, often focusing on the city. The major problem with this idea is that it believes that institutions are established by God and it therefore seeks a reformist track. Banks, corporations, multinationals, and nation-states may all have had elements within them, but they are ordained structures by God that Christians should participate within to fix. The theological error lies in a mistaken vision of God's sovereignty. Reformed theology, of which I am a representative, has tended to make God responsible for the *structure* of the present evil age, but not responsible for how people act within that structure. In its most pernicious forms, e.g., historical southern American Presbyterianism, it legitimized structures like slavery as God-given. God's sovereignty does not establish the form of the cosmos or the human institutions that compose it. Rather than God's sovereign reign, "As of yet, we do not see all things submitted to him."[25] Instead, God submitted for a time, and remains submitted for this time, to the power of human sinfulness for the sake of his mission of reconciliation.

Civilization is a sinful human construct, squarely the realm of Satan in the temptations of Jesus. As Jacques Ellul notes, when Jesus was tempted by Satan to receive all the kingdoms of the world by submitting to him, this was not an empty temptation. If it were outside of his power, it would not be a real temptation. Jesus would simply call his bluff and say, "Actually God rules it all." Instead Jesus refuses, thereby implying that Satan has offered something real.[26] Jesus's resistance and his confession that he must serve God alone, meant that he would not and could not receive the rulership of the kingdoms of the world without defeating the very power and structures that establishes and maintains them, i.e., Satan.

This means that civilization is not like a broken machine that Jesus came to fix, or that civilization is partnership with God in the great development project of the creation. There can be no redemption for that which God did not own in the first place, since redemption means a buying-back. We should not expect such a theology to lead the way in ecology because it seeks to repair the present but broken systems rather than see the fundamental structures of the myth of civilization as inherent to the problem of ecological disaster.

25. Heb 2:8.
26. Ellul, *Anarchy and Christianity*.

Embassy Examples

It is vital to not provide a *technē* for how an *ekklesia* should be structured. This should be based on local conditions and each community of Christ should develop its own local character, heightening diversity and local applicability. However, there are many practices that can be applied in your locale. Many of them focus first on eating. Bernard Charbonneau was an early ecologist who recognized the importance of intentionally eating well.[27] Norman Wirzba has dedicated an entire work to a theology of eating.[28] Education and the formation of the imagination is vital. Simply educating on the facts of ecological disaster is relatively ineffective because it produces obvious but all-too-small results, like voting differently, recycling, reducing plastic use, or switching to solar energy. While small, concrete practices are indeed important, of vastly more importance is a renewed imagination. This often takes serious work, long conversations, and individual relationships of trust. Simple practices need to be integrated into forming a renewed imagination.

Many others have focused on practices of worship. These can be useful provided they are integrated into a larger vision. But worship may prove counterproductive, if it fulfils an expectation of duty for a Christian. Ecologically conscious worship changes nothing and it, if confined to an hour or two per week, will have functionally little impact. But a renewed focus on word and sacraments in simple worship, rather than on a supposedly intense experience of the divine in highly orchestrated events, can help renew expectations for what God can and will do.

An *ekklesia* in an urban area can focus on community gardening, work with the poor, prisoners, addicts, and others who are the outcasts and downtrodden of civilization. A gathering that mixes apparent savages (those experiencing homelessness) with middle and upper class believers can have profound impacts on everyone involved. This is especially true for the wealthier Christians who, through individual relationships of love, may start to learn about systemic injustices inherent in the myth of civilization. But I would strongly encourage urban Christians to build relationships with local farms and rural communities. Simply developing practices of learning to see the costs of civilization can be transformative. Spending time in many of America's rural colonies and developing

---

27. Charbonneau, *The Green Light*, 158.

28. Wirzba, *Food and Faith*.

relationships within them could reframe the thinking of many in an urban context.

For most *ekklesia*-embassies the stages of exodus and wilderness will prove the most challenging. Convincing Christians of ecological problems is sometimes a tall order, let alone the need to challenge the myth of civilization in practical ways. But it is not too early to begin the process of forming communities in exile in rural or semi-rural and sustainable places that are capable of housing and hosting believers who want to experience a plausible, tangible, holy, and invasive environment. Creating communities focused on equipping leaders of new communities in a communal, church-seminary, garden/farm environment is feasible. In this way, church leadership can be equipped in an environment that embodies reconciliation with creation, as well as with other people.

Conclusion

This embassy-*ekklesia* has numerous resonances with Christian movements throughout history. It certainly sounds similar to monastic movements, particularly new monasticism of the past few decades. There is certainly a growing realization that Christians can no longer go along with the status quo in a post-Christendom era. This will certainly mean a reimagining of what church is and does. As the church approaches ecological issues it is met with challenges all around. Ecology is so politically charged that many church leaders fear addressing it. The church has little remaining political influence, which has meant that those who care about ecological issues have had to join non-Christian movements for climate justice, problematic as that is. That the church is not unified on at least taking seriously the groaning of creation reveals that the church has a great deal of inertia in its historical identities and particularities. But more than anything, I believe there is a broken imagination rampant in church institutions that seeks distractions in providing quality worship events, surviving institutional decline, prioritizing seemingly more pressing political issues like sexuality, gender, and abortion debates, while failing to understand the connection of these issues to each other and to ecology.

CHAPTER 14

To Nineveh

Engaging Civilization

THE *EKKLESIA,* OR THE embassy of the kingdom, must preach the gospel
of Jonah. We feel a great resistance to that. Some feel a great love for
Nineveh/Babylon, for the wealth, the technology, the speed and excite-
ment of the city. Others resist, like Jonah, because of hatred for "those
people" who should not be saved. Often that hatred is directed at the
"least of these"—the homeless and jobless. These are the real enemies of
civilization because their very presence is an outpost of chaos, of wild
people in the midst of the city. They are unaccounted for, a drain on the
local economy. "They should just get jobs, get a place to live, even if it be
a shelter." Sleeping outdoors is one of the great crimes, because it calls
civilization into question—that people can be human without any of the
trappings civilization claims makes us fully human. It is only acceptable
as recreation, as that sallying-forth from civilization to test our mettle
against the wild. Actually living *in* the land is often a crime. We are only
permitted to live *on* it. Living *on* the city is a crime, but living in it is the
chief end of humanity, according to the cosmos.

Jesus himself was a traveler, a wanderer, like his ancestors before
him. He was a wilderness man. In modern terms, he was homeless. He
"couch-surfed" and "slept rough." His great list of working for the least of
these includes providing food, drink, clothing, welcome as a guest, and
visitation to the sick and imprisoned.[1] He does not demand the development of housing projects, job creation, or integration into the cosmos.

1. Matt 25:35–45. See also Heb 10:34; 13:3.

These are systems that turn people into problematic categories that require saming solutions. Our responsibility to other people is not to make them self-sufficient. It is to create communities in which there shall be no poor among us by sharing.[2] This is only possible by discipleship and relationships of trust. What the embassy-*ekklesia* does for those outside of its community is the revelation of the values of the Creator in word and deed. This most assuredly does not mean reinforcing the structures of civilization, or the integration of outcasts into the world that has cast them out.

Ethics and a Christian Theology of Creation

Ethics begins in *axiology*, or the study of how we develop or find value. There is no point in elaborating a theory of what we should do without explaining why, and that why comes from value. We pursue what is valuable and avoid what is not. When it comes to ecology there are a number of places we could identify as the source of value.

The first possible location of value is in *human usage*. This is pragmatism. We value things that are useful to us. Ecologically speaking, this gives rise to an ethic of conservation. We should conserve valuable resources so that we can ensure they last and continue to give us value. This source of value also produces the most ecologically disastrous perspectives, because its only source of ecological value is the potential for future uselessness of the world. Within this perspective generally falls the concept of sustainability. If we cannot create a sustainable world, we cannot guarantee future value. That also means we cannot rely on our economic theories of value, which make future growth the source and security of value.

The second location of value is in *an authority or law*. This might be called legalism, or a form of deontology in which we do our duty in all situations. We might use this to construct an ethic that cares for the creation because God commands it, and it is our duty to look after it. The notion of stewardship comes from this location of value. We still act as the major arbiters of value, but we do so with a divine permission and a responsibility to answer to the lawgiver. This location of value generally proves useful only when the lawgiver is nearby with a clear threat of enforcing its will. Indeed, Jesus has a few parables about this

2. Deut 15:4, fulfilled in Acts 2:44.

kind of stewardship mentality that fails to motivate the people of God.[3] Knowledge that God will one day judge us for what we have done to his creation, while true, is not likely to motivate the complex world of civilization to radically transform its ways immediately, as Nineveh does in the book of Jonah.

The third location of value is in *a thing itself*. In the world of ecology this has been called "deep ecology." Deep ecology holds that all life has value in and of itself, and humans are only one form of life. While this has some similarities with the idea of a community of creation, given by Bauckham and others, deep ecology is problematic because any idea of inherent value is philosophically problematic. Intrinsic or inherent value is impossible to know, because we have no way of learning what value a thing has in itself. Furthermore, value exists only in a relationship. Value is not an absolute measurement, but a relative one. It helps us establish hierarchies of value. Value is not a thing to possess, it is a decision someone makes about an orientation or hierarchy. Thus, to believe in intrinsic value is an unjustifiable projection of human value onto a thing itself. Even if we are members of a community of creation, creatures that do not practice forms of judgment or discrimination are not capable of communicating value to us. We could say that an eagle values her chicks more than other chicks. This deer might value clover over grass to eat. These observable values are not deeply relevant for profound ethical deliberation because they do not help us compare the value of a deer and the value of an eagle's chicks. Nor is it given to us to make those value judgements.

The fourth location of value is *inherent in a thing as given by God*. Bouma-Prediger rightly explains that, "any ecocentric perspective must, from a Christian point of view, be transmuted into a theocentric perspective . . . ."[4] This is only a slight deviation from deep ecology, but an important one that allows for a meaningful hierarchization of value. But this view retains the problem that a thing cannot possess value, given that value is an action not a product. Put in terms of economics, we know that financial value does not exist in its physical representation. A one dollar bill and a ten dollar bill do not contain the value in themselves, but in the value people give to them through a collective will. Ecologically this means we will end up confusing our act of evaluation with the projected

---

3. Parable of the Wicked Tenants in Matt 21, Mark 12, Luke 20; Parable of the Talents in Matt 25; Parable of the Minas in Luke 19.

4. Bouma-Prediger, *For the Beauty of the Earth*, 127.

value that a thing ostensibly possesses. This tends to baptize preexisting value systems with divine legitimation.

To correct this, the final location of value is in *God* who actively values each individual creature in a relationship of judgment or evaluation. This is not a negative thing. Remember that judgment is simply a decision, not necessarily a negative decision. This relationship is rightly called love, though that is a very slippery term. In order for humans to rightly evaluate the creation, they must actively engage in a relationship with God and participate in his loving evaluation. In other words, reconciled communion with God is the source of joining in God's evaluative action for the creation. This does not mean we get to judge for ourselves.[5] It means we receive the evaluation of God and orient our lives accordingly. This is partly what the restoration of the image of God means. Because this knowledge of value is possible only in an active relationship of participation, such knowledge of value is inaccessible to those estranged from or in rebellion against God.

Ethics itself is problematic. Recall that judgment apart from God was precisely the temptation and original sin in the Bible. That very act was an attempt at becoming godlike. Karl Barth puts it thus, "It is our basic sin to take the place of the judge, to try to judge ourselves and others. All other sins, both small and great, derive ultimately from this source."[6] If this is correct, then the field of ethics itself is made problematic. It also means that cooperation between Christians and allies in ecological ethics is made challenging. While certain goods and values may overlap, like not letting the world be destroyed by human actions, the goal of each group is completely different. Such an alliance offers the possibility that Christians may convince others of the goodness of God. But it can also mean that Christians are tempted by expediencies to commit afresh the basic sin of judgment by collaborating with the judgments of other ecological voices. *Any properly Christian ethic must be centered in reconciliation with Christ.*

Thus, there is no real public ethics that Christianity has to offer to the world. The world of sinful rebellion is not capable of perceiving value rightly. So, while others may produce reasonable approximations of a reconciled ethic, like Aldo Leopold's Land Ethic, it will nonetheless remain problematic, as well as lacking motive, particularly for well-integrated

5. See Matt 7:1–2.
6. Barth, *Church Dogmatics*, IV/1 235.

people living in urban environments. And this is one of the major problems. Ecologically conscious Christians know that the creation is dying. We know that, if humans were reconciled to God, we would consequently desire to be reconciled to the creation; and we would even learn the mind of Christ so that we would learn to value others more than ourselves. But there is no rational means by which the mind of Christ can prevail over the pragmatism of the modern cosmos. We cannot logically convince the world to see things as reconciled people do, without reconciliation. This leaves us with a few ethical options.

The first option is the most obvious and basic one—*overpower*. If peace talks fail, war is the only other option. At least, that's how the reasoning generally goes for the world. If we cannot convince the world to be reconciled to God and thus to creation, we will have to *make* them. While this sounds a bit absurd at this point in Christian history, it has not always been. In fact, it has often proven too tempting an option, leading to forcible conversions. But there are other ways that overpower is manifest than in base violence. It is manifest in the attempt to ally Christian organizations and movements with political ones. For the majority of Christians who live in secular nations, this type of logic often seems to hold water. Perhaps we can vote in aspects of a Christian worldview, or Christian ethical principles. This has been the tactic of much of the anti-abortion movement in the United States. The problem is, the devil's tactics will not produce the kingdom of God. If the overpower tactic is successful, it produces subservient and embittered losers who see Jesus and Christianity as oppressors. If the overpower tactic fails, the revenge generally makes things worse than if the tactic had never been tried. The method of using power to assert one's will over another's is itself the devil's tactic, however. The mind of Christ is to serve, not to force submission. Indeed, the end of the Christ hymn in Philippians 2 sees that universal submission to the God is the future, but it is a future obtained precisely by self-emptying and disempowerment. The very reason we are not all dead, as in the flood of Noah, is that God will not use his power to overwhelm us.

A second option for a public ethical strategy is *to abandon the world*. While I have already argued for a form of this *as part of the movement of Christianity*, some take this as the final end or purpose of the church. There is a certain logic to escaping a world impossible to transform. We can build guarded survivalist outposts. But this shows another aspect of the inversion of the mind of Christ. Christ came to his enemies and died for them.[7] We are not to abandon the world any more than God himself did. We are ambassadors, and so we must engage the world. This does not negate forming communities outside of human civilization. In fact, it must involve that. But it means maintaining a continual movement away from and toward reentry into the world.

A third option for a public ethical strategy, and the one I believe to be correct, is *subversion*. Subversion involves dismantling structures of power by destroying the belief structures that uphold them. Perhaps the most vital point to communicate in this book is this—*civilization is a collective belief system that survives and thrives only by the collective desire of humans; and its continued existence will necessarily destroy God's creation that it systematically cannot perceive as real.* The task of Christians in this situation is to attack the myth of civilization by loving the enemies of God. But to do that, we have to be able to provide an alternate environment that proves the kingdom of God is a feasible alternative to the kingdoms of this world. So long as we merely preach a gospel of spiritual salvation and personal moral improvement, we do almost nothing. Christianity has preached a gospel far too small. It has, by its long submission to the power of human states, and by its long collusion with the narrative of civilizational progress, made the good news of Jesus a mockery among the nations. Christians have become tools of political movements. They have become key agents in the destruction of the creation by the advances of civilization. They have turned the kingdom of God into a promise of a personal paradise in the afterlife. All of these false beliefs offer no threat whatever to the principalities and powers of the world. The only ethical approach the kingdom of God has to offer is to expose the principalities and powers to shame. In other words, to show that the emperor has no clothes. Christians must find ways to demonstrate that the myth of power in politics, the myth of progress in technology, the myth of growth and wealth in economics, the myth of meaningful identity in human group-ings, and the myth of civilization in the city are false myths. None of them are capable of living up to their promises. They are built on false premises and demonstrably false rationale. We cannot demonstrate any of this by simply preaching about another world, about a life after death, or about how God is on our side in our movements of social justice. God is not on our side. Throughout the entire narrative of Scripture, the de-scendants of Cain are God's enemies. All of our nations, all of our cities,

7. Rom 5:8.

all of our attempts to leave creation for an artificially human constructed world, are rebellions against God. Our only ethical option is to live within these worlds as agents of another, actively working to sow the seeds of discontent.

Demythologizing and Transcending Civilization

This is not a return to Eden. We cannot get back to the garden we have so thoroughly plundered. Eden no longer exists as such. It has been paved over, its soil depleted, its climate changed, and its great trees turned into lumber. History cannot be reversed, and we cannot return to hunter-gatherer societies. Going forward in reconciliation means character development. This is not simply the development of virtues. Classical virtue is somewhat useful in theory, but many modern proponents of virtue ethics fail to grasp the determinative aspects of virtue and character. Those who integrate into one cosmos will define courage differently than those of another cosmos. Virtue, as the mean between the extremes, ends up being little more than the best possible means of adaptation to a cosmos in which the extremes of behavior are defined relative to the extremities of experience. Character formation, by contrast, is how a person learns from relationships and experiences. A mature person is capable of inhabiting different environments without necessarily integrating into them. In other words, civilizational virtues will militate against transcending civilization. But a mature character is able to rest entirely in the solid identity of being in Christ, and thus can pursue reconciliation no matter the cost, and no matter the difficulty of learning to live in a new post-civilizational environment.

But what does transcending civilization mean? It means consciously choosing to deconstruct first the *imagination* of civilization, and then its *structures*. To *transcend* civilization is to retain the lessons we have learned, while dismantling it in a wise fashion. To *reject* civilization, by contrast, would be the simple desire to return to a supposedly unfallen hunter-gatherer stage of existence, and impose this on all others. Such a revolution would, of course, require massive depopulations. It is somewhat useless to give a utopian framework of what this would look like, though that will be the most obvious request. Time and again one hears the critique against those who question a system, that they are not offering a better option for replacement. That is the essential point. Transcending civilization does not mean reshaping it. It means understanding what the whole project of creating a socially constructed world means, and consciously choosing to reject it. It does not mean destroying the machines any more than God destroyed Babel. Babel was not destroyed. The mission of reconciliation is not to destroy computers, for example. The mission is to transform the mind through reconciliation such that computers and their logic are understood, but no longer needed, nor desired.

In that way, it is important that Christians understand the aspects of civilization. We must understand economics, technology, political systems, systems of identity-construction, the processes of simplification, and the whole humanly constructed world as a whole. We must be able to understand the motives and rationale behind these structures, and choose to go beyond them.

Re-Narrating Ecology

If the problem of ecology is a broken imagination, and its solution is the renewal of the mind in Christ, then we need to retell the story of ecology and disaster for the world. This will involve the terms we have used throughout this book: chaos, cosmos, civilization.

Ecology is about putting people in their rightful place. That rightful place is within the creation as reconciled subjects and representatives of God. The human role and task is not to manage the creation, but to reveal to it the character of God as shown to us in Jesus Christ and in his self-humbling.

Ecology tells the story of chaos in the forms of climate change, soil depletion, pollution, and mass species extinction. Climate change, for example, has been called, by the actor Harrison Ford, a monster that needs to be slain. Others have taken up this call to recast climate change in the language of a Joseph Campbell style hero story in which we can be the heroes who collectively slay this dragon.[8] But "climate change" is a projected concept. That is, the climate is changing, of course, but that is not really the problem. The climate has no will. We do. Climate change is not a dragon to be slain. *We* are. We can never be the heroes, even if we change our ways to stop climate change. Heroes cannot be responsible for the disaster that they then solve! That would be a new kind of myth in which the villain engages down a long road to total destruction, only to repent,

8. Townshend, "The Epic Story of Solving Climate Change."

and work to fix all the damage he has done. At best we can be repentant villains. But this doesn't fit the myth of civilization. We are supposed to be the heroes. The earth is the problem. It is simply not advanced enough to hold us in. We need to leave it behind and pursue our fortunes away from our mother's crib, now that we are nearly mature enough to do so. If we are talking about myths, this sounds far more like Oedipus than a classic hero story. We have slain God our father, brought shame to our "mother" earth, and brought plague upon ourselves and the world. And now? Oedipus repented and renounced the kingship. Will we?

Humans are chaos monsters, parasites, the earth's most successful invasive mammal. Whatever disasters befall us are deserved and good for the hopeful restoration of creation. In the dragon-slaying hero myth, we are the dragons, and the climate is the hero who may just conquer us. Like the dragon, we deserve what comes to us. But it is not humanity as such that is evil. We have a broken imagination. Our imaginations of civilization, of politics, economics, technology, identity, and urbanism need to be slain. Then will there be hope of a restored cosmos. Who knows what new order could be made out of the corpse of the myth of civilization? If Christians are to take part in this, we must work for the kingdom of God to be what comes from the corpse of civilization. From God's perspective, however, humans are not chaos monsters. We are rebels. The solution is not to kill us as chaos monsters, as in the great flood of Noah. The solution is reconciliation.

Christian thinking on ecology must begin with a renewed imagination and a re-narration of the problem. The *ekklesia* ought to be on the front lines of a radical project of imaginational transformation. We must call the world to transcend civilization, not the environment. At this point, only civilizational-level transformations seem likely to make a difference. As the saying goes, desperate times require desperate action.

Conclusion

Plundering Civilization

EDEN, THE CREATION OF God that he declared "very good" and in line with his intention, has been plundered. It is now at great risk of death. The only reasonable course of action is to investigate the most deep-level reasons for this situation with a humility that will do whatever it takes to prevent this. I am, as yet, unaware of anyone publicly calling for such radical change. Political calls to action, even those of protest movements, pursue greater control by asking governments to enact change. Greater human management and the further progression of civilization will seal the fate of both humanity and the creation, as humanity shows no ability to escape its broken and parasitic imagination.

Such radical change must begin with the submission of the human imagination to the kingship of the Creator through reconciliation. It then must change its ways to whatever extent is demanded by this reconciliation. For us today, this is a transformation of every aspect of civilization. Like those at Babel, we must give up on the task of trying to make a name for ourselves by refashioning the world in our image through construction. We have seen that economics, politics, technology, identity, and the city all create no-exit situations. They are false hopes and false solutions built upon a foundational irrationality endemic to the human mind.

The solution is not to return to primitive ways, nor destroy technology. The solution is to continue the process of maturation. Many call our time the Anthropocene, others talk about humans coming to maturity, or have visions of continued progress. All of these beliefs demonstrate an adolescent imagination, one in which humans believe they have attained independence and mastery while remaining blind to the deep dependencies and relationships that give life. Ecological problems reveal a collective "failure to launch." Our civilizational imaginations remain

childish and irresponsible, dreaming of a carefree lifestyle with no consequences. We try to seek our freedom and self-assertion by rejecting any
determination by God our Father and our "mother" earth. We imagine
that we can do it all for ourselves, that we can be anything we want to
be, that we don't need anyone. Like teenagers, we have a rather skewed
self-understanding, believing that we are far more mature than we really
are. We have merely traded being determined by local communities and
environments for global, technological, pseudo-communities and pseu-
do-environments, which have decimated local communities and diverse
ecological environments. Our supposed freedom has come at the cost of
enslaving the creation and ourselves to systems over which none have
control, but whose existence rests entirely on collective human belief.

Growing up involves the psychological pain of realizing that we cannot be anything we want to be. It involves learning our limits after a period of learning our capabilities. It means learning how we are emplaced
within a time and place, destined to grow weaker and die. Growing up
means learning to live in a community in which we are not the masters
or managers. We are members of a fellowship, each imposed upon by the
other. Growing up means learning to share, to place the needs of others
ahead of one's own desires, to seek the good of others before our own.
Growing up means giving up the faith of our fathers.

True maturity is seen in the picture of God incarnate, suffering
at the hands of his creatures, dying a miserable and humiliating death
so that his creation may be rescued. God demonstrates maturity by his
taking on a lower form and limiting himself to the determinants of that
form. Jesus lived as a man without any recourse to the benefits of high
technology. He sweated and shivered. He cried and laughed. He walked
instead of driving or being driven. He lived as *this* man, in *this* community, within *this* family, speaking *this* language, eating *this* food, being hated by *this* people. He demonstrated love by limiting his power,
increasing his responsibility beyond himself and his people. He showed
his love by building a community of those who would follow his example,
uniting them by his Spirit and the call to suffer as he did, so that we could
become mature in his image.[1]

Civilization will "collapse" as it has before in human histories. What
lessons have we learned already? What can we take into a future of human diminishment? What moderated and mature self-understanding

1. Eph 4.

can be formed by this? What can be plundered from the corpse of the chaos monster that is collective humanity and civilization?

The answer must not be the things we currently value, the things that prevent maturity. Much of our *techne* must be left behind. Our economic imaginaries and their systems must die. Our political dreams of global unity through systems of impersonal governance must perish. Our notions of self-created identity have no place in the maturity that appreciates the givenness of relationships. And we must abandon our cities, both in imagination and in reality.

The only solution to a plundered Eden is the subversive plundering of Babylon, of civilization by the invasion of the kingdom of God. Anything less than total transformation of the human imagination will be no transformation at all. We have doomed God's creation to death as humans killed God in Jesus Christ. The only reasonable counter-imaginary to the juvenility of the Anthropocene is the maturity of the kingdom of God.

Bibliography

Arendt, Hannah. *Eichmann in Jerusalem*. London: Penguin, 2006.

Attfield, Robin. *Environmental Ethics*. Cambridge: Polity, 2014.

Bahnson, Fred, and Norman Wirzba. *Making Peace with the Land*. Downers Grove, IL: IVP, 2012.

Barth, Karl. *Church Dogmatics*. Translated by Geoffrey W. Bromiley and Thomas F. Torrance. London: T. & T. Clark, 2009.

Bates, Matthew W. *Salvation by Allegiance Alone: Rethinking Faith, Works, and the Gospel of Jesus the King*. Grand Rapids: Baker Academic, 2017.

Bauckham, Richard. *Bible and Ecology: Rediscovering the Community of Creation*. London: Darton, Longman, & Todd, 2010.

Berger, Peter L. *The Desecularization of the World: Resurgent Religion and World Politics*. Grand Rapids: Eerdmans, 1999.

———. *The Sacred Canopy: Elements of a Sociological Theory of Religion*. New York: Anchor, 1990.

Berger, Peter L., and Thomas Luckmann. *The Social Construction of Reality: A Treatise in the Sociology of Knowledge*. New York: Anchor, 1990.

Berry, Wendell. *A Place on Earth*. Berkeley, CA: Counterpoint, 2009.

———. *Jayber Crow*. Berkeley, CA: Counterpoint, 2001.

———. *That Distant Land*. Berkeley, CA: Counterpoint, 2005.

———. *What I Stand on: The Collected Essays of Wendell Berry 1969–2017*. New York: Library of America, 2019.

———. *The World-Ending Fire*. Berkeley, CA: Counterpoint, 2019.

Blanchard, Kathryn D., and Kevin J. O'Brien. *An Introduction to Christian Environmentalism: Ecology, Virtue, and Ethics*. Waco, TX: Baylor University Press, 2014.

Bonhoeffer, Dietrich. *Creation and Fall; Temptation: Two Biblical Studies*. New York: Simon and Schuster, 1997.

Bouma Prediger, Steven. *For the Beauty of the Earth: A Christian Vision for Creation Care*. Grand Rapids: Baker Academic, 2010.

Brock, Brian. *Christian Ethics in a Technological Age*. Grand Rapids: Eerdmans, 2010.

Brown, Dee. *Bury My Heart at Wounded Knee*. New York: Owl, 2007.

Brunner, Daniel L., Jennifer L. Butler, and A. J. Swoboda. *Introducing Evangelical Ecotheology*. Grand Rapids: Baker Academic, 2014.

Caillois, Roger. *Man and the Sacred*. Translated by Meyer Barash. Urbana, IL: University of Illinois Press, 2001.

———. "Paris, a Modern Myth." In *The Edge of Surrealism: A Roger Caillois Reader*, 173–89. Durham, NC: Duke University Press, 2003.

Calvin, John. *Commentary on Daniel.* Vol. 1. Grand Rapids: Christian Classics Ethereal Library. https://www.ccel.org/ccel/calvin/calcom24.i.html.

Cavanaugh, William T., ed. *Fragile World: Ecology and the Church.* Eugene, OR: Cascade, 2018.

Campbell, Joseph. *The Hero with a Thousand Faces.* Novato, CA: New World Library, 2008.

Charbonneau, Bernard. *The Green Light.* Translated by Christian Roy. London: Bloomsbury Academic, 2018.

Chesterton, G. K. "A Defence of Detective Stories." *The Defendant*, 74–77. 1901. Reprint, Mineola, NY: Dover, 2012.

Chomsky, Noam. *Understanding Power.* New York: New Press, 2002.

Dalley, Stephanie. *Myths from Mesopotamia.* Oxford: Oxford University Press, 2000.

Davis, Ellen F. *Scripture, Culture, and Agriculture: An Agrarian Reading of the Bible.* New York: Cambridge University Press, 2009.

Dawkins, Richard. *The Selfish Gene.* Oxford: Oxford University Press, 2016.

Dreher, Rod. *The Benedict Option.* London: Penguin, 2017.

Duranton, Gilles, and Matthew A. Turner. "The Fundamental Law of Road Congestion: Evidence from Us Cities." *American Economic Review* 101.6 (2011) 2616–52.

Durkheim, Emile. *The Elementary Forms of Religious Life.* Translated by Carol Cosman. Oxford: Oxford University Press, 2001.

Eliade, Mircea. *The Sacred and the Profane: The Nature of Religion.* New York: Harcourt Brace, 1959.

Ellul, Jacques. *Anarchy and Christianity.* Translated by Geoffrey W. Bromiley. Grand Rapids: Eerdmans, 1991.

———. *Autopsy of Revolution.* Translated by Patricia Wolf. New York: Knopf, 1971.

———. *The Ethics of Freedom.* Translated by Geoffrey W. Bromiley. Grand Rapids: Eerdmans, 1976.

———. *The Humiliation of the Word.* Translated by Joyce Main Hanks. Grand Rapids: Eerdmans, 1985.

———. *The Meaning of the City.* Translated by Dennis Pardee. Grand Rapids: Eerdmans, 1970.

———. *The New Demons.* Translated by C. Edward Hopkin. New York: Seabury, 1975.

———. *The Political Illusion.* New York, Knopf, 1967.

———. *The Politics of God and the Politics of Man.* Translated by Geoffrey W. Bromiley. Grand Rapids: Eerdmans, 1972.

———. *Presence in the Modern World: A New Translation.* Translated by Lisa Richmond. Eugene, OR: Cascade, 2016.

———. *Propaganda: The Formation of Men's Attitudes.* Translated by Konrad Kellen and Jean Lerner. New York: Knopf, 1965.

———. *The Reason for Being: A Meditation on Ecclesiastes.* Grand Rapids: Eerdmans, 1990.

———. *The Subversion of Christianity.* Translated by Geoffrey W. Bromiley. Grand Rapids: Eerdmans, 1986.

———. *The Technological Bluff.* Translated by Geoffrey W. Bromiley. Grand Rapids: Eerdmans, 1990.

———. *The Technological Society*. Translated by John Wilkinson. New York: Knopf, 1964.

———. *The Technological System*. Translated by Joachim Neugroschel. New York: Continuum, 1980.

Foot, Philippa. *Virtues and Vices and Other Essays in Moral Philosophy*. Oxford: Oxford University Press, 2002.

Francis, Pope. *Laudato Si*. Vatican City: Libreria Editrice Vaticana, 2015.

Gadamer, Hans-Georg. *Truth and Method*. Translated by Joel Weinsheimer, and Donald G. Marshall. New York: Continuum, 2004.

Girard, René. *The Scapegoat*. Baltimore: Johns Hopkins University Press, 1986.

———. *Violence and the Sacred*. Baltimore: Johns Hopkins University Press, 1977.

Gooley, Tristan. *How to Read Nature: Awaken Your Senses to the Outdoors You've Never Noticed*. New York: Experiment, 2017.

———. *The Lost Art of Reading Nature's Signs*. New York: Experiment, 2015.

Graeber, David. *Debt: The First 5,000 Years*. Brooklyn, NY: Melville House, 2012.

———. *The Democracy Project: A History, a Crisis, a Movement*. New York: Spiegel & Grau, 2013.

———. *Toward an Anthropological Theory of Value: The False Coin of Our Own Dreams*. New York: Palgrave, 2001.

Harlan, Jack R. *Crops and Man*. 2nd ed. Madison, WI: American Society of Agronomy, 1992.

Heidegger, Martin. *Being and Time*. Translated by John Macquarrie, and Edward Robinson. New York: HarperPerennial, 2008.

Johnson, Elizabeth A. *Creation and the Cross*. Maryknoll, NY: Orbis, 2019.

Kant, Immanuel. *Religion within the Bounds of Mere Reason*. Edited by Allen Wood and George di Giovanni. Cambridge: Cambridge University Press, 2018.

Leeman, Jonathan. *Political Church*. Downers Grove, IL: InterVarsity, 2016.

Leopold, Aldo. *A Sand County Almanac*. Oxford: Oxford University Press, 2001.

Lints, Richard. *Identity and Idolatry: The Image of God and Its Inversion*. Downers Grove, IL: IVP Academic, 2015.

Longman III, Tremper, and John H. Walton. *The Lost World of the Flood: Mythology, Theology, and the Deluge Debate*. Downers Grove, IL: IVP Academic, 2018.

Loss, Scott R., Tom Will, Sara S. Loss, and Peter P. Marra. "Bird-Building Collisions in the United States: Estimates of Annual Mortality and Species Vulnerability." *The Condor* 116.1 (2014) 8–23.

Marx, Karl. *Capital: A Critique of Political Economy*. Translated by Ben Fowkes. Harmondsworth, UK: Penguin, 1988.

Moo, Douglas J., and Jonathan A. Moo. *Creation Care: A Biblical Theology of the Natural World*. Grand Rapids: Zondervan, 2018.

Niebuhr, H. Richard. *Christ and Culture*. San Francisco: Harper, 2001.

Nielsen, Karen Margrethe. "Economy and Private Property." In *The Cambridge Companion to Aristotle's Politics*, edited by Marguerite Deslauriers, 67–91. Cambridge: Cambridge University Press, 2013.

Nietzsche, Friedrich. *Thus Spoke Zarathustra*. Translated by Graham Parkes. Oxford: Oxford University Press, 2008.

Preston, Richard. *The Hot Zone*. New York: Anchor, 1995.

Rosset, Peter. "The Multiple Functions and Benefits of Small Farm Agriculture in the Context of Global Trade Negotiations." *Development* 43.2 (2000) 77–82.

Scott, James C. *Against the Grain: A Deep History of the Earliest States*. New Haven, CT: Yale University Press, 2018.

———. *Seeing Like a State: How Certain Schemes to Improve the Human Condition Have Failed*. New Haven, CT: Yale University Press, 1999.

———. *Two Cheers for Anarchism*. Princeton: Princeton University Press, 2014.

Seaford, Richard. *Cosmology and the Polis: The Social Construction of Space and Time in the Tragedies of Aeschylus*. Cambridge: Cambridge University Press, 2015.

———. *Money and the Early Greek Mind: Homer, Philosophy, Tragedy*. Cambridge: Cambridge University Press, 2004.

Smith, Adam. *The Wealth of Nations*. New York: Bantam Classic, 2003.

"Soil Is a Non-Renewable Resource" Food and Agriculture Organization of the United Nations, accessed October 29, 2019, http://www.fao.org/fileadmin/user_upload/soils-2015/docs/EN/IYS_fact_sheets_preservation_en_PRINT.pdf.

Stone, Brad. "Jeff Bezos Wants to Send You to Space Too." Bloomberg, accessed November 16, 2018. https://www.bloomberg.com/news/features/2018-07-26/amazon-s-jeff-bezos-wants-to-send-you-to-space-too.

Sturluson, Snorri, and Jesse L. Byock. *The Prose Edda*. London: Penguin, 2005.

Taylor, Charles. *Modern Social Imaginaries*. Durham, NC: Duke University Press, 2004.

———. *A Secular Age*. Cambridge, MA: Belknap, 2007.

Townshend, Solitaire. "The Epic Story of Solving Climate Change." *Forbes*, September 14, 2018, https://www.forbes.com/sites/solitairetownsend/2018/09/14/why-climate-storytelling-must-change.

Trotsky, Leon, Slavoj Žižek, and Henry Noel Brailsford. *Terrorism and Communism: A Reply to Karl Kautsky*. New York: Verso, 2007.

Tull, Patricia K. *Inhabiting Eden: Christians, the Bible, and the Ecological Crisis*. Louisville, KY: Westminster John Knox, 2013.

Twiss, Richard. *Rescuing the Gospel from the Cowboys*. Downers Grove, IL: InterVarsity, 2015.

"UN Report: Nature's Dangerous Decline 'Unprecedented'; Species Extinction Rates 'Accelerating.'" United Nations, accessed 31 July 2019, https://www.un.org/sustainabledevelopment/blog/2019/05/nature-decline-unprecedented-report/.

Wagenfuhr, G. P. "Jacques Ellul and Charles Taylor on the Sacrality of Secularism." In *Political Illusion and Reality*, edited by David W. Gill, and David Lovekin, 115–25. Eugene, OR: Pickwick, 2018.

———. *Plundering Egypt: A Subversive Christian Ethic of Economy*. Eugene, OR: Cascade, 2016.

———. "Religion Comme Jeu: La Situation Au XXième Siècle." In *Comment Peut-on (Encore) Être Ellulien Au XXième Siècle*, 209–10. Paris: La Table Ronde, 2014.

———. *Unfortunate Words of the Bible*. Eugene, OR: Cascade, 2019.

Walton, John H. *The Lost World of Genesis One: Ancient Cosmology and the Origins Debate*. Downers Grove, IL: IVP Academic, 2009.

———. *Old Testament Theology for Christians: From Ancient Context to Enduring Belief*. Downers Grove, IL: IVP Academic, 2017.

Walton, John H., and J. Harvey Walton. *The Lost World of the Israelite Conquest: Covenant, Retribution, and the Fate of the Canaanites*. Downers Grove, IL: IVP Academic, 2017.

Wirzba, Norman. *The Essential Agrarian Reader*. Berkeley, CA: Counterpoint, 2004.

————. *Food and Faith: A Theology of Eating*. Cambridge: Cambridge University Press, 2018.

————. *From Nature to Creation: A Christian Vision for Understanding and Loving Our World*. Grand Rapids: Baker Academic, 2015.

————. *The Paradise of God: Renewing Religion in an Ecological Age*. Oxford: Oxford University Press, 2007.

Wright, N. T. *The Day the Revolution Began: Reconsidering the Meaning of Jesus's Crucifixion*. New York: HarperOne, 2016.

————. *How God Became King: The Forgotten Story of the Gospels*. New York: HarperOne, 2016.

————. *Jesus and the Victory of God*. Minneapolis: Fortress, 1997.

————. *The New Testament and the People of God*. Minneapolis: Augsburg Fortress, 1996.

————. *Paul: A Biography*. New York: HarperOne, 2018.

————. *The Resurrection of the Son of God*. Minneapolis: Fortress, 2003.

————. *Surprised by Hope: Rethinking Heaven, the Resurrection, and the Mission of the Church*. New York: HarperOne, 2008.

————. *Virtue Reborn*. London: SPCK, 2010.

Žižek, Slavoj, and John Milbank. *The Monstrosity of Christ: Paradox or Dialectic?* Cambridge, MA: MIT Press, 2009.

Name/Subject Index

Scripture Index

☙

NEW TESTAMENT

CPSIA information can be obtained
at www.ICGtesting.com
Printed in the USA
LVHW041114270423
745481LV00015B/155